Pekka Abrahamsson   Nilay

Lean Enterprise
Software and Systems

First International Conference, LESS 2010
Helsinki, Finland, October 17-20, 2010
Proceedings

 Springer

Volume Editors

Pekka Abrahamsson
University of Helsinki
Department of Computer Science
Gustaf Hällströminkatu 2b, P.O. Box 68
FI-00014 University of Helsinki, Finland
E-mail: Pekka.Abrahamsson@cs.helsinki.fi

Nilay Oza
VTT Technical Research Centre of Finland
Vuorimiehentie 3, P.O. Box 1000
FI-02044 Espoo, Finland
E-mail: nilay.oza@vtt.fi

Library of Congress Control Number: 2010936297

ACM Computing Classification (1998): D.2, K.6

ISSN   1865-1348
ISBN-10   3-642-16415-3 Springer Berlin Heidelberg New York
ISBN-13   978-3-642-16415-6 Springer Berlin Heidelberg New York

springer.com

© Springer-Verlag Berlin Heidelberg 2010
Printed in Germany

Typesetting: Camera-ready by author, data conversion by Scientific Publishing Services, Chennai, India
Printed on acid-free paper   06/3180   5 4 3 2 1 0

Preface

The LESS 2010 conference was the first scientific conference dedicated to advancing the "lean enterprise software and systems" body of knowledge. It fostered interactions by joining the lean product development community with the agile community coupled with innovative ideas nurtured by the beyond budgeting school of thinking. The conference was organized in collaboration with the Lean Software and Systems Consortium (LSSC). The conference is established as a conference series. The idea of the conference was to offer a unique platform for advancing the state of the art in research and practice by bringing the leading researchers and practitioners to the same table. Indeed, LESS 2010 attracted a unique mix of participants including academics, researchers, leading consultants and industry practitioners. The aim of the conference was to use this diverse community to advance research and practical knowledge concerning lean thinking within the field of software business and development. LESS 2010 had more than 60% of its speakers come from the industry and the remaining from academia. LESS is poised to grow as we advance into future iterations of the conference and become the conference for lean thinking in systems and software development. Its growth and credibility will be advanced by the communities and knowledge exchange platform it provides. LESS offers several avenues for knowledge exchange to create a highly collaborative environment. Each year, we aim to bring novelty to a program that fosters collaboration, letting new ideas thrive during and after the conference.

Lean is a new word hitting software companies. Many consider it as the next step after agile. Several methods and tools have already been proposed that present a blend of agile and lean practices. We in the LESS conference aim to evolve bottom-up by bringing different communities who have two common denominators—lean and software or systems. This cannot be done without consideration of how any business is run. For these purposes, the beyond budgeting school of thinking fits nicely into the conference scope. Beyond budgeting is about rethinking how we manage contemporary organizations where innovative management models represent the only sustainable competitive advantage. In a holistic sense, beyond budgeting aims at releasing people from the burdens of stifling bureaucracy and suffocating control systems, trusting them with information and giving them time to think, reflect, share, learn and improve. Similarly, agile was originally started as a movement towards lighter weight process models and ways of working. Lean thinking promotes a holistic system-like philosophy that encompasses the whole organization. LESS builds on these schools to move forward—towards the software organization of the 2010s.

The LESS conference had mainly two types of submissions—academic submissions with full or short papers and industry submissions with mostly short talk proposals. Industry submissions attracted several leading consultants and practitioners from large companies. All the full and short paper proposals (irrespective of whether they were academic or industry based) were reviewed by at least two Program Committee members. All the talk proposals were reviewed by Track Chairs. Track

Chairs were fully empowered to design their tracks. The LESS conferences will continue to build upon this value of trust and empowerment of communities to develop novel, engaging avenues. The selected papers represent a diverse range of experiences, studies and theoretical angles. The selected talks represent some of the most eminent speakers from their respective communities. LESS 2010 was organized in three tracks: (1) Scaling Agile to Lean, (2) Lean Product Development and Innovation and (3) Beyond Budgeting. Furthermore, our distinguished keynote speakers included Deborah Nightingale from MIT, Duc Truong Pham from Cardiff Manufacturing Centre and Martin Curley from Intel. The conference also hosted a range of other engaging avenues including tutorials, workshops, panels, open spaces, lightning talks and social networking programs.

We would like to extend our deep gratitude to all those who contributed to the organization of the LESS 2010 event. The authors, the sponsors, the chairs, the reviewers, and all the volunteers: without their help this event would have not been possible. Nonetheless, we thank the lean, agile and beyond budgeting communities, whose integral role made this conference an exciting platform for sharing and presenting innovative research. These proceedings continue that LESS journey, which started in Helsinki, Finland.

August 2010   Pekka Abrahamsson
                                                                      Nilay Oza

Conference Organization

 UNIVERSITY OF HELSINKI University of Helsinki, Department of Computer Science

 Lean Software & Systems Consortium

Executive Organizing Committee

Program Chairs

Pekka Abrahamsson   University of Helsinki, Finland and
Nilay Oza   VTT Technical Research Center of Finland

Organizing Chairs

Fabian Fagerholm   University of Helsinki, Finland and
Petri Kettunen   University of Helsinki, Finland

Lean Product Development and Innovation Track Chairs

Jayakanth "JK" Srinivasan MIT, USA and
Karl Scotland   Rally Software, UK

Scaling Agile to Lean Track Chairs

Vasco Duarte   Nokia, Finland and
Kieran Conboy   NUI Galway, Ireland

Beyond Budgeting Track Chairs

Peter Bunce   Beyond Budgeting Partnership LLP, UK and
Bjarte Bogsnes   Statoil, Norway

Executive Track Chair

Frances Paulisch   Siemens

Program Committee

Noura Abbas	University of Southampton, UK
M. Ali Babar	IT University of Copenhagen, Denmark
Bjarte Bogsnes	Statoil, Norway
Jan Bosch	Intuit, USA
Nils, Brede Moe	SINTEF, Norway
Peter Bunce	BBRT, UK
Torgeir Dingsoyr	SINTEF, Norway
Jutta Eckstain	IT Communication, Germany
Ola Ellnestam	Agilcal AB, Sweden
Christian Engblom	Ericsson, Finland
Tor Erland Fegri	Sintef, Norway
Steve Fraser	Cisco Systems, USA
Juan Garbajosa	UPM, Spain
Gabor Gunyho	F-Secure, Finland
Harri Haapasalo	University of Oulu, Finland
Geir Hanssen	Sintef, Norway
Rob Hathaway	Indigo Blue, UK
Jeremy Hope	BBRT, UK
Juho Jäälinoja	Nokia, Finland
Pankaj Jalote	IIIT, India
Kari Känsälä	Nokia, Finland
Karlheinz Kautz	Copenhagen Business School, Denmark
Allan Kelly	Software Strategy, UK
Petri Kettunen	University of Helsinki, Finland
Mikko Korkala	VTT Technical Research Center of Finland, Finland
Raija Kuusela	VTT, Finland
Michael Lang	NUIG, Ireland
Stig Larsson	Mälardalen University, Sweden
Garry Lohan	NUIG, Ireland
Kalle Lyytinen	Case Western Reserve University, USA
Olav Maassen	Xebia, The Netherlands
Chris Matts	Independent, USA
Frank Maurer	University of Calgary, Canada
Orla McHugh	NUIG, Ireland
Jürgen Münch	Fraunhofer IESE, Germany
Gustaf Naeser	BWin, Sweden
Frances Paulish	Siemens, Germany
Minna Pikkarainen	VTT, Finland
Charlie Poole	Poole Consulting, USA

Ken Power	Cisco, Ireland
David F. Rico	George Washington University, USA
Kurt Schneider	University of Hannover, Germany
Deb Secor	Rockwell Collins, USA
Alberto Sillitti	Free University of Bozen-Bolzano, Italy
Mattias Skarin	Crisp AB, Sweden
Darja Smite	Blekinge Institute, Sweden
Dragan, Stokic	ATB-Bremen, Germany
Joakim Sunden	Avega Group, Sweden
Daniel Sundmark	Mälardalen University, Sweden
Marko Taipale	Huitale, Finland
Dave Thomas	Bedarra Research Labs, USA
Joe Tidd	University of Sussex, UK
Xiaofeng Wang	NUIG, Ireland

Sponsors (as of August 23, 2010)

Title Sponsor

Reaktor

Platinum Level

HOUSTON
INC.

Other Sponsors

IEEE Software (Media sponsor), Tivit Oy, Tekes, VTT Technical Research Centre of Finland, University of Helsinki

Table of Contents

Beyond Budgeting

Panels

Keynotes

Scaling Agile to Lean – Track Summary

Kieran Conboy[1] and Vasco Duarte[2]

[1] National University of Ireland, Galway
kieran.conboy@nuigalway.ie
[2] Nokia Corporation
vasco.duarte@nokia.com

There are many books, journals and articles explaining agile and to a much lesser extent lean software development methods. Technical competences such as software architecture, automated testing and quality assurance are key focal areas of these materials on agile and lean methods. While some are prescriptive, there is often a substantial difference between the textbook 'vanilla' version of the method and the method actually enacted in practice. Prescribed practices are inevitably interpreted in diverse ways or tailored to suit the specific needs of teams. The constantly evolving technological environment that software development projects are enacted in also highlights the need to tailor prescribed agile practices to work in emerging deployment models, such as cloud computing and mobile computing. Quite a few empirical studies focus on how agile methods were adopted, tailored and used in real-world contexts (e.g., Rasmusson, 2003, Fitzgerald et al., 2006). However, there is a distinct absence of lean software development cases, and cases of agile deployment tend to be weak in terms of theoretical foundation, fail to build on previous lessons, and often lack consistency and coherence (Abrahamsson et al., 2009, Conboy, 2009). In the absence of sound, systematic research, there are few lessons learned across studies, and thus the existing body of knowledge is somewhat fragmented and inconclusive. A systematic and insightful understanding of agile adoption, tailoring and execution is yet to be achieved, and research on lean software development is yet to begin.

Meanwhile, there is a need to investigate the true extent to which agile and lean software development creates business value and return on investment (ROI). This is an important relationship since project failures are common: for example, the Standish Group's 2009 Chaos report finds that 32 percent of IT projects were considered successful, 24 percent of IT projects were considered failures and 44 percent were considered challenged in terms of time, budget, and features – a worsening situation compared with the 2006 survey results. Agile and lean software development, with its emphasis on simplification and iterative development and a set of guiding principles, has been embraced by many as a way of securing IT project outcomes that create business value. However, despite the rising popularity of agile methods, and the emergence of lean, rigorous empirical research into business value and ROI of agile and lean is distinctly absent, which means that companies have to rely on anecdotal evidence and make an act of faith when adopting agile and lean methods.

P. Abrahamsson and N. Oza (Eds.): LESS 2010, LNBIP 65, pp. 1–2, 2010.
© Springer-Verlag Berlin Heidelberg 2010

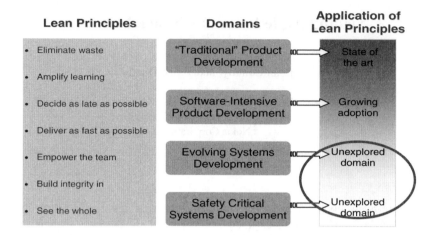

Fig. 1. The Research Gap: Lean Principles in Evolving and Safety-critical Systems Development

Therefore, a systematic and insightful understanding of agile adoption, tailoring and execution, proposed by this research, is highly desirable. Our talks, papers and panels make significant progress toward achieving these goals. Firstly we identify problems with agile and where agile is simply not sufficient in resolving all of our software development problems. Kati Vilkki deals directly with this issue in her talk "When Agile is Not Enough". We also look at the concepts of agile and lean and really question what the benefits are, moving beyond simple acceptance of the often purported benefits. JurgenAppelo's talk on Complexity versus Lean and the panel "Why Agile? Why Lean?" Both contribute to this. Scaling of agile and lean is also a big issue tackled in this track. David Rico examines the scaling of agile and lean to large projects and then on to programs, while talks by Ken Power, David Joyce, and Dennis Stevens all talk about taking agile and lean beyond the team, focusing on ways in which these concepts can be applied at an organisational level.

References

Abrahamsson, P., Conboy, K., Wang, X.: "Lots Done, More To Do": The Current State of Agile Systems Development Research. European Journal of Information Systems 18, 1–7 (2009)

Conboy, K.: Agility From First Principles: Reconstructing The Concept of Agility in Information Systems Development. Information Systems Research 20, 329–354 (2009)

Fitzgerald, B., Hartnett, G., Conboy, K.: Customising Agile Methods to Software Practices. European Journal of Information Systems 15, 197–210 (2006)

Rasmusson, J.: Introducing XP into Greenfield Projects: Lessons Learned. IEEE Computer 20 (2003)

Agile Transformation Study at Nokia – One Year After

Maarit Laanti

Nokia, P.O. Box 407, 00045 Nokia Group, Finland,
Tel.: +358 7180 8000
maarit.laanti@nokia.com

Abstract. Many organizations have started to deploy agile methods but only few extensive surveys exist on the impacts of these methods. In this study, we wanted to see if there is any change in the practitioners' opinions after one year of appliance, and if any real trends can be found from the data. The data were collected using two questionnaires. The population of the first study contains more than 100 respondents from three different continents (Europe, North America, and Asia) and seven different countries and the second study 500 respondents from the same organization. The results reveal that most respondents are satisfied agile way of working and would like to stay in agile mode. They also think using agile methods is important for the future. In two consecutive studies we can see that the opinions of the people who have actual experience on agile methods have stayed the same and that the general opinion towards agility has remained extremely positive. We also show that the opinions are reflecting the actual experience on agile methods.

Keywords: software engineering, agile software development, software processes, agile deployment.

1   Introduction and Related Literature

1.1   Current Status of Agile Adoption

According to a Forrester study, agile has reached mainstream: according to their survey, 35% of respondents are stated that agile most closely reflects their development methods [1]. The growth of the usage of agile methods in last three years (from 17%) has been remarkable [2]. This implies that the benefits of agile methods have been widely recognized in the software industry. In addition, the existing numerous publications on agile methods in both scientific and non-scientific forums mainly seem to report positive impacts of agile adoption. However, adoption of agile methods has proven to be a challenging task [3]. It has been claimed that agile adopters are often unaware of what agile adoption really means, and how broad a change is actually required [2]. This paper is trying to reveal with statistical methods what is happening in agile adoption in one specific organization. It is a study of two surveys conducted one year apart (April 2008 and April 2009) in a large telecom software organization (Nokia) during the course of agile transformation. The main agile model used can be defined as scaled-up Scrum [4] as defined in [5] and [6]. In total, the 2008 survey data

P. Abrahamsson and N. Oza (Eds.): LESS 2010, LNBIP 65, pp. 3–19, 2010.

include more than 1000 and 2009 survey data more than 500 responses regarding different aspects of agile development from the viewpoint of various organizational stakeholders. The goal of this paper is to study if a linkage can be found between a person's attitude toward agility and the experience (time) in applying agile methods in practice. The paper should provide useful insight for organizations going though similar transformations.

1.2 Background

The fundamentals of agile methods, i.e., the values and principles behind the methods (http://agilemanifesto.org/), define the underlying aspiration of agility. Agile Manifesto highlights the values of communication and collaboration, responsiveness, and focusing on the implementation of working software. In agile principles, several more detailed ambitions for agile methods have been defined.

Some studies report that the adoption of individual agile practices, or certain fundamentals of agile software development, has been undertaken to complement the organization's existing processes [7]. Often, the adoption of existing agile methods may require their radical modification to fit the operative context [8]. Thus, it is no surprise that several case studies report challenges in the adoption of agile software development methods [3]. It has been reported that agile adopters are often not aware of what agile adoption really means, and how broad a change is actually required [2]. Most large-scale adopters have had also to mix agile with their currently existing methods, and compromise the agile orthodoxy [1]. This is in line with the thinking that just having shorter iterations resulting in better quality may not be sufficient for large companies producing complex software; a more holistic view on agility may be needed [9].

Various success and failure factors have been proposed to be significant in the agile adoption phase ([10][11]). For example, it has been suggested [11] that for various reasons, agile methods seem to polarize people and stakeholder groups into opponents and supporters having very different standpoints regarding the usefulness of agile methods for the organization. To overcome this, a fundamental change of philosophy and the development of new behaviors are claimed to be required across the organization [11]. A recent study proposes that the appreciation of agile methods seem to increase once they have been adopted and applied in practice [10], which indicates that while there is likely to be resistance among the agile adopters in the organization, time and experience in applying the methods will have a positive effect on this resistance.

It has been claimed that organizations that have failed in planning agile adoption in systematic manner will generate sporadic results across the organization [11]. Kettunen and Laanti have proposed a framework [9] for understanding the multidimensional nature of agility that could be used as a basis for software process improvement (SPI). Not all problems in software projects can be solved by software process methodologies, but during agile transformation an organization can be seen as a force field consisting of forces for and against agility [9]. Kettunen and Laanti have described this force field as *goals* (what we try to achieve with agility), *means* (what we need to put in place in order to be agile) and *enablers* (what needs to be in place before agility can happen). They also present the outline for an agility evaluation grid containing hundreds of attributes collected from literature and categorized into *goals*, *means*, and *enablers*.

This paper is structured as follows: Section 2 discusses research aims, context, and data collection and analysis methods. Section 3 contains results with representative statistics, research questions, qualitative analysis, and limitations. Section 4 covers discussion of the main results and items for future study with final remarks.

2   Research Approach

In this section, the research aims, context, and data collection and analysis methods are presented.

2.1   Research Aims

The level of success in software process improvement can be characterized in terms of personnel satisfaction and whether the new process is actually used [12]. An efficient process may be disliked by personnel, but such a process would not be compliant with the agile value of team empowerment [4] and proper balance of decision making centralization and decentralization [13]. Thus, it is of major importance to study and understand the underlying factors affecting the satisfaction of stakeholders towards agility in organizations adopting agile methods.

Currently, there seems to be a lot of hype related to agile methods yet limited empirical evidence to support their usefulness [14]. Thus, it is important to evaluate how sound agile methods really prove to be. The assumption here is that if agile is only hype and provides no real improvement, adopters would initially be eager but would then turn pessimistic after experiencing agile methods in practice. Alternatively, if following agile methods would prove to be very difficult in practice, they might first be quite optimistic and then become realistic, seeing it as something laborious but necessary.

In this study, we first see how strongly a person's background – i.e., the length of the person's experience with agile methods — impacts to perceptions of and satisfaction with agile methods. The assumption is that when the study population is large enough there is enough cases of successful agile adoption and we will be able to study the general trends. Secondly, we want to study how these opinions have changed during one year timeframe – i.e. whether the satisfaction towards agile methods has more of a permanent nature or not. From a broader perspective, this provides us a way to find out whether agility seems to be making a permanent entrance or if it will prove to be another form of hype that will fade away. Thus the first research aim of this study is to determine respondents' opinions and attitudes toward agility and how they change as the person gains more and more experience in using agile methods. The following two research questions guide the quantitative analysis of the study:

R1)   How does the respondents' length of experience using agile methods in practice impact to their attitudes and opinions toward agile methods?

R2)   How have the respondents' attitudes developed during the one-year follow-up period?

2.2 Research Context

In the year 2008 survey we had more than 1000 respondents from 3 different continents (Europe, North America, and Asia) and 7 different countries. 90% of the respondents represented Research and Development (R&D), while the rest represented mainly Marketing, Design, or other support organizations. The total response rate was 33% from the population of the study. The year 2009 survey was done to same organization. However, the response rate in the current year 2009 survey was much lower – in spite of our best attempts we only got 576 responses, which is significantly lower than the year before. Was this because of the "agile" was already yesterday's news, and not so controversial topic as a year before? Or was this because people had lost their interest in agility?

When comparing the respondent's backgrounds from both surveys, we can see that there is slightly more respondents with other than agile roles and bit less respondents with scrum roles (product owner, scrum master and scrum team member). This could be that only those people who thought the topic was new, important or controversial answered the year 2009 survey; people who were less or more happy with the agile methods in use and who were more concerned with everyday questions in did not bother to answer. The left side of Figure 1 represents the background data from year 2008, and the right side of Figure 1 represents the background data of year 2009 survey.

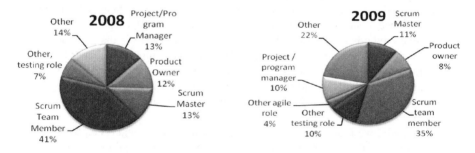

Fig. 1. Left side: Respondents' agile role (of those who reported they had an agile role) in year 2008 survey. Right side: Respondents' agile role in year 2009 survey.[1]

2.3 Data Collection and Analysis

This research was conducted as a questionnaire-based survey. The year 2008 questionnaire was conducted in March 2008 and it was open in web for two weeks in April 2008. The year 2009 survey was conducted in March 2009, and it was open for two weeks. Both studies were extensive in figuring out the respondents' background, opinions towards agility and the perceived benefits. In this study, we limit ourselves to study only the attitudes towards agility and the respondent's agile background.

---

[1] Many people claim that Project/Program manager is not a scrum or agile role. However the terms used here vary, the terms Project/program manager are wblished unlike e.g. scrum of scrum of scrum manager.

First, the attitudes are compared with the respondents' agile background with Kruskal-Wallis H test [15]. Kruskal-Wallis H test is a nonparametric test that does not assume normality. It is testing the equality of population medians among the groups. Instead of using the variance, it is replacing the actual values with ranks – otherwise it is identical to parametric test one-way ANOVA (analysis of variance). Kruskal-Wallis H test is like Mann-Whitney U test, but it can be used with multiple values (Mann-Whitney U is limited to nominal variables with only two values).

In addition to Kruskal-Wallis test, we performed X^2 test of independence between respondents' agile background and attitudes. In the Chi-Square test of Independence [15], the frequency of one nominal variable is compared with different values of the second nominal variable. The Chi-square test of Independence is used when we have two nominal variables. Like many other nonparametric tests, Chi-Square test of Independence does not assume normality of the data, and can also take multiple variable values.

3 Results of the Study

3.1 Representative Statistics

Attitude towards the use and deployment of agile methods

The year 2008 and 2009 surveys repeated same attitude questions:

1. How important you consider agile & iterative development in the future?
2. How satisfied you are with agile & iterative development within your own work?
3. Would you prefer going back to the old way of working?

In year 2008 the attitude question 1 was a multiple-choice question with a scale from 1 (very important) to 5 (not important at all). Question 2 was also a multiple-choice question with a scale from 1 (very satisfied) to 5 (very dissatisfied). Question 3 had the following options: 1= YES, 2= I see no difference, 3= NO.

The year 2009 survey was done differently: For attitude question 1 (importance) the respondents were offered a choice of text strings of ordinal nature: *very important, important, neutral, not very important* and *not important at all*. For attitude question 2 (satisfaction) there was a similar selection of text strings: *very satisfied, satisfied, neither satisfied or dissatisfied, dissatisfied* and *very dissatisfied*. For attitude question 3 (would you go back) there were selections: *yes, no* and *I see no difference* just like in the last year's survey but also a new one "*I do not know as I have never worked in waterfall mode*".

In year 2008 the attitude towards agile development could be considered very positive. For example, 75% of all respondents considered agile as important or very important (Figure 2, left side), and nearly 60% would not like to go back to the old (Figure 4, left side). The satisfaction towards agile development within respondents' own work (Figure 3, right side) was not as positive; only 47% were either "satisfied" or "very satisfied."

Interestingly, respondents with no agile experience seem to be more neutral in their answers than people with some agile experience. This is clearly visible in Figures 2, 3 and 4.

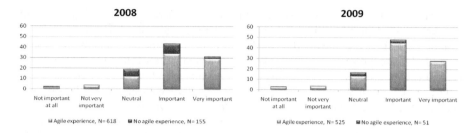

Fig. 2. Statistics on the questions, "How important you consider agile & iterative development in the future" categorized by agile experience

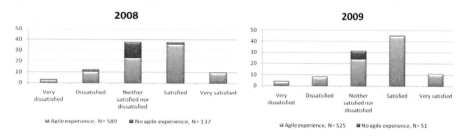

Fig. 3. Statistics on the questions, "How satisfied you are with agile methods" categorized by agile experience

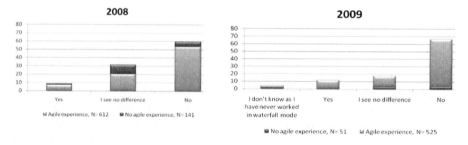

Fig. 4. Overall distribution of responses to the question, "Would you like to go back to the old way of working", categorized by agile experience

The results of the year 2009 survey show similar results. As we can see in Figure 2 right side, 76% of respondents think agile is important or very important, and only 7 percent think it is not. The satisfaction towards agile methods seems to slightly increase: not only 57% are rather satisfied than dissatisfied (year 2008 47%), see Figure 3 right side, but also the number of dissatisfied or very dissatisfied persons has decreased, being now 13 % (year 2008 16%). The number of those who would like to stay in agile has increased, being now 67% (year 2008 60%) but also the group who would like to go back has increased, being now 12% (year 2008 9%). This could be explained by smaller number of neutral responses as seen in Figure 4 right side.

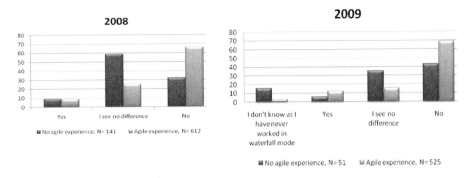

Fig. 5. Percentage of answers to question "would you go back" calculated from total answers of two groups: respondents with and without agile experience

Figure 5 shows the percentages of respondents separately to year 2008 and 2009 data divided to two groups: respondents with agile experience equal to 100% and respondents with agile experience equal to 100%. Illustrating the data this way lets us better compare the distribution of opinions of those having agile experience and those having no agile experience and enables detection of trends. This enables us to study how the opinions of those with no previous agile experience have changed. In year 2008 study respondents with no agile experience were mostly neutral to the change, whereas now the majority is positive (Figure 5). However, if the new category "I don't know" is counted as neutral answers, the year 2008 and 2009 responses are almost identical.

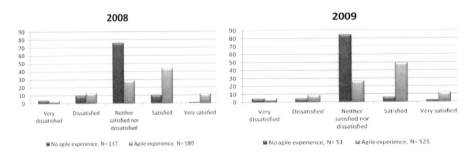

Fig. 6. Percentage of answers to question "how satisfied you are with agile methods" calculated from total answers of two groups: respondents with and without agile experience

Figures 6 and 7 describe the respective confidence intervals of how satisfied people are to their work and how important they see agile methods having similar scales. From these we can see that there is no change in satisfaction towards the agile methods but contrast between experienced and inexperienced respondents have grown regarding the importance of agile methods (in year 2009 majority of non-experienced are neutral in their opinions whereas the "experienced" curve has remained the same). This could be because agile deployment is already "yesterday's news" – or that those who have not yet been exposed to agile methods will not see it affecting their work (both surveys have some respondents from the supporting functions).

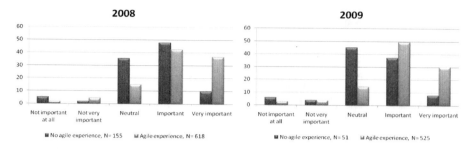

Fig. 7. Percentage of answers to question "how important you consider agile & iterative development in the future" calculated from total answers of two groups: respondents with and without agile experience

3.2 Kruskal-Wallis H Test for Agile Experiences and Attitude

Year 2008 survey
The impact of actual experience on agile methods to attitudes was studied with Kruskal-Wallis H test. With Kruskal-Wallis H test the mean ranks of samples from the populations are expected to be the same, i.e.:

$$H_0: \mu_1 = \mu_2 = \mu_3$$

$$H_A: \mu_i \neq \mu_j$$

The mean ranks in Table 1 of appendix A indicate that the longer agile experience people have, the more important they consider agile development and the more satisfied they are and less likely they would go back to old methods. Table 2 in Appendix A shows that the differences are significant for all the attitudes tested, so the *null hypothesis* of means being equal should be rejected.

From the results we can see that the means of different groups having different agile background are unequal regarding the importance (H= 60.499, 5 d.f.[2], P < 0.05), satisfaction towards agile methods (H= 73.278, 5 d.f., P < 0.05) and whether people would like to back to old methods or not (H=52.914, 5 d.f., P < 0.05).

Year 2009 survey
Kruskal-Wallis H test was done also to year 2009 survey data. The mean ranks are shown in Table 3 in Appendix A and the test results in Table 4 in Appendix A.

From the results, we can see that the means of different groups having different agile background are unequal regarding the importance (H= 36.3, 5 d.f., P <0.05), satisfaction towards agile methods (H= 35.2, 5 d.f., P < 0.05) and whether people would like to back to old methods or not (H= 25.2, 5 d.f., P < 0.05). Comparing against year 2008 values we can see that the differences between different groups have become smaller. There may be various explanations to this phenomenon, see Appendix C.

---

[2] d.f. = degree of freedom.

3.3   Relation of Agile Experience to Attitudes

We further study the *independence* of attitude and agile experience variables. The *null hypothesis* is there is no relationship between the two variables. This is done by comparing the observed frequencies:

$$H_0 : f_0 = f_A$$

$$H_A : f_0 \neq f_e,$$

where f_0 is the observed and f_e is the expected frequency.

The results for importance and attitudes from year 2009 data are shown in Table 5 in Appendix B. Notice that in some of the cases the cell count has been less than 5 which mean that the sampling distribution is too small to use Chi-squared test. However, the statistical software used in the calculations has then automatically replaced the Chi-square test with Fisher's exact test [15].

The Chi-squared test indicated that the difference was significant: X^2 (1, N=20)= 69.7, $p < 0.05$. For satisfaction X^2 (1, N=20)= 92.0, $p < 0.05$ (Table 6 Appendix B) and for would like to go back X^2 (1, N=15)= 55.9, $p < 0.05$ (Table 7 Appendix B). For year 2008 data the respective values are: importance and agile experience X^2 (1, N=20) =85.6, $p < 0.05$ (Table 8 Appendix B), satisfaction X^2 (1, N=20)= 148.8, $p < 0.05$ (Table 9 Appendix B) and for would you like to go back X^2(1, N=10)= 76.7, $p < 0.05$ (Table 10 and Figure 8 in Appendix B). The results indicate that respondents' experience on agile methods is related to attitudes.

3.4   Limitations of the Study

This study is scoped only into few questions in two consequent surveys and their relation to respondents' agile background. The reported benefits and problems with agile methods are scoped out from this study. Also the survey was done in one organization (Nokia) only, so it might be biased by the organization culture and the specific interpretation of agility; so there is a question for external validity, i.e. how largely these results can be generalized. It could well be e.g. that the resistance to agile methods has some relation to the speed of the transition, and the deployment method itself. This can only be verified by making similar studies in other organizations. However, the survey was sent to the same organization and people in both cases and the possibility of other explaining factors have been ruled out as carefully as possible (contributing to internal validity of the study).

Although the two surveys show some changes in the attitudes, it is impossible to show the change of attitude specific to a person as both of the surveys were done anonymously. This kind of study would require maybe a smaller group of respondents, and a systematic follow-up of attitude development.

The impact of applicability of agile model to respondents' role is also scoped out from the study, even though agile impact to some roles have definitely been bigger than to some other roles.

4 Conclusions

In this study, we compared results from two consecutive agile satisfaction surveys to each other. The first survey was done in March-April 2008, and the next one year after. The research questions set for the study were: R1) How does respondents' length of experience using agile methods in practice impact opinions toward agile methods and R2) How have the respondents' attitudes developed during the one-year follow-up period?

The key finding in this study is that all the attitudes (importance of agile development, satisfaction towards agile methods and if one would like to go back to the old methods) vary based on how long agile expertise the respondent has in all cases – Kruskal-Wallis H test done in both year's data give the same result. The second key finding is that these variables (how important respondent see agile development for the future, how satisfied they are with agile development and would they like to go back to the old way of working) are not independent from the agile expertise that the respondent has but that the Chi-square test done in both year's data indicate a significant difference in all the attitudes when comparing different respondents with different length of experience in agile methods.

For Research Question 2, we can see that the attitudes regarding the overall satisfaction towards agile methods, how important agile methods are considered and whether people would like to go back to old have not dramatically changed. When comparing the year 2008 and 2009 data on a detailed level, it looks like the opinions of different groups have approached each other. However, the trend figures show that opinions of those who are experienced with agile methods have only changed little and maybe come a bit closer to each other while the contrast still remains between those who have agile experience and those who have not. That leads to the third key finding of this study: it is recommended that agile methods will be tried out in practice.

The narrowed opinion-neutral population and significantly smaller response rate could be a result of the fact that those who are facing problems with agile methods have more likely answered the 2009 survey than those who are content. The fact that opinions of people with different experience on agility seem to approach each other during the one-year period is suggesting that as the people are communicating with each other and sharing experiences, the satisfaction towards agile methods might be growing as the company makes progress in the *New Technology Adoption Curve* [16]. A third sample would be needed to estimate *Individual-level Cumulative Adoption Likelihood Curve* [17]. Because of the many reported benefits of agile methods, it is not plausible that we would just be going still upwards yet another *Hype Cycle* [18]. Because the adoption of agile methods has not been based on free will, the *Roger's S-curve of Cumulative Adoption of Technology* might not be quite suitable to study how the opinions develop [16]. The authors would like to see social – and behavioral sciences to answer this challenge.

Before the first survey the authors were hesitant at if the agile methods are having a positive impact on Nokia. After the first and second survey the authors were convinced that a systematic way to do agile deployment[3] is needed, and the critical voices

---

[3] This change is reflected to the language used in Nokia: after these studies we started systematically talk about *agile deployment* instead of more passive but more widely used *agile adoption.*

are a minority and possibly caused by people going though their own change transition curves or some specific problems in the deployment itself. This would be one possible area of future studies.

Acknowledgements

The authors would like to thank Ms Kirsi Korhonen from *Nokia Siemens Networks* for her valuable comments related to the statistical methods used, Dr. Harri Kiljander for language proofing and Dr. Outi Salo for her contribution.

References

1. West, D., Grant, T.: Agile Development: Mainstream Adoption Has Changed Agility. Forrester Research (2010)
2. Schwaber, K., Laganza, G., D'Silva, D.: The truth about agile processes: frank answers to frequently asked questions. Forrester Report (2007)
3. Svensson, H., Höst, M.: Introducing an agile process in a software maintenance and evolution organization. In: Proceedings of 9th European Conference of Maintenance and Reengineering (2005)
4. Schwaber, K., Beedle, M.: Agile Software Development with Scrum. Prentice-Hall, Inc., Englewood Cliffs (2002)
5. Laanti, M.: Implementing program model with agile principles in a large software development organization. In: Proceedings of 32nd Annual IEEE International Conference on Computer Software and Applications, Compsac 2008 (2008)
6. Leffingwell, D., Aalto, J.-M.: A Lean and Scalable Information Model for the Agile Enterprise. Whitepaper (2009)
7. Manhart, P., Schneider, K.: Breaking the ice for agile development of embedded software: an industry experience report. In: Proceedings of the 26th International Conference on Software Engineering, ICSE 2004 (2004)
8. Grenning, J.: Launching XP at a Process-Intensive Company. IEEE Software, 3–9 (November/December 2001)
9. Kettunen, P., Laanti, M.: Combining agile software projects and large-scale organizational agility. Software Process: Improvement and Practice 13, 183–193 (2008)
10. Chow, T., Cao, D.: A survey study of critical success factors in agile software projects. Journal of Systems and Software 81, 961–971 (2008)
11. Norton, D.: Five reasons organizations fail to adopt agile methods. Gartner 9 (2008)
12. Abrahamsson, P.: Measuring the success of software process improvement: the dimensions. In: Proceedings of European Software Process Improvement Conference, EuroSPI 2000 (2000)
13. Reinertsen, D.: The principles of Product Development Flow. In: Second Generation lean Product Development. Celeritas Publishing (2009), ISBN-10: 1935401009
14. Dybå, T., Dingsøyr, T.: Empirical Studies of Agile Software Development: A Systematic Review. Information and Software Technology 50, 833–859 (2008)
15. Field, A.: Discovering Statistics using SPSS, 3rd edn. Sage Publications Ltd., Thousand Oaks (2009), ISBN 978-1-84787-906-6
16. Rogers, E.: Diffusion of Innovations, 4th edn. Free Press, New York (1995)

17. Fichman, R., Kemerer, C.: The Illusory Diffusion of Innovation: An Examination of As-similation Gaps. Information Systems Research 10(2), 255–275 (1999)
18. Linden, A., Fenn, J.: Understanding Gartner's Hype Cycles. Gartner Strategic Analysis Report (2003)

Appendix A

Table 1. Attitudes mean ranks grouped by agile experience

	How important you consider agile & iterative development in the future?		How satisfied you are with agile & iterative development within your own work?		Would you go back to the old way of working?	
Experience from agile in practice	**N**	**Mean Rank**	**N**	**Mean Rank**	**N**	**Mean Rank**
Not at all	155	448.57	137	431.69	141	254.06
1 - 3 months	90	358.69	87	353.56	89	343.67
4 - 6 months	136	321.51	129	318.08	134	351.26
7 - 11 months	196	334.41	188	305.48	195	365.33
1 - 2 years	97	300.23	92	257.75	95	397.51
> 2 years	29	250.12	27	224.24	29	382.97
Total	**703**		**660**		**683**	

Table 2. Kruskal-Wallis H test results for attitudes and agile experience

Test Statistics[a,b]

	How important you consider agile & iterative development in the future?	How satisfied you are with agile & iterative development within your own work?	Would you go back to the old way of working?
Chi-Square	60.499	73.278	52.914
Df	5	5	5
Asymp. Sig.	.000	.000	.000

a. Kruskal Wallis Test

b. Grouping Variable: experience from agile in practice

Table 3. Attitudes mean ranks grouped by agile experience

	How important you consider agile & iterative development in the future?		How satisfied you are with agile & iterative development within your own work?		Would you go back to the old way of working?	
Experience from agile in practice	N	Mean Rank	N	Mean Rank	N	Mean Rank
Not at all	51	394.41	51	403.93	51	220.96
1 - 6 months	67	325.83	67	310.95	67	250.84
6 - 12 months	142	288.52	142	280.38	142	284.29
1 – 2 years	219	265.36	219	266.59	219	313.46
2 - 5 years	89	258.99	89	272.02	89	297.73
> 5 years	8	262.00	8	292.00	8	323.38
Total	576		576		576	

Table 4. Kruskal-Wallis H test results for attitudes and agile experience

Test Statistics[a,b]

	How important you consider Agile development in the future?	How satisfied you are with Agile development within your own work?	Would you go back to the old (non-agile) ways of working?
Chi-Square	36.335	35.160	25.160
df	5	5	5
Asymp. Sig.	.000	.000	.000

a. Kruskal Wallis Test

b. Grouping Variable: 6. How long experience do you have from agile development?

Appendix B

Table 5. Importance attitude compared tested with agile experience, year 2009 data

Chi-Square Tests

	Value	df	Asymp. Sig. (2-sided)
Pearson Chi-Square	69.749[a]	20	.000
Likelihood Ratio	70.188	20	.000
Linear-by-Linear Association	24.912	1	.000
N of Valid Cases	576		

a. 12 cells (40.0%) have expected count less than 5. The minimum expected count is .24.

Table 6. Satisfaction attitude compared tested with agile experience, year 2009 data

Chi-Square Tests

	Value	df	Asymp. Sig. (2-sided)
Pearson Chi-Square	92.020[a]	20	.000
Likelihood Ratio	90.719	20	.000
Linear-by-Linear Association	16.018	1	.000
N of Valid Cases	576		

a. 9 cells (30.0%) have expected count less than 5. The minimum expected count is .33.

Table 7. "Would you go back" attitude compared tested with agile experience, year 2009 data

Chi-Square Tests

	Value	df	Asymp. Sig. (2-sided)
Pearson Chi-Square	55.944[a]	15	.000
Likelihood Ratio	52.321	15	.000
Linear-by-Linear Association	20.765	1	.000
N of Valid Cases	576		

a. 6 cells (25.0%) have expected count less than 5. The minimum expected count is .33.

Table 8. Importance attitude compared tested with agile experience, year 2008 data

Chi-Square Tests

	Value	df	Asymp. Sig. (2-sided)
Pearson Chi-Square	85.568[a]	20	.000
Likelihood Ratio	93.502	20	.000
Linear-by-Linear Association	40.335	1	.000
N of Valid Cases	703		

a. 10 cells (33.3%) have expected count less than 5. The minimum expected count is .70.

Table 9. Satisfaction attitude compared tested with agile experience, year 2008 data

Chi-Square Tests

	Value	df	Asymp. Sig. (2-sided)
Pearson Chi-Square	1.488E2	20	.000
Likelihood Ratio	155.905	20	.000
Linear-by-Linear Association	53.222	1	.000
N of Valid Cases	660		

a. 7 cells (23.3%) have expected count less than 5. The minimum expected count is .82.

Table 10. Would you go back attitude compared tested with agile experience, year 2008 data

Chi-Square Tests

	Value	df	Asymp. Sig. (2-sided)
Pearson Chi-Square	76.685[a]	10	.000
Likelihood Ratio	74.427	10	.000
Linear-by-Linear Association	31.835	1	.000
N of Valid Cases	683		

a. 1 cells (5.6%) have expected count less than 5. The minimum expected count is 2.63.

Appendix C

Figure 8 represents Boxplot figure [15] of how satisfied year 2008 survey respondents are with agile & iterative development. In a Boxplot figure, the median value is represented with a bar, surrounded by a box within which 50% of the observations fall. Sticking out of the top and bottom of the box are two whiskers which extend to the most and least extreme scores respectively [15].

Looking the distribution of answers in each category, it looks like "Not at all" and "> 2 Years" are different to other groups as "1-3 Months" is falling in between of "Not at all" and "4-6 months". Because of this distribution, we wanted to have more detailed view on the group "> 2 Years" and thus changed agile experience categories in year 2009 survey.

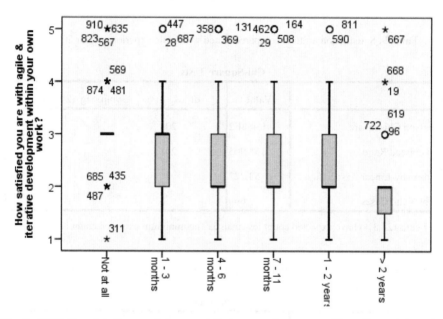

Fig 8. 2008 Boxplot figure of how satisfied respondents are with agile and iterative development categorized by agile experience

The Boxplot figure of a similar agile satisfaction data is represented in Figure 9. "Not at all" category is still different to all other categories. Answer distribution of categories "1-6 months", "6-11 months", "1-2 years", "2-5 years" are more similar to each other, which might be due to deletion of category "1-3 months". Interestingly, distribution of answers in category "> 5 years" is quite different from other categories. It would be interesting to study if this is a real opinion difference that is shown here, or a denial of true expertise (it may be hard for a recognized expert who has worked several years in software industry to admit to be new in agile methods).

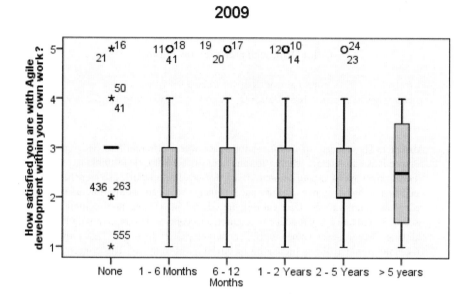

Fig. 9. 2009 Boxplot figure of how satisfied respondents are with agile and iterative development categorized by agile experience

The Role of the User Story Agile Practice in Innovation

Colm O'hEocha and Kieran Conboy

National University of Ireland Galway
coheocha@agileinnovation.eu, kieran.conboy@nuigalway.ie

Abstract. The concept of an innovation space where different knowledge and perspectives can interact leading to innovation is central to lean thinking. The SECI framework of organizational knowledge creation identifies five enabling conditions which impinge on this space, namely intent, autonomy, fluctuation, redundancy and variety. User Stories, introduced in XP and now commonly used in Scrum, are a key practice in requirements capture. In common with lean thinking, they are user value centric, encourage rich dialogue between project stakeholders and avoiding premature specification of solutions. This conceptual paper examines user stories through the dual lenses of an innovation space and the five SECI enablers. The authors conclude that expressing user needs as user stories can support the development of innovative solutions, but that care must be taken in the design of the user stories and their application. This paper concludes with a set of recommendations to support innovation through user stories.

Keywords: agile methods, user stories, innovation space, lean thinking, knowledge creation, SECI.

1   Introduction

One of the seminal events for the development of the agile software development movement was the 1986 publication in Harvard Business Review of "The New New Product Development Game" (Nonaka and Takeuchi 1986). Describing lean production principles applied to new product development, the paper introduced the metaphor of a rugby team where a clear goal, overlapping skill sets and joint accountability allow teams dynamically adapt and self-organize to achieve their objectives despite unforeseen setbacks and challenges. From this, the term scrum was used by Sutherland and Schwaber in 1995 to describe an incremental, team based approach to software development. In this way, agile development and innovating new products share a common lineage.

Agile methods have long been advocated in supporting innovation (Highsmith 1999). Proponents argue they explicitly call for self-reflection and improvement of the method through retrospection. Close customer contact and an understanding of the business problem to be solved can help the development team create more innovative solutions than if they were coding to a static functional specification. Advocates have written of 'hyper-productive' scrum exhibiting 'punctuated equilibrium' leading to discontinuous or radical innovations (Sutherland, Downey et al. 2009).

P. Abrahamsson and N. Oza (Eds.): LESS 2010, LNBIP 65, pp. 20–30, 2010.

User stories are a common practice in agile methods for feeding user requirements into the development process. Unlike traditional requirements engineering approaches, they do not call for comprehensive specification of the solution 'up-front' but instead encourage rich dialogue between customers and the technical team at implementation time to arrive at the best solution. As the name implies, user stories express user centric functionality, and are written in a story style. They reflect what the user would like the system to do, rather than how it should do it.

This lack of specificity introduces considerable uncertainty and ambiguity to requirements management. Both uncertainty and ambiguity are held to foster innovation and are considered essential ingredients in developing novel solutions and supporting organizational learning (Kline and Rosenberg 1986; Nonaka 1991; Lester and Piore 2004). Deploying these elements in an innovation space, 'ba' (Nonaka 1991) or 'conversation' (Lester and Piore 2004), along with other recognized innovation enablers (Nonaka 1991) suggests the user story practice should support innovation. However, as far as we are aware, little rigorous research has focused on how exactly user stories facilitate innovation. Using the concepts of an innovation space and the organizational knowledge creation framework (Nonaka and Takeuchi 1995) – commonly referred to as SECI after its four core processes of Socialisation, Externalisation, Combination and Internalisation, this paper will examine further how user stories enhance the ability of agile methods to support innovation. The aim of the paper is to establish aspects of user stories that are likely to support the emergence of innovative solutions from the agile development team.

Section 2 describes the concept of an innovation space and summarizes some of the approaches to it described in the literature. Section 3 provides an overview of the SECI framework, particularly the 5 enabling conditions necessary for organizational knowledge creation, while section 4 describes the agile user story practice in further detail. Section 5 then discusses how this practice provides an innovation space and supports and constrains the 5 enablers. This discussion draws on both the authors experience as agile practitioners, and on theoretical arguments. Finally, section 6 summarizes conclusions and recommendations for the use of user stories in supporting innovation within Information Systems Development (ISD) teams. Note that this paper is conceptual in nature and these conclusions have yet to be tested empirically.

2   Innovation Space, Knowledge Creation and Variability

The concept of an 'innovation space' (Figure 1) is widely evident in the literature. It represents a mental space where an understanding of both the problem to be solved and the components of a solution available can be brought together to create an environment where a more innovative solution can emerge (Hippel 2005). An associated concept is that of boundary objects (Carlile 2002) which serve as *"as a means of representing, learning about, and transforming knowledge"* across boundaries, such as the problem and solution domains. Agile user stories can be used to create an innovation space and serve as boundary objects in supporting innovation. This section explores these concepts further with the aim of examining exactly how user stories can positively impact innovation.

In plan-driven ISD methods, the problem and solution domains are represented by two different functions in the organization, and usually by two different teams with different skill sets. The problem is articulated by customers, users and analysts, usually in terms of a solution which they believe will solve the problem. That is, requirements are normally expressed in terms of software features described in various levels of detail, even down to screen layouts, data fields and menu structures. This is passed to the designers, developers and operations teams who implement such a solution based on the technologies available. In this case the innovation space can be very restricted – the requirements as expressed can reflect a limited understanding of the possible opportunities offered by the available technologies. This in turn leads to sub-optimal solutions which can reflect previous patterns of application already familiar to those in the problem domain. The technologists similarly gain little understanding of the business problem being addressed, and therefore are not in a position to pursue alternate, more effective solutions offered by the solution space but not considered by the customer. This reflects the demarcation of roles underpinning many traditional product development methods which results in a tendency to identify 'what' the customer wants, rather than 'why' the customer wants it (Reinertson 1998). Indeed, many waterfall methods explicitly advocate the separation of the problem and solution spaces by requiring full and final requirements be 'signed-off' by the customer or business. Even the term 'requirement', used universally to mean features to be included, implies they are mandatory and non-negotiable (Cockburn 2007). This is accompanied by 'change management systems' which minimize variability in the design, development and delivery phases. In summary, waterfall methods do not nurture an innovation space – on the contrary, they tend to severely restrict or even eliminate it.

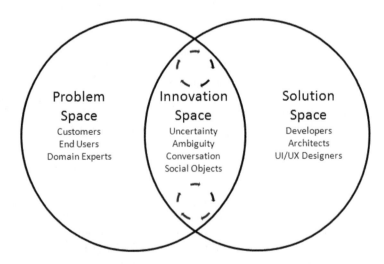

Fig. 1. Innovation Space

In knowledge creation literature, Nonaka and Konno introduce the concept of 'ba' which they describe as "a shared [physical, mental or virtual or any combination] space for emerging relationships" for the purposes of knowledge creation (Nonaka and Konno 1998). Building on this existentialist concept they contend that knowledge exists in a tacit, intangible form within ba and becomes information when detached from it. Ba is the "frame [...] within which knowledge is activated as a resource for creation" and is essential to both individual and collective knowledge creation and therefore learning. Lean thinking argues that the objective of product development is to 'out-learn the competition' (Reinertson 1998) indicating that knowledge creation, and the associated 'ba', is essential for product innovation.

Innovation and product development literature also highlight the importance of uncertainty and variability in innovation. The chain-link theory of innovation (Kline and Rosenberg 1986) stresses the iterative nature of the innovation process, rejecting the linear, deterministic model driven by scientific discovery and invention and underlying the traditional R&D organizational structure and process. Uncertainty is an inherent trait in innovation and structures or processes which try to constrain or deny it have been thoroughly discredited. This view is further developed in information theory which positively values variability, and consequently 'failure' in terms of not conforming to predetermined plans, as being the source of information creation (Reinertson 1998). The value of such information is increased where it is created early and is efficiently absorbed and used in creating new knowledge which can contribute to innovation. Indeed, a process without variability cannot create new information, and cannot therefore develop new learning and products. That is, while repeatability may be a virtue in production, it renders development utterly sterile.

Another concept contributing to innovation is that of ambiguity and the conversation required to resolve it (Fonseca 2002; Lester and Piore 2004). Precise specification of a requirement limits or even eliminates the opportunity to interpret it from a different perspective. Ambiguity can be used positively to accommodate the variability essential to innovation. Progressing from such ambiguity to a precise specification involves conversation between those representing the problem and the solution domains.

From the above we can see that innovation and knowledge creation literature identify an 'innovation space' as a key element in arriving at novel solutions. This space brings together and activates knowledge from both the problem and solution domains and nurtures productive conversations which leverage variability and ambiguity to arrive at novel solutions. We discuss later how the user story practice can be used to enable many of these factors in ISD. One specific description of an innovation space is ba which forms part of the SECI knowledge creation framework and is discussed next.

3   Organizational Knowledge Creation

The SECI theory of organizational knowledge creation has enjoyed "paradigmatic status" (Gourlay 2003) since first elaborated by Nonaka and Takeuchi (Nonaka and Takeuchi 1995). In the following text the major components of the theory are described, focusing particularly on the five "enabling conditions" which support an innovation space, or ba.

SECI is based on two underlying constructs. Epistemologically there exist two forms of knowledge – tacit and explicit. Ontologically, knowledge is formed by individuals and the interactions common within organizations which can develop, refine, clarify and amplify it. Using these two 'dimensions' of knowledge creation, SECI proposes a spiral model where tacit and explicit knowledge are in continuous dialogue within a ba, transforming through the four processes of socialization, externalization, combination and internalization.

Socialization represents conversion of knowledge from tacit to alternate tacit forms and can occur through shared experience (for example apprenticeship). This can rarely be achieved through abstracting knowledge into an external form, can even occur without language and therefore requires close face to face interaction. *Externalization* uses metaphors to convert tacit knowledge to explicit form – it is the articulation of knowledge. The writing of poetry could be regarded as a highly sophisticated example of this whereby complex and nuanced knowledge is transferred through metaphor to an explicit form for communication to others. *Combination* of multiple externalized knowledge sources through meetings and conversations can lead to the creation of new knowledge by bringing together existing explicit forms. Finally, *internalization* involves the conversion of explicit knowledge to a tacit form through 'action based' learning. Taken together, these transformations create, develop and disseminate knowledge within the various organizational levels from individuals to entire value chains.

SECI identifies 5 enabling conditions (**Fig. 2**) for these processes, and the ba in which they occur. For an individual to acquire knowledge, Nonaka proposes they must be 'committed'. That is, they must have an *intention*, an action oriented concept which forms their approach to the world. The value of information, and the knowledge to which it can contribute, depends on the intention of the receiver, and not purely on the nature of the information itself. Therefore, the perception, context and prior knowledge of the individual affect the possibility and form of meaning derived from it. Additionally, *autonomy* at both individual and group level is essential to provide the freedom to absorb new knowledge – this does not need to be absolute freedom, but reflect a 'minimum critical specification' (Morgan 1986). Autonomy reflects empowerment where authority, guided by a clear understanding of intention, is delegated to where it can be most effectively exercised. Thirdly, knowledge creation requires *fluctuation* whereby there are discontinuities in the interaction of an individual's knowledge with their perceived reality, leading to the re-evaluation of assumptions underlying their current knowledge. Such breakdowns or contradictions therefore contribute to the creation of new knowledge. Fourthly, *information redundancy* facilitates efficient knowledge flow and absorption, as well as empowerment of the team through participation of members on the basis of consensus and common understanding. This reflects the use of knowledge to facilitate the absorption of additional learning which can in turn enable innovation (Cohen and Levinthal 1990). Redundancy also creates resiliency within the team through the "principle of redundancy of potential command" (McCulloch 1965 quoted in Nonaka and Takeuchi 1995) and supports the development of trust between team members. And finally, SECI proposes Ashby's principle of *'requisite variety'* (Ashby 1957) in balancing the creation of knowledge and its effective processing. According to this principle, the diversity of knowledge at any point in the organization should match the diversity it must process.

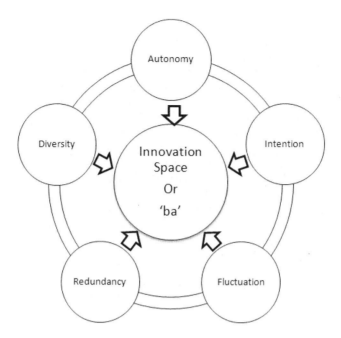

Fig. 2. SECI Enabling Conditions

The SECI theory is pre-dominant in the field of knowledge creation. It provides a comprehensive framework for the evaluation of the agile practice of user stories in creating an innovation space and enabling that space for knowledge creation and innovation.

4   Agile Practice – User Stories

The concept of user stories were first introduced to software development with the publication of Kent Beck's eXtreme Programming book in 1999 (Beck 1999). User Stories represented a technique of establishing a shared understanding of software requirements using a low-overhead, user centric and flexible approach. This concept was later developed further and extended to apply to other agile methods such as scrum (Cohn 2004). Although not universally accepted as the best way to capture software requirements (Cockburn 2007) they are widely used and are therefore treated here as a common agile practice.

The user story format has three elements often articulated as Card, Conversation and Confirmation (Jeffries 2001). The *card*, so called as its often written on an index card, is a small number of sentences used to describe the intent of the story. The card serves as a token, summarizing intent and acting as a placeholder for a conversation which will elaborate on the detail closer to the time it is required. As implied by the name user story, this description should be both user centric in terms of the language used and the need expressed. It should be written in the form of a story. A format commonly used by agile teams takes the form '*As a <role> I want to <action> so that <result>*'. An example would be "*As an online customer I want to enter a product name so that I can view details of that product*". The card can also capture initial estimates of the value of the story to the customer and the cost in implementing it. The *conversation* represents a discussion between the team, customer, end users and other stakeholders, which clarifies the details of the requirement and frames the solution design to be used. The term conversation reflects the verbal nature of the interaction – negotiation around the requirement is through rich, highly interactive dialogue, using a shared vocabulary understandable by both customers and the development team, and not necessarily resulting in written specification. *Confirmation* represents the acceptance criteria or tests which must be satisfied before the story can be considered fully implemented. Unlike the conversation, such tests are normally written down for later reference (often on the reverse of the story index card), though ideally they represent the intent agreed rather than precisely how a feature will be implemented. By ensuring these tests pass, the development team should be confident that the value of the story has been delivered to the customer.

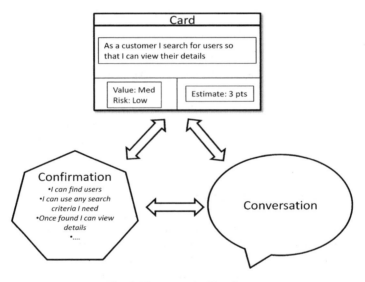

Fig. 3. Elements of a User Story

The user story format is advocated in agile methods as it is lightweight, reduces design in process, encourages late commitment, facilitates iteration planning and supports a shared understanding of the business value and design of software features. The latter of these concerns knowledge creation in an innovation space and will be discussed further in terms of the effect of the user story technique on innovation.

5   Discussion

User stories support the coming together of problem and solution domain knowledge in a shared innovation space, or ba. The user story card holding a summary of the intent, and optionally, an initial estimate of effort and value, is used primarily for planning purposes – it is not intended to be sufficient for implementation. It is the conversation represented by the card which positions the 'whole team' (Beck 2005) to develop a shared mental model of the optimum solution based on a mutual understanding of the problem and solution domains. This conversation within the cross-functional team should include all perspectives and skills, including the customer, product owner, designers, developers and other stakeholders. By representing the requirement in terms of the customer's intent, a user story card maintains the ambiguity and uncertainty until the solution space can be appropriately explored – the opportunity to arrive at a novel solution is not closed down prematurely.

In evaluating the capability of the user story practice in creating new knowledge and innovation, the five enabling conditions proposed by SECI are here used as a lens.

Intention: The user story is designed to capture only the *intent* of the user at a high level – a succinct description in one or two sentences of what the user wants to achieve, and a set of criteria to help determine if the need has been satisfied. This contrasts with traditional requirement specification techniques which encourage the comprehensive specification of the *solution* by those in the problem space (usually the customer or end user), leaving little room for negotiation, learning or participative and emergent design. User stories communicate the business intent clearly to those with the technical skills to design a solution. That is, a user story expresses the *intention* of the user and is a simple mechanism to place that intention within the innovation space, where various stakeholders can interact through the conversation and arrive at a mutually agreed solution.

Autonomy: Within the conversation on a user story the design approach and exact scope can be negotiated by those that best understand the constraints and solution technologies. Autonomy supports self-organization and accountability, which in turn helps motivate individuals to work together to find better solutions (Nonaka 1991). The conversation provides the space in which this autonomy can be exercised. The accountability conferred on the team by this same autonomy can also lead to fluctuation, as a sense of responsibility for developing an effective solution motivates the team to evaluate novel approaches.

Fluctuation: With the rich interactive communication surrounding the focus of discussion – namely the user story, comes knowledge transfer and learning. As each individual learns more about the business problem being addressed, the possible ways value can be generated and the technical solutions available, they experience a changing understanding of the user story. This can lead to changing understandings and perspectives by all parties as pre-conceived ideas are abandoned or altered. This can induce a 'creative chaos' whereby participants are moved to adjust their views of the story based on input from others, leading to a state of uncertainty, ambiguity and fluctuation wherein innovation flourishes.

Information Redundancy: The rich conversation invoked by the user story format both requires and contributes to information redundancy. To communicate effectively and internalize others perspectives requires 'absorptive capacity' (Cohen and Levinthal 1990), a depth of knowledge allowing appreciation of the others point of view.

Through the four SECI knowledge transformation processes active in the group conversation, new knowledge relating to different perspectives is created and disseminated across the team, thereby increasing information redundancy. In the agile literature, this has led to the term 'generalizing specialists' to describe team members who have great depth of expertise in one or more areas, but some knowledge of many other areas allowing them work effectively as part of an integrated team. In more traditional approaches lacking this conversational element, little learning occurs leading to the common 'silo' effect where past solutions are re-applied to new problems thereby limiting innovation.

Requisite Variety: The concept of cross-functional teams, often referred to as feature teams in the agile literature, bring a variety of knowledge and perspectives to the user story conversation, allowing novel solution designs to emerge (Campion, Medsker et al. 1993; Lee and Xia 2010). However, literature suggests (though it has not been empirically demonstrated) that such diversity may come at a price in terms of the efficiency of the team in exploring different possibilities, in communicating effectively and in arriving at shared decisions (Lee and Xia 2010). Therefore, diversity within the team should be balanced with the need for efficiency – it should be appropriate to handling the variety of customer needs and technical solutions likely to be encountered by the team. Assigning a high level estimate to a user story before the conversation occurs may bound the possible solutions investigated and helps achieve this balance in diversity.

6   Conclusions and Recommendations

User stories are widely used in agile methods. Their focus on small increments of functionality of short term value to the user is sympathetic with lean thinking. The card, conversation and confirmation elements of the user story format are particularly conducive to developing innovative user solutions. Sometimes described as a 'placeholder for a conversation' (Highsmith 1999) a user story can serve as a boundary object facilitating the transfer and creation of new knowledge within a shared innovation space. Through the card and confirmation elements the format of a story includes the user's intention in taking a defined action. Through the conversation element, it fosters information redundancy in the team through sharing of perspectives and leverages team diversity in exploring possible solution design. Similarly, by allowing the solution design emerge from the team conversation, the autonomy of the team is supported while fluctuation or 'creative chaos' can be encouraged by the lack of predefined solution guidelines. In the remainder of this section we describe some recommendations for maximizing the contribution of user stories to solution innovation.

By separating the business intent and value of the story from its logical and technical design, the space provided for a cross-functional team to explore and develop solutions is maximized. However, this can be constrained where the <action> of the user story is prescriptive, defining 'how' the user will achieve their objective and not confining itself to 'why'. But the <action> is important in providing context to the story – it relates under what circumstances the <result> should occur. Therefore, a careful balance of contextualizing the intent of the user while avoiding unnecessary specification of a solution by describing what the user action might be can help maintain space for novel solutions to be developed. Similarly, within the confirmation element of the user story, by specifying only acceptance rather than systems tests, the users intent can be expressed in the broadest terms possible, without constraining the solution space. The system tests should relate to the intent of the story, rather than the specific actions the user must take to achieve that intent.

The user story form has been criticized for being too granular and thereby lacking full context of the user experience in pursuing the intent of the story (Cockburn 2007). To facilitate exploration of novel solutions, understanding the wider context of interaction within which the user story exists can be key – therefore, approaches such as user story mapping (Patton 2008) are recommended. Where possible, initial user stories should be described at a high level (sometimes referred to as epics (Cohn 2004)) and collaboratively developed into a series of user stories small enough to be elaborated, developed and tested in short iterations.

The conversation called for by the practice creates an innovation space where the stakeholders in the story can leverage the five innovation enablers proposed by SECI. Factors such as a clear intent, team autonomy in how a solution is developed, a sense of creative chaos, continuous learning and redundancy and diversity within the team all contribute to an innovative environment. In this way, the user story practice is central to the innovation capability of agile teams. However, in practice these benefits are often reduced for localized efficiency by assigning specialists within the team to design and estimate stories without collaboration (O'hEocha, Conboy et al. 2010). It is recommended that where possible the design of solutions, especially at the high levels of epics or themes, are collaborated upon by a diverse set of team members. This can help prevent past techniques being automatically applied to new problems and foster continuous questioning and novel approaches.

In summary, careful use of the practice, such as ensuring solutions are not framed before the conversation occurs, or are embodied into the confirmation criteria, are necessary to maintain space for innovation. In addition, the intent of the story, as well as the larger strategic intent of the organization, must be clearly articulated to ensure the appropriate learning takes place. Information redundancy and team diversity must be managed to ensure balance between the efficiency of converging on a solution quickly and closing down the conversation prematurely and thwarting the emergence of novel solutions.

The aim of this paper is to establish aspects of user stories that are likely to support the emergence of innovative solutions from the agile development team. It has been argued above that, if implemented appropriately, the practice is likely to significantly contribute to the development of novel solutions, and indeed to the learning and thereby innovative capability of the agile team. Further possible research will include testing these conclusions empirically.

References

Ashby, W.R.: An Introduction to Cybernetics. Chapman and Hall, New York (1957)

Beck, K.: Extreme Programming Explained: Embrace Change. Addison-Wesley, Reading (1999)

Beck, K.: Extreme Programming Explained - Embrace Change. Pearson Education, New Jersey (2005)

Campion, M., Medsker, G., et al.: Relations Between Work Group Characteristics and Effectiveness: Implications for Designing Effective Work Groups. Personnel Psychology 46(4) (1993)

Carlile, P.R.: A Pragmatic View of Knowledge and Boundaries: Boundary Objects in New Product Development. Organisation Science 13(4) (2002)

Cockburn, A.: Agile Software Development: The Cooperative Game. Pearson, Boston (2007)

Cohen, W.P., Levinthal, D.A.: Absorptive Capacity: A New Perspective on Learning and Innovation. Administrative Science Quarterly 35(1) (1990)

Cohn, M.: User Stories Applied. Pearson, Boston (2004)

Fonseca, J.: Complexity and Innovation in Organisations. Routledge, New York (2002)

Gourlay, S.: The SECI Model of Knowledge Creation: Some Empirical Shortcomings. In: Proceedings of the 4th European Conference on Knowledge Management, Oxford (2003)

Highsmith, J.: Adaptive Software Development. Dorset House, New York (1999)

Hippel, E.v.: Democratising Innovation. MIT Press, Cambridge (2005)

Jeffries, R.: Essential XP: Card, Conversation and Confirmation. XP Magazine (2001)

Kline, S.J., Rosenberg, N.: An Overview of Innovation. In: Landau, R., Rosenberg, N. (eds.) The Positive Sum Strategy, pp. 275–306. National Academy Press, Washington (1986)

Lee, G., Xia, W.: Toward Agile: An Integrated Analysis of Quantitative and Qualitative Field Data of Software Development Agility. MIS Quarterly 34(1) (2010)

Lester, R., Piore, M.: The Missing Dimension. Harvard University Press, Boston (2004)

Morgan, G.: Images of Organization. Sage Publications, Beverly Hills (1986)

Nonaka, I.: The Knowledge-Creating Company. Harvard Business Review 69(6), 96–104 (1991)

Nonaka, I., Konno, N.: The concept of ba: building a foundation for knowledge creation. California Management Review 40(3), 40–54 (1998)

Nonaka, I., Takeuchi, H.: The New New Product Development Game. Harvard Business Review 64(1) (1986)

Nonaka, I., Takeuchi, H.: The Knowledge-Creating Company. Oxford University Press, New York (1995)

O'hEocha, C., Conboy, K., et al.: So you think you're agile? In: XP 2010, Trondheim, Norway. LNBIP, vol. 48, pp. 315–324. Springer, Heidelberg (2010)

Patton, J.: The new user story backlog is a map (2008),
http://www.agileproductdesign.com/blog/the_new_backlog.html

Reinertson, D.: Managing the Design Factory: A Product Developers Tool Kit. The Free Press, New York (1998)

Sutherland, J., Downey, S., et al.: Shock Therapy: A Bootstrap for Hyper-Productive Scrum. In: Agile 2009, Chicago. IEEE Computer Society, Los Alamitos (2009)

Lean/Agile Software Development Methodologies in Regulated Environments – State of the Art

Oisín Cawley, Xiaofeng Wang, and Ita Richardson

Lero-The Irish Software Engineering Research Centre,
University of Limerick,
Ireland
{Oisin.Cawley,Xiaofeng.Wang,Ita.Richardson}@lero.ie

Abstract. Choosing the appropriate software development methodology is something which continues to occupy the minds of many IT professionals. The introduction of "Agile" development methodologies such as XP and SCRUM held the promise of improved software quality and reduced delivery times. Combined with a Lean philosophy, there would seem to be potential for much benefit. While evidence does exist to support many of the Lean/Agile claims, we look here at how such methodologies are being adopted in the rigorous environment of safety-critical embedded software development due to its high regulation. Drawing on the results of a systematic literature review we find that evidence is sparse for Lean/Agile adoption in these domains. However, where it has been trialled, "out-of-the-box" Agile practices do not seem to fully suit these environments but rather tailored Agile versions combined with more plan-based practices seem to be making inroads.

Keywords: Software Development, Regulated Environment, Lean, Agile, Medical Device, Embedded-Software, Safety-critical.

1 Introduction

In this report we investigate the contemporary practices of Lean/Agile Software Development methodologies, as practiced in the regulated safety-critical domains. Of particular interest to us is how applicable these methodologies are within the domain of medical device software development, and whether the benefits that have been reaped from *Lean manufacturing* [1] can be achieved in this specific domain. We aim to identify areas which require further investigation and which will assist companies in understanding and adopting such beneficial software development practices.

1.1 Lean and Agile Software Development

Lean Software Development can be viewed as the application of the concepts and principles, which drive Lean Manufacturing [1] and [2], to the practice of developing software. Robert Charette - the originator of Lean Development - sees it as a key

P. Abrahamsson and N. Oza (Eds.): LESS 2010, LNBIP 65, pp. 31–36, 2010.

component in building a change tolerant business [3]. The key difference he says between Lean and Agile is that Agile is a bottom up approach while Lean is a top down approach. He developed the 12 principles of Lean Development [3] which have very close similarities with the Agile manifesto, and so we see this as the point where Lean concepts meet Agile software development practices. By applying the specific Lean principles [2] within the context of the software development domain, we can see how many of the Agile software development techniques support them [4],[5] and [6].

As a result the boundary between Lean Software Development and Agile Software Development is something that is currently being debated. We view Agile methods as supportive practices of a Lean software development philosophy, and so for the purpose of this report we treat them as one while bearing the distinction in mind.

1.2 Regulation

The increasing complexity of electronic devices is making the hardware and software development processes much more interlinked and so any software development methodology used must take that into consideration. These hardware-software systems are playing an increasing role in our everyday lives, and the obvious safety element is of paramount concern. Various standards have been introduced to help ensure the highest level of confidence in the safe functioning of such systems, and while the regulatory standards are quite rigorous, they are not necessarily prescriptive. Standards, such as the RTCA's[1] DO-178B standard [7] for the aviation industry, and ISO 13485:2003 [8] for medical devices, do not impose any particular software development methodology. The important thing is that the processes, activities and tasks, as identified by the regulations, are being implemented.

2 Analysis of the Literature

The information presented here is mostly drawn from the results of a Systematic Literature Review (SLR)[2] into the practices of Lean/Agile development in the medical device industry. The SLR was carried out following the guidelines by [9] and quickly showed there to be a lack of published material in this specific area. In order to progress our investigation we widened our review to cover regulated safety-critical embedded-software development in general.

The Agile methodologies most reported throughout the literature were XP and SCRUM (Fig. 1), but one of the areas we were interested in investigating was the 'flavour' of Agile being adopted/trialled in these domains (Fig. 2). From the data there are clear indicators in support of a combination of Agile and more traditional planned-type (Agile-Planned) software development practices.

---

[1] Radio Technical Commission for Aeronautics (www.rtca.org)
[2] http://staff.lero.ie/ocawley/Publications/Lean-Agile-in-medical-devices/

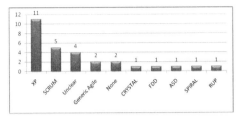

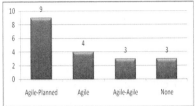

Fig. 1. Methodologies reported   **Fig. 2.** Agile 'Flavour' being reported
(Y-Axis shows the number of publications)

2.1 State of Methodology Adoption

There are many reports supportive of the use of Lean/Agile methodologies in embedded-software development, including regulated environments such as medical devices. Within the Aerospace industry for example, [10] found that nearly all Agile practices can be mapped to the DO-178B [7] regulatory standard and yet the Aerospace industry has been slow in adopting them. Similar mappings were performed [11] [12], finding that while most of the DO-178B requirements can be mapped to XP, SCRUM, CRYSTAL practices, some are outside the scope of these methodologies and some need to be re-interpreted. [11] found that, similar to other embedded-software domains, the further on in the life-cycle you are, the less agility it is possible to maintain. The final stage of certification is where they see the least amount of agility possible. Interestingly, the Open-DO Initiative[3] is calling for a more lean and open-source approach to aviation software development. They state that:

"By leveraging on lean approaches and agility we aim... to shift the focus of safety-critical software development to more continuous and incremental certification approaches."

Specifically in relation to the medical device industry, our industry involvement within a medical device manufacturing plant is demonstrating that interest is being expressed in a more lean approach. This is not surprising since the development lifecycle of a medical device is typically measured in years, and so any mechanism that will help reduce this, and thereby provide a competitive edge, is worth investigating. The literature has reports of successful Agile implementations but, as with the embedded-software domain in general, there are caveats which have led to 'flavours' of Agile methods being implemented. [13] took a cautious approach at first followed by a full SCRUM implementation. [14], developing software for a specific medical device, note the most important thing for Food and Drugs Administration (FDA) approval is the need to perform formal review and approval steps. They implemented a hybrid Planned-Agile methodology in order to get the benefits of agility while maintaining discipline around certain areas such as documentation.

[15] implemented Agile (XP and Scrum) in Medtronic, a company developing class III medical device[4] software. They found that the practices of pair-programming and test-driven development provided early feedback and better quality. [16] discuss

---

[3] http://www.open-do.org/about/
[4] High risk devices whose failure or misuse would likely cause serious patient injury (EU council directive 93/42/EEC)

the successful implementation of Agile practices within Abbott's diagnostic division, and concluded that: "*...an agile approach is the approach best suited to development of FDA-regulated medical devices*". A strong endorsement indeed. [17] made use of a combination of XP, Scrum and Organisational Patterns to overcome system constraints and regulatory issues related to safety.

Deciding how to begin adopting Agile development in this context is another source of uncertainty. [18] developed a comparative process selection model, while more recently [19] proposed six recommendations when considering Agile adoption in embedded systems development. Specifically related to mission and life-critical systems, [20] developed a three-stage process to help determine the applicability of agile practices to a company's specific environments.

2.2 Some Issues Encountered

As we might expect in a regulated environment, there is a burden of proof which must be met in demonstrating compliance. The validation and verification steps are obvious areas which are focused on. [21] suggests that XP's focus on automating testing can benefit critical systems, but suggests that it should be tried and evolved further to meet the specific needs. To facilitate the requirements of safety demonstrations throughout the lifecycle, [22] developed a formal specification language for nuclear engineering applications. [23] reduced the testing effort in Guidant by between 25% and 90% by means of a Pattern-Oriented Scenario-Based testing approach which supports a Lean/Agile process.

Similarly, issues with refactoring are highlighted, such as the potential to invalidate earlier certification (credit) [12], or to introduce timing issues [24]. A workable configuration management system combined with relentless testing can help.

From a regulation point of view, it is imperative that there is full traceability right throughout the development lifecycle. [25] suggests that the Agile practice of single sourcing information greatly simplifies requirements traceability within regulated development. [6, 25] point to source control management (SCM) as being a fundamental best practice which assists traceability, while [26] propose building upon the practice of TDD to produce a requirements traceability matrix as a direct by-product of the TDD process.

Any Lean or Agile strategy can only succeed if the people involved are organised and motivated appropriately. [27] identified a collection of practices for Lean governance of software development projects. [25] says that in his experience there are quality-oriented Agile development practises which are much better suited to regulated environments than traditional practices. Management training [28], "Making Allies and Friends" [15] are ways used to help in the transformation. If the right attitudes and management supports are not in place, the effort may be doomed from the start [29].

3 Conclusions and Further Work

We found only a small number of publications which could indicate a very low-level of adoption of Lean/Agile methods in regulated, safety-critical domains, however, it may simply indicate a reluctance of companies in these domains to make their internal practices public. A noticeable lack of reference to the concept of "Lean Software Development" (LSD) was evident. We feel however that due to its relatively recent growth in popularity, LSD has not had time to be adequately defined, evaluated and trialled. The potential of LSD for safety-critical regulated domains needs further detailed investigation.

Starting down the Lean/Agile road can be difficult. We believe it would be very useful to look at developing a roadmap for such companies to trial specific Lean/Agile practices within the constraints of their environments while minimising the risk to compliance.

While much focus is given to the more physical practices, very little is said about what corporate operating procedures are needed to be in place [30]. It would be useful to look at the governance of Lean/Agile software development in these domains with a view to identifying how to design policies and product lifecycles which support the software development teams in a Lean/Agile manner.

Finally, we noticed very little reference to the issues associated with Global Software Development (GSD). We feel that while GSD is currently well researched, it would be worthwhile to examine GSD issues within the safety-critical regulated industry.

Acknowledgements. This research is supported by Science Foundation Ireland (SFI) through the Principal Investigator Programme, grant no. 08/IN.1/I2030, and grant no. 03/CE2/I303.1 within Lero - the Irish Software Engineering Research Centre (http://www.lero.ie),

References

1. Womack, J.P., Jones, D.T., Roos, D.: The Machine That Changed The World: How lean production revolutionized the global car wars. Simon & Schuster Ltd., New York (2007)
2. Liker, J.: The Toyota Way. McGraw-Hill, New York (2003)
3. Highsmith, J.: Agile Software Development Ecosystems. Addison-Wesley, Reading (2002)
4. Poppendieck, M., Poppendieck, T.: Lean Software Development: An Agile Toolkit. Agile Software Development. Addison-Wesley Professional, Reading (2003)
5. Poppendieck, M., Poppendieck, T.: Implementing Lean Software Development From Concept to Cash. Addison-Wesley Professional, Reading (2006)
6. Hibbs, C., Jewett, S.C., Sullivan, M.: The Art of Lean Software Development, p. 128. O'Reilly Media, Sebastopol (2009)
7. RTCA, DO-178B: Software Considerations in Airborne Systems and Equipment Certification. RTCA, Radio Technical Commission for Aeronautics (1992)
8. ISO, ISO 13485:2003: Medical devices – Quality management systems – Requirements for regulatory purposes. International Organisation for Standardisation (2003).
9. Kitchenham, B., Charters, S.: Guidelines for performing Systematic Literature Reviews in Software Engineering (2007)
10. VanderLeest, S.H., Buter, A.: Escape the waterfall: Agile for aerospace. In: IEEE/AIAA 28th Digital Avionics Systems Conference, DASC 2009 (2009)

11. Wils, A., Van Baelan, S., Holvoet, T., De Vlaminck, K.: Agility in the avionics software world. In: Abrahamsson, P., Marchesi, M., Succi, G. (eds.) XP 2006. LNCS, vol. 4044, pp. 123–132. Springer, Heidelberg (2006)
12. Chisholm, R.A.: Agile Software Development Methods and DO-178B Certification. In: Division of Graduate Studies and Research. Royal Military College of Canada (2007)
13. Rottier, P.A., Rodrigues, V.: Agile Development in a Medical Device Company. In: AGILE 2008 Conference, pp. 218–223. IEEE Computer Society, Los Alamitos (2008)
14. Lin, W., Fan, X.: Software development practice for FDA-compliant medical devices. In: The International Joint Conference on Computational Sciences and Optimization, China (2009)
15. Spence, J.W.: There has to be a better way! In: AGILE Conference, Denver, CO, USA, pp. 272–278. IEEE Computer Society, Los Alamitos (2005)
16. Rasmussen, R., Hughes, T., Jenks, J.R., Skach, J.: Adopting Agile in an FDA Regulated Environment. In: Agile Conference, pp. 151–155. IEEE Computer Society, Los Alamitos (2009)
17. Cordeiro, L., Barreto, R., Barcelos, R., Oliveira, M., Lucena, V., Maciel, P.: TXM: an agile HW/SW development methodology for building medical devices. ACM SIGSOFT Softw. Eng. Notes 32(6), 4 (2007)
18. Kettunen, P., Laanti, M.: How to steer an embedded software project: tactics for selecting the software process model. Information and Software Technology (2005)
19. Srinivasan, J., Dobrin, R., Lundqvist, K.: State of the Art' in Using Agile Methods for Embedded Systems Development. In: Computer Software and Applications Conference (2009)
20. Sidky, A., Arthur, J.: Determining the Applicability of Agile Practices to Mission and Life-Critical Systems. In: Proceedings of the 31st IEEE Software Engineering Workshop (2007)
21. Grenning, J.: Extreme programming and embedded software development. In: Embedded Systems Conference (2002)
22. Yoo, J., Cha, S., Kim, C.H., Song, D.Y.: Synthesis of FBD-based PLC design from NuSCR formal specification. Reliability Engineering & System Safety (2005)
23. Tsai, W.T., Paul, R., Yu, L., Wei, X.: Rapid Pattern-Oriented Scenario-Based Testing for Embedded Systems. In: Yang, H. (ed.) Software Evolution with UML and XML (2005)
24. Ronkainen, J., Abrahamsson, P.: Software development under stringent hardware constraints: do agile methods have a chance? In: 4th International Conference on Extreme Programming and Agile Processes in Software Engineering (2003)
25. Ambler, S.W.: Imperfectly agile: You too can be agile! Dr. Dobb's Journal 31(10), 82–84 (2006)
26. Huffman Hayes, J., Dekhtyar, A., Janzen, D.S.: Towards traceable test-driven development. In: Proceedings of the ICSE Workshop on Traceability in Emerging Forms of Software Engineering, pp. 26–30. IEEE Computer Society, Los Alamitos (2009)
27. Ambler, S.W., Kroll, P.: Best practices for lean development governance (2007), http://www.ibm.com/developerworks/rational/library/jun07/kroll/
28. Van Schooenderwoert, N.: Safety-Critical Applications Built via Agile Discipline (2008), http://www.boston-spin.org/slides/boston_spin_slides_2008_09.pdf
29. Mueller, G., Borzuchowski, J.: Extreme embedded a report from the front line. In: OOPSLA 2002 Practitioners Reports (2002)
30. Poppendieck, M.: XP in a Safety-Critical Environment. Cutter IT (2002)

Lean and Agile Project Management:
For Large Programs and Projects

David F. Rico

Severn, Maryland, USA
dave1@davidfrico.com

Abstract. This talk discusses how agile methods can be used for managing high-risk, time-sensitive R&D-oriented new product development (NPD) projects with demanding customers and fast-changing market conditions. It establishes the context, provides a definition, and describes the value-system for lean and agile project management. It provides a brief survey of popular lean and agile project management approaches and illustrates the mechanisms for scaling the lean and agile project management model up to large-scale, distributed projects. It also illustrates a few key agile project management case studies as well as basic, burnup/burndown, cost estimating, business value, earned value management, and advanced metrics for agile methods including real options. Finally, this talk addresses the critical differences between agile and traditional non-agile project management paradigms, as well as the debate surrounding the pros and cons of agile certification.

Keywords: Lean thinking; lean development; agile methods; agile project management; complex adaptive systems; systems thinking; flexibility; high-performance teams; adaptive, iterative, incremental, collaborative, participative, and rolling wave planning; real options; business value; return on investment; costs and benefits; earned value management; metrics; models; measurements.

1 APM Introduction

Agile Project Management (APM) is a new paradigm for managing high-risk, time-sensitive, research and development-oriented new product development projects [1]. APM seems to be the ideal model for modern, post-industrial information age knowledge workers. In reality, however, APM has a long and rich history and lineage. Tenets of APM can be traced back to the principles of experimentation used by Louis Pasteur in the 1800s and Thomas Edison in the early 1900s, organismic biology by Bertalanffy in the 1920s, cybernetics by Weiner in the 1940s, systems theory by Boulding in the 1950s, systems dynamics by Forrester in the 1960s, double-loop learning by Argyris in the 1970s, learning organizations by Senge in the 1980s, adaptive planning by Highsmith in the 1990s, and many others who are too numerous to mention here [2]. The fundamental notion or theory underlying APM is that modern systems are complex, not well-understood, subject to the forces of dynamic and unstable market conditions, technology intensive, and constantly changing [3].

P. Abrahamsson and N. Oza (Eds.): LESS 2010, LNBIP 65, pp. 37–43, 2010.
© Springer-Verlag Berlin Heidelberg 2010

Counter to the principles of complex adaptive systems are traditional methods based on scientific management principles pioneered by Adam Smith and Frederick Taylor in the British and American industrial revolutions of the 1800s and 1900s [4]. Key ideas emerging from this paradigm were division of labor, specialization, time and motion, Gantt charts, mass production, hierarchical organizations, and most other principles associated with 20th century manufacturing. The basic notion behind traditional methods is that all system requirements can and should be documented, work breakdown structures should be carefully constructed, all activities should be defined and scheduled, cost and effort estimated, and then meticulously detailed project plans should be carefully controlled using techniques such as earned value management to within a 5% or 10% level of precision [5]. After software-intensive systems reached crisis proportions in the 1960s, the term software engineering was coined, and many people began applying principles of traditional methods to software development as a means of controlling project scope, time, and cost.

While the proponents of Taylorism attempted to control chaos with scientific management principles, others began to rediscover the job-shop practices used by highly creative and innovative individual artisans, mathematicians, and scientists throughout the ages [6]. Part of this rediscovery included the formation of the human school of management in the 1930s and 1940s, autonomous work groups in the 1950s, computerized manufacturing in the 1960s, flexible manufacturing in the 1970s, new product development in the 1980s, and lean thinking in the 1990s [7]. Although the leading thinkers had already discovered that incremental planning was superior to long-term strategic planning in the 1970s, it wasn't until 1994 that traditional methods were officially declared obsolete [8]. The basic notion behind modern ideas is that inductive thinking is better than reductionism, chaos can't be controlled, planning should be done a little bit at a time, planning should be participative with the key stakeholders it affects, products should be built in smaller chunks, and projects should be frequently re-planned to dynamically adapt to changing market conditions [9].

2   Types of Major APM Models

As large, heavyweight traditional methods including SW-CMM, CMMI, ISO 9001, ISO 12207, ISO 15288, PMBoK, SEBoK, and SWEBoK were in their golden age, agile methods finally emerged in the 1990s and 2000s [10]. Agile methods didn't appear out of thin air, but were firmly based on autonomous work groups from the 1950s, end user involvement from the 1960s, iterative development from the 1970s, and rapid application development from the 1980s [11]. The major ones emerged in this order, Crystal Methods, Scrum, Dynamic Systems Development Methodology, Feature-Driven Development, and finally Extreme Programming (XP). XP emerged in 1998 and took the world by storm. In 2001, the creators of these methods formed what is known as the Agile Manifesto, which was a common set of operating principles. It was based on four broad values: (1) customer collaboration, (2) iterative development, (3) self-organizing teams, and (4) adaptability to change [12]. Shortly on their heels emerged the paradigm of APM, with models such as release planning, sprint planning, radical project management, extreme project management, and APM.

2.1 Sprint Planning

Scrum, one of the earliest forms of agile methods, was created by Jeff Sutherland at Easel circa 1993 [13]. Scrum is generally comprised of four broad stages, sprint planning, sprints, sprint review meetings, and sprint retrospective meetings. However, more emphasis has been placed on the project management components of Scrum. One view of Scrum divides its project management model into two broad phases, initial planning and the sprint cycle. The initial planning sub-phase consists of a discovery session when projects are initiated, scoped, and organized. It also consists of a release planning sub-phase when a project backlog is formed consisting of prioritized user needs and a general timeline for multiple development sprints. The sprint cycle phase consists of a sprint planning sub-phase, the development sprint itself, daily team meetings, sprint reviews, and retrospectives.

2.2 Release Planning

XP, one of the most popular agile methods, was created by Kent Beck at Chrysler circa 1998 [14]. Scrum influenced the creation of XP, although Scrum's project management model was refined based on XP. Originally, XP was comprised of 13 practices: planning game, small releases, metaphor, simple design, tests, refactoring, pair programming, continuous integration, collective ownership, on-site customer, 40-hour weeks, open workspace, and just rules. However, XP's project management model is comprised of two broad phases, release planning and iteration planning. The release planning phase consists of three sub-phases, exploration, commitment, and steering. During this phase, user needs are captured, prioritized, and a release plan is formed with a timeline for multiple iterations. During the iteration planning phase, technical tasks are formed, estimated, and executed to build the product.

2.3 Extreme Project Management

Extreme Project Management (XPM) was created by Doug DeCarlo of the Cutter Consortium circa 2004 for all types of projects [15]. XPM's design was influenced by Rob Thomsett's Radical Project Management model, Jim Highsmith's APM model, and Kent Beck's XP model. Its motivation came from chaos theory and complex adaptive systems, and resembles a lightweight project management model for new product development. XPM consists of five broad phases: visionate, speculate, innovate, re-evaluate, and disseminate. A broad vision for the project and product is formed during the visionate phase. The output of the speculate phase is a project plan and the innovate phase is used to iteratively develop the solution. Finally, the project's and product's status are assessed during the re-evaluate phase and products are distributed to customers in the disseminate phase if they are successful.

2.4 Agile Project Management I

Another APM model was created by Sanjiv Augustine, then of CC Pace, circa 2004 [16]. Sanjiv's model was influenced by Jeff Sutherland's Scrum model, Kent Beck's XP model, and Jim Highsmith's APM model. Sanjiv's model focused on two broad areas, a leadership model to establish the organizational culture for agile methods and a broad framework for managing agile projects. There are three broad phases in Sanjiv's model: foster alignment and cooperation, encourage emergence and self organization, and learning/adaptation. The first phase consists of establishing organic teams and an overall project and product vision. The second phase consists of establishing simple rules, a climate of open information exchange, and light-touch for just the right balance of flexibility and discipline. The last phase focuses on learning and adaption at both the organizational and project levels.

2.5 Agile Project Management II

An influential model of APM was created by Jim Highsmith of the Cutter Consortium circa 2004 [17]. The design of Jim's model was influenced by Rob Thomsett's Radical Project Management model, Jeff Sutherland's Scrum model, and Kent Beck's XP model. Jim's model is based on four major ideas, establishing a project and product vision, planning for multiple releases, using agile practices for product development, and bringing administrative closure to a project. There are two broad phases in Jim's model, innovation lifecycle and iterative delivery. The first phase consists of envisioning a product, speculating or creating a release plan, exploring the product's development, launching a successful product, and closing it out administratively. The second phase consists of technical planning, product development, operational testing, adaptation, deployment, and a variety of other activities such as continuous integration.

3   Scaling APM to Large Programs and Projects

As use of agile methods spread, traditional methodologists felt they were only for very small projects, although they were never designed with this limitation in-mind [18]. Literature emerged that exhibited the applicability and scalability of agile methods to large programs and projects. Some of the major techniques for doing so included multi-level teams, plans, backlogs, coordination, and governance [19]. Multi-level teams are comprised of product management teams who primarily interface to the customer, release management teams who plan agile projects, and feature teams who are responsible for managing day to day development. Multi-level plans consist of product roadmaps, release plans for multiple iterations, and iteration plans for day to day activity. Multi-level backlogs consist of capabilities or epics, feature sets or themes, and user stories or system-level requirements. Multi-level coordination consists of capability teams, feature-set teams, and feature teams (also known as a Scrum of Scrums). Multi-level governance also consists of governing, functional, and feature teams for establishing program and project policies, standards, processes, tools, and non-functional requirements. Numerous other scaling techniques are emerging from the literature on distributed teams.

4   Metrics and Models for APM

Many seek to identify the right blend of metrics and models for APM [20]. For some, the goal is to map traditional metrics to those of agile methods. For instance, basic metrics for size, effort, productivity, complexity, quality, testing, and reliability apply to agile projects as well as traditional ones. However, size and productivity may be measured in terms of story points, which is similar to function points. Productivity or velocity refers to story points per sprint or iteration, and are tracked using burndown or burnup charts. This gives a basic measure of work completed within a two to four week period. Basic effort and cost models are starting to emerge based on lines of code, function points, and user stories per hour [21]. Business value is measured in terms of costs, benefits, breakeven point, benefit to cost ratio, return on investment, net present value and real options [22], [23]. Some are willing to adopt the use of agile methods, so long as they can apply earned value management, which led to the emergence of AgileEVM [24]. However, agile project plans have a much shorter time horizon than traditional ones, and change frequently. While traditional projects are designed for small changes, agile projects are designed for larger size, cost, and scope changes, as long as it results in greater business value.

5 APM Case Studies

Thousands of projects are now using agile methods on a world-wide basis. As a result, hundreds of APM case studies have emerged over the last 20 years. While it is not the purpose to analyze all of them, five agile case studies will be examined here, by Google, Primavera, FDA, FBI, and the U.S. DoD, in order to illustrate the range of industries applying APM. As an illustration of electronic commerce, Google used Scrum on one of its largest projects, Ad words, in order to improve project planning, estimation, and quality [25]. As an example of the shrink-wrapped software industry, Primavera used Scrum on a 100 person team to achieve dramatic quality improvements and cycle time reductions [26]. As an example of the highly-regulated healthcare market for safety-critical systems, Abbott used Extreme Programming to achieve significant cost, schedule, staff-size, and quality improvements [27]. As an example of a large, traditional civilian law enforcement government agency's enterprise-scale data warehouses, HPTI used Extreme Programming to achieve dramatic productivity and quality improvements [28]. Finally, as an example of a large, traditional U.S. DoD government agency enterprise-level web services, FGM used Extreme Programming to improve teamwork, productivity, and quality [29].

6 APM Summary

APM is a fundamentally new paradigm, and is not simply a lighter weight traditional project management approach. At its core, APM is also based upon the four major values of agile methods: (1) customer collaboration, (2) iterative development, (3) self-organizing teams, and (4) adaptability to change. Therefore, new metrics should be used to reflect these four values, rather than simply applying traditional measures. On average, APM results in 50% improvements in cost, schedule, quality, and personnel resources [30]. Agile certification is a topic of debate, although it helps form a common understanding of processes and terminology, create a more disciplined workforce, show a commitment to its values, and result in recognition

[31]. Common agile myths are slowly being disproven: they are only for small co-located software teams, they don't scale up to large projects, and they are undisciplined. A frequently asked question is "When is it appropriate to use traditional versus agile methods?" Early theories asserted that traditional methods were better for large projects, while agile methods were for small ones [32]. Also, it's important to remember that agile methods were designed to address the uncertainty and instability of large projects (and they were created to overcome the high failure rates associated with using traditional methods on projects of all sizes).

References

1. Thomsett, R.: Radical Project Management. Prentice-Hall, Upper Saddle River (2002)
2. Rico, D.F.: Effects of Agile Methods on Website Quality for Electronic Commerce (2007), http://davidfrico.com/rico07q.pdf
3. Chin, G.: Agile Project Management: How to Succeed in the Face of Changing Project Requirements, Amacom, Broadway (2004)
4. Pine, B.J.: Mass Customization: The New Frontier in Business Competition. Harvard Business School Press, Boston (1992)
5. PMBoK Guide: A Guide to the Project Management Body of Knowledge. Technical report, Project Management Institute (2008)
6. Thomke, S.: Experimentation Matters: Unlocking the Potential of New Technologies for Innovation. Harvard Business School Publishing, Boston (2003)
7. Shafritz, J.M., Ott, J.S.: Classics of Organization Theory. Wadsworth, New York (2001)
8. Mintzberg, H.: The Rise and Fall of Strategic Planning. Free Press, New York (1994)
9. Reinertsen, D.G.: The Principles of Product Development Flow: Second Generation Lean Product Development. Celeritas, Redondo Beach (2010)
10. Highsmith, J.A.: Agile Software Development Ecosystems. Addison-Wesley, Boston (2002)
11. Rico, D.F., Sayani, H.H., Field, R.F.: History of Computers, Electronic Commerce, and Agile Methods. In: Zelkowitz, M.V. (ed.) Advances in Computers: Emerging Technologies, vol. 73, pp. 3–55. Elsevier, San Diego (2008)
12. Agile Manifesto (2001), http://www.agilemanifesto.org
13. Schwaber, K.: Agile Project Management with Scrum. Microsoft Press, Redmond (2004)
14. Beck, K., Fowler, M.: Planning Extreme Programming. Addison-Wesley, Upper Saddle River (2001)
15. DeCarlo, D.: Extreme Project Management: Using Leadership. In: Principles and Tools to Deliver Value in the Face of Volatility. Jossey-Bass, San Francisco (2004)
16. Augustine, S.: Managing Agile Projects. Pearson Education, Upper Saddle River (2005)
17. Highsmith, J.A.: Agile Project Management: Creating Innovative Products. Pearson Education, Boston (2009)
18. Boehm, B.W.: Get Ready for Agile Methods with Care. IEEE Computer 35, 64–69 (2002)
19. Leffingwell, D.: Scaling Software Agility: Best Practices for Large Enterprises. Pearson Education, Boston (2007)
20. Jones, C.: Estimating Software Costs: Bringing Realism to Estimating. McGraw-Hill, New York (2007)
21. Rico, D.F.: What is the ROI of Agile vs. Traditional Methods? TickIT International 10, 9–18 (2008)

22. Rico, D.F.: ROI of Software Process Improvement: Metrics for Project Managers and Software Engineers. J. Ross, Boca Raton (2004)
23. Rico, D.F., Sayani, H.H., Sone, S.: The Business Value of Agile Software Methods: Maximizing ROI with Just-in-Time Processes and Documentation. J. Ross, Ft. Lauderdale (2009)
24. Sulaiman, T., Barton, B., Blackburn, T.: Agile EVM: Earned Value Management in Scrum Projects. In: Agile Conference, pp. 7–16. IEEE Press, New York (2006)
25. Striebeck, M.: Ssh: We are Adding a Process. In: Agile Conference, pp. 193–201. IEEE Press, New York (2006)
26. Schatz, B., Abdelshafi, I.: Primavera Gets Agile: A Successful Transition to Agile Development. IEEE Software 22, 36–42 (2005)
27. Rasmussen, R., Hughes, T., Jenks, J.R., Skach, J.: Adopting Agile in an FDA Regulated Environment. In: Agile Conference, pp. 151–155. IEEE Press, New York (2009)
28. Babuscio, J.: How the FBI Learned to Catch Bad Guys One Iteration at a Time. In: Agile Conference, pp. 96–100. IEEE Press, New York (2009)
29. Fruhling, A., McDonald, P., Dunbar, C.: A Case Study: Introducing Extreme Programming in a U.S. Government System Development Project. In: 41st Annual Hawaii International Conference on System Sciences, pp. 464–473. IEEE Press, New York (2008)
30. Mah, M.: Measuring Agile in the Enterprise. In: Agile Conference, IEEE Press, New York (2008)
31. Ambler, S.W.: Coming Soon: Agile Certification. Dr. Dobb's Journal 32, 67–69 (2007)
32. Boehm, B., Turner, R.: Balancing Agility and Discipline: A Guide for the Perplexed. Addison-Wesley, Boston (2004)

When Agile Is Not Enough

Kati Vilkki

Nokia Siemens Networks, Linnoitustie 6, FI-02600 Finland
Kati.Vilkki@nsn.com

Abstract. Agile provides a good framework for improving software development, but it is not enough to get true improvement in the way the whole organization functions or to get significant business benefits. Very seldom an organization's biggest problems are in software development. More often they are in interfaces of different functions or not understanding well enough what business the organization is in and what do customers really want. For these purposes, it is argued, that lean thinking gives better tools to understand and address the underlying problems. It is shown that lean and agile complement each other in many areas, but there are also challenges in combining the two approaches. Lean addresses the role of management, which agile mostly omits. It is argued that combining lean thinking with Scrum means actually going to the roots of Scrum; Scrum has been influenced by lean thinking, so there is no inherent conflict.

Keywords: Lean thinking, lean software development, agile software development, Scrum.

1 Introduction

Agile provides a good framework ´for improving software development, but in my experience it is not enough to get true improvement in the way the whole organization functions or to get significant business benefits. Agile is just not enough when software is only part of the product, in very large-scale development (i.e., tens of teams, systems of systems development), or when there is need to improve the way the whole organization works. Yet, this is the case most often.

Very seldom an organization's biggest problems are in software development,. Rather, more often they are in interfaces of different functions, or not understanding well enough what business the organization is in and what do customers really want. Even though it very often looks like we have an "R&D problem" or "software quality problem" the root causes of these problems are somewhere else than R&D or software. Lean thinking approaches the problem more holistically and thereby offers better tools to understand and address the underlying problems.

This paper is based on experiences gathered from several years of agile transformation in a multi-technology, multi-site, multi-cultural and large software development organization. The transformation begun in 2005 and still continues. The author has been the responsible leader of the transformation since its inception. Over

P. Abrahamsson and N. Oza (Eds.): LESS 2010, LNBIP 65, pp. 44–47, 2010.

the years, significant progress has been done from a single or few team experiments to the transformation of several business units from waterfall based software development to agile and lean development. We have now come to an understanding how far a transformation can carry with the operational and thinking tools offered by agile methods.

2   Comparing and Contrasting Agile and Lean Approaches

It is not fair to blame "agile of not being enough"; agile methods are meant for software development and the thinking behind is very much team and software oriented, so it is not possible for agile to cover all the needed areas. Therefore, we decided to combine lean thinking to our agile adaptation.

We have experienced that lean and agile complement each other in many areas, but there are also challenges in combining these two. Since agile is team oriented, a bottom-up approach works well in the agile adaptation. However, the limits of one team and the bottom-up approach are very soon reached in large organizations. This is especially the case when interfaces of different functions should be changed or the whole organization should be seen as one system. One team simply does not have the needed knowledge or power to influence.

Lean requires a top-down approach, involvement of larger organizations and the management. Of course lean thinking and many lean tools can be used also on team level, but again, to get the full benefits of lean, team level changes are not enough.

So the question is how to combine a bottom-up with top-down approaches in agile and lean transition. This is an interesting question since it is actually the same question as how to combine self-organized teams and the ability of the whole organization to move towards the same direction and work together. Based on my experience, I think this is the reason the question has proven to be very difficult for organizations to answer. In fact, I claim that many have been unable to answer it at all, which is one reason for the failed or only partially successful agile and lean transitions.

Combining the two approaches requires a deep understanding of the lean thinking from the managers of the organization. If they do not take the time to learn about lean principles and what they mean for the whole organization and especially for leadership and management practices, there is little chance for real improvement.

The management and leadership practices are closely connected to the role of managers, which agile and lean view very differently. In agile methods, for example, the line managers are omitted completely, and many organizations in agile transition struggle with what is the role of line managers in agile – or even if there is any role.

Scrum has become the *de facto* agile method or at least the agile management framework, because of its seeming simplicity and the fact that it tries to address some issues connected to management roles. Two new roles – i.e. Product Owner and Scrum Master – are introduced with Scrum, but what happens to the existing manager roles? Just adding two new management roles and thus increasing management overhead is likely to cause conflict between new and old management roles. Thereby, in my experience, this is not a good solution. Neither the removal of all the old management roles is feasible because in large organizations the two Scrum roles are simply not enough. While, some Scrum enthusiasts may claim differently, scaling up the Scrum roles is at least needed, e.g. Enterprise Scrum Master and head Product Owner roles.

Software forms only a part of the product in many systems development endeavors, or in large organizations altogether. Therefore, scaling up only a few roles is not sufficient. The teams are seldom truly cross-functional or they would have an end-to-end responsibility or even visibility. Rather, they are cross-functional within R&D or one part of the R&D, but they do not cover sales, manufacturing, delivery etc. It is easy to say that the solution is to make the teams truly end-to-end, but with products that require thousands of people to develop, involve tens of factories in building the products, a cross-functional team approach is not the solution.

Lean gives much better answers to role of management; lean addresses the role of management, which agile mostly omits. Combining lean thinking with Scrum means actually going to the roots of Scrum; Scrum has been influenced by lean thinking, so there is no inherent conflict.

Mary Poppendieck [e.g., 1] calls the two main management roles in lean product development the Product Champion (vs. Product Owner) and competency leader, which is a coaching line manager role and can be combined with Scrum master role at least after the first step of agile transition.

The Product Champion provides an engaging vision and direction to the teams involved in developing and delivering the product. The coaching line manager is focused in helping individuals and team to grow to their full potential.

There is one issue where both agile and lean thinking are unanimous about: the traditional role of command and control managers is not needed. This is might be very difficult for organizations to give up. R&D line managers very often complain that they don't have any time for the truly important issues – with which they mean coaching people or keeping up the technical excellence of the product or the teams. Instead all their time goes to reporting, planning and having useless meetings. Many managers find the idea of self-organizing team a relief after the initial shock and are able to find themselves a meaningful role as a coach or a technical leader.

But managers find it very often difficult to change their role to a more meaningful one because of management processes and organizational expectations towards manager role. An individual manager can feel powerless when facing the whole corporate machinery. We have noticed that in order for the teams to be self-organized, also managers need to empower themselves to start challenging dysfunctional organizational practices and policies. For this a whole new management philosophy is needed. Changing organizational practices is much easier to do when the whole management team working together on this, as a team. We have got the best results of coaching whole management teams instead of individual managers.

3 Conclusions

This paper has maintained that agile provides a good framework for improving software development, but it is not enough to get true improvement in the way the whole organization functions or to get significant business benefits. Lean thinking gives better tools to understand and address the underlying problems. Lean and agile complement each other in many areas, but there are also challenges in combining the two approaches. One of the more serious concerns raised was the role of other functions than software development.

In order for a successful agile and lean transition, many of the traditional financial, planning and human resource practices need also be changed. They do not support the new line manager role, empowerment or a lean way of working. Neither agile nor lean address these corporate level management issues very clearly. Due to these issues we are now experimenting with bringing in some thoughts from Beyond Budgeting [e.g., 2] school of thinking.

In conclusion, so agile is not enough, we need a change in the whole management philosophy. Agile, lean and beyond budgeting complement each other nicely and are based on sufficiently similar principles of customer focus, understanding where the value comes from, empowering front line people and making decisions where the knowledge is.

References

1. Poppendieck, M., Poppendieck, T.: Leading Lean Software Development. Addison-Wesley, Reading (2009)
2. Bogsnes, B.: Implementing Beyond Budgeting: Unlocking the Performance Potential. John Wiley & Sons, Inc, Hoboken (2009)

Refactoring the Organization

Ken Power

Cisco Systems, Inc, Galway, Ireland
ken.power@gmail.com

Abstract. Every organization has a design. As an organization grows, that design evolves. A decision to embrace agile and lean methods can expose weaknesses in the design. The concept of refactoring as applied to software design helps to improve the overall structure of the product or system. Principles of refactoring can also be applied to organization design. As with software design, the design of our organization can benefit from deliberate improvement efforts, but those efforts must have a purpose, and must serve the broad community of stakeholders that affect, or are affected by, the organization. Refactoring to agile and lean organizations demands that we have a shared vision of what the refactoring needs to achieve, and that we optimize the organization around the people doing the work.

Keywords: agile, lean, organization design, stakeholder, stakeholder management, refactoring, metaphor, Jazz, artful making, organization patterns.

1 Introduction

Any organization can be viewed as a set of social structures. As firms grow, people make choices about how to structure themselves. Organizations within organizations emerge or are created. As with software designs, the organization design that emerges is not always what was envisioned. As organizations embrace agile and lean development we find we need to refactor our organization structures so they are optimized to support, rather than control, the people who do the work. We need to question traditional management philosophies about how to organize and manage work. We need to acknowledge that everyone involved in the development of our products, from concept to cash, has some stake in the outcome of what we do. We need to adopt effective strategies that help us identify and engage with those people that influence, or are influenced by, our organizations and processes. This paper, and the accompanying talk, brings together a set of concepts that help with organization design and refactoring.

2 Refactoring

Refactoring has a long tradition in the field of Object-Oriented software development. Martin Fowler described refactoring the design of existing code [1]. Refactoring is one of the technical practices of XP [2]. Although Fowler's refactorings talk about code and software design, we can take the concept of refactoring and apply it to

P. Abrahamsson and N. Oza (Eds.): LESS 2010, LNBIP 65, pp. 48–51, 2010.

organizations. The process of refactoring a software design is typically performed one refactoring at a time, with a vision of what the end result will look like, and with a goal of not breaking the system. This talk will discuss some refactorings that can be applied to organizations, where the organization is anything from a team to a business unit, to an entire firm.

3 Stakeholders

Although the term stakeholder is often used in software development, it is often limited to customers, end-users, or project sponsors. Where there is deeper mention of stakeholders, they typically treat the development team or 'the customer' as a single stakeholder. Stakeholder management provides us with a set of tools for identifying and engaging with the broad group of stakeholders that affect, or are affected by our organizations, and helps us understand what their stake is [3]. Applying principles of stakeholder management helps our agile and lean organizations to be successful, and gives us a context in which to apply organization-level refactorings. Any changes made to the organization are done so to balance the needs of multiple stakeholders. Freeman identifies seven techniques or strategies for creating value for stakeholders, including stakeholder assessment, stakeholder behavior analysis, understanding stakeholders in more depth, assessing stakeholder strategies, developing specific strategies for stakeholders, creating new models of interaction for stakeholders, developing integrative value creation strategies [3]. To successfully ship a product or deliver a service, it helps to understand who has a stake in our product, our services, and our organizations. It also helps to understand that the nature of that stake or claim changes over time. Related research shows how stakeholder management principles can be applied to help organizations create structures that support Scrum teams [4].

4 Metaphors as a Tool for Engaging Stakeholders

When creating or changing organization structures to support agile and lean development, it is often difficult to know when we are 'done'. Indeed, if we truly embrace agile and lean principles then we are never 'done'. Rather, we are in a state of continuous deliberate improvement. Metaphors provide a powerful way to develop a shared vision, and can help shape how people perceive an idea. This is particularly useful when discussing organization design. The eventual outcome may not be clear or easy to articulate. It helps to have a guiding metaphor, or set of metaphors.

4.1 Jazz Improvisation

Barrett describes what we can learn from Jazz as an enabling metaphor for creativity and innovation in organization learning [5]. He describes seven features of jazz improvisation that organizations can apply to create more innovative and adaptive environments. The first of these is *provocative competence*. Organizations will routinely fall back on hold habits and established routines, unless they deliberately embed experimentation and create structures that inspire alternative possibilities. The second feature is *embracing errors as a source of learning*. Errors are a vital source of learning, yet organizations can grow to discourage errors and minimize risk-taking. The third feature is *minimal structures that allow maximum flexibility*. Large bureaucratic organizations with too many rigid rules stifle innovation and creativity. The fourth feature is what Barrett describes as *distributed task*: continual negotiation toward dynamic synchronization. The fifth feature is *reliance on retrospective sense-making*. The sixth feature is *"Hanging out": Membership in communities of practice*. The idea of communities of practice is taking root in agile development circles too, and is seen as an alternative to traditional functional hierarchies. The seventh feature is *alternating between soloing and supporting*. Jazz ensembles usually rotate the leadership role. Members each get an opportunity to develop an idea, and are supported by the rest of the group.

4.2 Collaborative Arts

Artful Making proposes a framework for knowledge work that draws inspiration from the world of collaborative arts and theatre production. Austin and Devin note that "*as business becomes more dependent on knowledge to create value, work becomes more like art*" [6]. The Artful Making framework is iterative, not sequential, and involves repeated cycles of talking with the customer about the product, creating incremental versions of the product, and showing the product to the customer for feedback. The environment required to support an artful making process is similar to that required to support teams in an agile and lean organization. There are four basic attributes, or qualities, of an artful making process. The first is called *release*, and is a form of control that expects wide variation within known parameters. The second attribute is *collaboration*, and relies on experienced, skilled professionals coming together in a spirit of openness where they allow new and unpredictable ideas to emerge. Collaboration is not the same as compromise. The third quality is *ensemble*, where people come together in collaboration to create something that is more than the sum of the individual parts; more than any individual party could have conceived off alone. The fourth quality is *play*, and is the quality exhibited by the interactions between the customer and the group creating the product.

5 Organization Patterns

The organization patterns identified by Coplien and Harrison address specific stakeholders, and the relationships between stakeholders [7]. Viewed in this context the patterns provide guidance on building effective stakeholder relationships within software development organizations. The authors consider an organization as a social system with structures, and in that context they identify patterns that have helped software companies to achieve improved efficiencies in organization and performance. They group the patterns into four pattern languages, each of which addresses a particular set of problems. There is a pattern language for project management, growth of the product and process, organization style and role relationships, and people and code.

6 Conclusion

Organization design can benefit from principles of refactoring. Our organizations have stakeholders. In product development we often take too narrow a view of who those stakeholders are, and what their stake really is. The principles of stakeholder management help us to identify, understand and engage with the many diverse range of stakeholders. When refactoring an organization's design to support agile and lean development, we aim to optimize the structures of the organization around the people who are doing the work. To be meaningful, refactoring must have a purpose. Metaphors provide a useful tool to communicate that purpose. Jazz improvisation and Artful Making are two useful enabling metaphors for understanding the rich and complex interactions between the many and varied stakeholders in a product development organization. Finally, Organization Patterns provide a rich body of knowledge that compliments agile and lean, and that provides proven patterns for engaging stakeholders and guiding changes in the design of our organization.

References

1. Fowler, M.: Refactoring: improving the design of existing code. The Addison-Wesley Object Technology Series. Addison-Wesley, Reading (1999)
2. Beck, K.: Extreme programming explained: embrace change. Addison-Wesley, Reading (2000)
3. Freeman, R.E., Harrison, J.S., Wicks, A.C.: Managing for stakeholders: survival, reputation, and success. The Business Roundtable Institute For Corporate Ethics Series in Ethics and Leadership, New Haven, Conn., Yale University Press, London (2007)
4. Power, K.: Stakeholder Identification in Agile Software Product Development Organizations. In: Agile Conference 2010. IEEE Computer Society, Orlando (2010)
5. Barrett, F.J.: Creativity and improvisation in jazz and organizations: implications for organizational learning. Organization Science 9, 605–622 (1998)
6. Austin, R.D., Devin, L.: Artful making: what managers need to know about how artists work. Financial Times Prentice Hall. Financial Times/Prentice Hall, Upper Saddle River (2003)
7. Coplien, J.O., Harrison, N.: Organizational patterns of agile software development. Pearson Prentice Hall, Upper Saddle River (2004)

A Journey to Systemic Improvement

David Joyce

ThoughWorks Australia
dpjoyce@googlemail.com

Abstract. Various Agile methods focus on delivering "value" or "valuable working software" or "delivering quality code" but what if we are just doing the wrong thing righter? A more recent development has been the popularity of "Lean" thinking for IT. However there is far more to a successful intervention than mapping value streams and finding then removing "waste". I also see a series of anti patterns forming:

- Traditional IT leaves "knowledge of the work" to a mixture of Business Analysts, Product Owners, proxy customers and managers views.
- Those within IT often point to meeting the needs of the "business" as if they are the ones who produce revenue for the organisation. The customer becomes forgotten.
- The approach of IT implementation is "push" - here is the new IT system, now how do we get people to use it?

I believe decisions about the use of IT should be taken from a position of knowing the "what and why" of current performance as a system. In the Systems Thinking approach IT is "pulled", the people doing the work understand the "what and why" and "pull" IT into parts of the work, knowing what to expect. The first part of this talk is an overview of Systems Thinking theory, and more specifically how it can be applied to IT and what benefits this will bring. Part two of this talk revolves around a series of experience reports using the Systems Thinking Method in both IT and non-IT areas within BBC worldwide.

David Joyce

David is an agile coach with 12 years technical team management and coaching experience, and 20 years software development experience. In recent years, using Scrum and XP, David has coached onshore and offshore teams and successfully launched an internet video startup from inception to launch. More recently David has coached teams on Lean, Kanban and Systems Thinking at BBC Worldwide in the UK. David currently works for Thoughtworks as a principal consultant and is a Systems Thinker, Lean practitioner, Kanban coach and certified Scrum Master. David recently received the Lean SSC Brickell Key award for outstanding achievement and leadership.

P. Abrahamsson and N. Oza (Eds.): LESS 2010, LNBIP 65, p. 52, 2010.

Complexity vs. Lean, the Big Showdown

Jurgen Appelo

Author/CIO
jurgen@noop.nl

Abstract. Agile software development is (in part) based on the idea that software teams are complex adaptive systems (CAS), and many experts (like Jeff Sutherland, Jim Highsmith, Sanjiv Augustine, Joseph Pelrine) have borrowed terms from complexity theory ("self-organization", "emergence") to explain how software teams work. During a panel session at the Scan-Agile 2009 conference in Helsinki I asked panel members Mary Poppendieck (lean development) and Dave Snowden (complexity theory) what the difference is between complexity thinking and lean thinking. Is there a difference? How do Complexity and Lean "see" each other? Unfortunately, due to some confusion, the question never got answered and the conference moved on. Afterwards Mary Poppendieck told me honestly that she didn't really know how to answer that question. And maybe the other panel members had the same problem. ☺ Now I suggest that I try to answer that question myself. My upcoming book about complexity science and management of software teams has made me think a lot about topics like these. I think I have some interesting ideas that would lead to good discussions. Some examples:

1. Lean software development promotes removing waste as one of its principles. However, complexity science seems to show that waste can have various functions. In complex systems things that look like waste can actually be a source for stability and innovation;
2. Lean software development preaches optimize the whole as a principle, and then translates this to optimization of the value chain. However, I believe that complexity science shows us a value chain is an example of linear thinking, which usually leads to sub-optimization of the whole organization because it is a non-linear complex system;

My suggestion is therefore to organize a talk and discussion where I present the concepts of complexity theory, and how this relates to Lean thinking. I will then try and "challenge" a few basic assumptions in Lean software development as a Devil's Advocate. The audience will discuss the issues with me, and either they decide that my "challenges" don't hold, or they agree with me and accept some nuance to the basic Lean principles. Either way, we will all learn and have fun!

Jurgen Appelo

Jurgen is a writer, speaker, developer, entrepreneur, manager, blogger, reader, dreamer, leader, freethinker, and... Dutch guy. After studying Software Engineering at the Delft University of Technology, and earning his Master's degree in 1994,

P. Abrahamsson and N. Oza (Eds.): LESS 2010, LNBIP 65, pp. 53–54, 2010.
© Springer-Verlag Berlin Heidelberg 2010

Jurgen Appelo has busied himself starting up and leading a variety of Dutch businesses, always in the position of team leader, manager or executive.

Jurgen's current occupation is Business Unit Manager at Sociotoco, and Chief Information Officer at ISM eCompany. With 200 employees it is one of the leading e-commerce solution providers in The Netherlands. As a manager, Jurgen has experience in leading a horde of 100 software developers, development managers, project managers, business consultants, quality managers, service managers and kangaroos, some of which he hired accidentally.

Jurgen is primarily interested in software engineering, quality improvement and complexity theory, from a manager's perspective. As a writer he has published a number of papers and articles in several magazines, including Dr. Dobb's, Software Quality Professional, Methods & Tools, The Software Practitioner, StickyMinds, Software Development Network, Computable and Automatisering Gids. He is also a speaker, being regularly invited to talk at seminars and conferences about agile software development, project management, process improvement, and development management.

However, sometimes he puts all writing, speaking and managing aside to do some intensive programming himself, or to spend time on his ever-growing collection of science fiction and fantasy literature, which he stacks in a self-designed book case, which is 4 meters high.

Lean Product Development and Innovation – Track Summary

Jayakanth Srinivasan[1] and Karl Scotland[2]

[1] Lean Advancement Initiative, Massachusetts Institute of Technology, USA
jksrini@mit.edu
[2] EMC Consulting, United Kingdom
kjscotland@googlemail.com

Abstract. The words lean, product development, and innovation have unique implications for software organizations. Most lean software implementations have focused on the individual work practices rather than attempt to take a system approach. This is consistent with the evolution on lean thinking. Similarly even though innovation is the lifeblood of software organizations, few are successful at sustaining their innovation efforts. We believe that lean product development serves as a bridge to connect lean enterprise thinking and innovation in a mutually reinforcing manner. The program we have put together focuses on blending research and practice to provide the conference attendee with immediately usable tools, tips and techniques, and at the same time create the foundation for creating a lean system of innovation.

Keywords: lean enterprise, product development, agile software development, innovation.

1 Introduction

Lean and Innovation have both been touted as transformational strategies that are essential to long term survival of organizations – and yet there remains a perception that they are often at odds with each other. In this paper, we briefly touch upon some of the key ideas from both streams of knowledge, and discuss how the research and practice presented in this track aim to extend our understanding of lean innovation, and present ways of seeing them as approaches that are complementary and mutually reinforcing.

1.1 From Lean Production to Lean Enterprises

The elevation of classical lean practices from production to the enterprise level can be traced back to the first widely published academic paper [1] on the Toyota production system in 1977. At the heart of Toyota's successful evolution from a supplier of trucks to the US Army in Japan post World War II to the largest automotive manufacturer in the world is the combination of an efficient and effective production system, and a system for growing human capital. While lean principles and practices

P. Abrahamsson and N. Oza (Eds.): LESS 2010, LNBIP 65, pp. 55–59, 2010.
© Springer-Verlag Berlin Heidelberg 2010

were taking hold in Japan at that time, there was little evidence that these concepts could be applied outside either the Japanese or the manufacturing context. The groundbreaking IMVP study that resulted in the 'Machine that Changed the World' [2], highlighted the successes that Toyota was having in steadily increasing their market share, while at the same time lowering costs and improving quality. The focus of the early lean work was on understanding the production system alone, lead to the common misunderstanding that the practices were best suited to, and successful in the manufacturing shop-floor. Womack and Jones [3] provided one of the first attempts at generalizing the understanding of the Toyota Production System (TPS) through their five principles of lean thinking. Although their ideas were drawn from studying the automotive industry in general, other researchers began to test the applicability of the principles in other domains. Their emphasis on waste-elimination led to the proliferation of tools ranging from value stream mapping to kanban systems.

The work of Murman et al. [4] in applying lean principles to the aerospace industry resulted in five lean enterprise principles that reframed lean efforts as being focused on value creation as opposed to solely waste elimination. 'Lean Enterprise Value' was one of the first books to advocate the need for an understanding of the enterprise value proposition as a basis for transformation efforts. Their research across government and industry reemphasized the need to connect production processes to human-oriented processes. The continued research in the Lean Advancement Initiative at MIT on enterprise transformation resulted in the development of the seven enterprise transformation principles [5]. The emphasis on principles is driven by the fact that they are flexible and capable of adaptation to the appropriate level. We are beginning to see lean be applied in the software context, but a majority of efforts have been focused on work practices rather than on taking a holistic systems approach.

1.2 Understanding Innovation

The importance of innovation for organizational success can be traced back to Schumpeter [6], wherein he defines innovation as:

> "Changes of the combinations of the factors of production as cannot be effected by infinitesimal steps or variations in the margin. They consist primarily in changes in the methods of production and transportation, or in the production of a new article, or in the opening up of new markets or of new sources of materiel."

This definition of innovation has stood the test of time, and while ideas like entrepreneurship have emerged in more recent time, the essence of innovation remains the same. As Drucker [7] points out almost 50 years after Schumpeter when discussing innovation:

> "It is the means by which the entrepreneur either creates new wealth-producing resources or endows existing resources with enhanced potential for creating wealth."

In other words, innovation can be in the product or the process [8]. It can be classified based on the whether it is incremental or radical [9], or modular or architectural [10]. At the heart of the innovation puzzle is the ability to connect the strategy and tactics associated with the macro perspective, with the mechanics of effectively transitioning ideas into finished products and services at the micro-level. The four factors that Van de Ven identified in 1986 as being key to successful innovation [11], namely, the human problem of managing attention, the process problem of managing good ideas into good currency, the structural problem of managing part-whole relationships, and the strategic problem of institutional leadership, remain relevant today. For software organizations, these questions are magnified when operating under the constraints of billable hours, and blurring identities between the client organization and the developer organization (when the project is outsourced/offshored).

1.3 Lean Product Development

Lean Product Development brings the two ideas of lean and innovation together to enable organizations to achieve sustainable competitive advantage. Hoppmann integrated a detailed literature review (the included [12], with an extensive survey of 113 companies to identify the eleven practices that collectively comprised the state of the art on lean product development [13]. The eleven practices: Strong Project Manager, Set-based Engineering, Process Standardization, Specialist Career Path, Product Variety Management, Workload Leveling, Supplier Integration, Responsibility-based Planning and Control, Cross-project Knowledge Transfer, Rapid Prototyping, Simulation und Testing, Simultaneous Engineering when clustered and ranked, provide a roadmap for organizations that are attempting to adopt lean product development.

In more recent work, Gordon et al. [14] surveyed 300 employees across North America and Europe in the automotive, high-tech and medical devices industries to understand if there were unique characteristics for product development success. The data from 28 organizations showed that the ones with the best track record for product development: a. had a set of clear project goals early in the lifecycle, they nurtured a strong project culture, and maintained contact with their customers throughout the project's lifecycle. For software organizations that have adopted agile methods successfully, the last two are already taking place, but the first is a function of customer-driven uncertainty, rather than team driven uncertainty. Gordon et al found that teams that embraced the three tactics were 17 times as likely as the laggards to have projects come in on time, five times as likely to be on budget, and twice as likely to meet their company's return-on-investment targets. These numbers highlight the importance of effectively transitioning to a lean product development system.

2 Blending Research and Practice

The research papers in this track can be broadly partitioned into two themes: understanding holistic system level challenges, and gaining deeper insights into specific principles and practices. Kettunen highlights the challenge faced by most software organizations – current product development approaches are often inadequate for delivering high performance even in the face of changing requirements. Given the limited empirical evidence of the performance effects of lean practices, the paper develops a roadmap and a framework for future research. Rudolph and Paulisch capture rich data using a single case study of how lean is interpreted within a project within the Automation business unit at Siemens. They used the four lenses of product portfolio, technical architecture, process, and people & organizations, to understand the dynamics of value creation and delivery. Their analysis highlighted the need for a value-oriented requirements process, and the need for an incremental development process with product quality.

Given that waste elimination is a fundamental tenet of classical lean thinking, actually achieving minimal waste is challenging. Although the importance of leadership in successfully driving change is recognized, Ikonen focuses on an underexplored aspect of waste elimination – the impact of adding leadership at the cost of project resources. Using a quasi-controlled experiment in two projects, the research showed that waste can be reduced with the right leadership even in self-organized teams. Following the waste theme, Mandic et al. focus on understanding flow in the software development process as a means of improving performance. They define the generalized concept of value creation points, and the associated system of three axioms that capture the unique aspects of software development. They emphasize that understanding the nature and diversity of decisions is critical for understanding flow in software development.

The nine practice oriented talks and tutorials are focused on providing participants with a broad based understanding of the frameworks, practices and tools that are in use today. The case studies that will be discussed in the track include large aerospace and defense organizations like Rockwell Collins, online automotive markets like mobile.international, and startups like Huitale. The tutorial sessions include understanding single piece flow, the latest output of the lean systems engineering working groups, aspects of kanban systems, the clean delivery system and developing a systems approach to product development

3 Takeaway

This track was focused on connecting the dots between the classical lean, lean enterprises, product development, and innovation. Our goal in blending together research and practice is to create a program that will provide immediate benefits to the conference attendee and at the same time plant the seed of reflection to guide holistic evolution of discrete practices into lean systems of innovation.

References

1. Sugimori, Y., Kusunoki, K., Cho, F., Uchikawa, S.: Toyota production system and kanban system materialization of just-in-time and respect-for-human system. International Journal of Production Research 15(6), 553–564 (1977)
2. Womack, J.P., Jones, D.T., Roos, D.: The machine that changed the world. Rawson Associates, New York (1990)

3. Womack, J.P., Jones, D.T.: Lean Thinking: Banish waste and create wealth in your organisation. Simon and Shuster, New York (2003)
4. Murman, et al.: Lean Enterprise Value: Insights from MIT's Lean Aerospace Initiative. Palgrave MacMillan, China (2004)
5. Nightingale, D.N., Srinivasan, J.: Lean Enterprise Thinking: Driving Enterprise Transformation. AMACOM Press (2011)
6. Schumpeter, J.: The explanation of the business cycle. Economica, 286–311 (1927)
7. Drucker, P.: The discipline of innovation–the innovative enterprise. Harvard Business Review 63(3), 67–73 (1985)
8. Tushman, M.L., Nadler, D.A.: Communication and technical roles in R&D laboratories: an information processing approach. Management of Research and Innovation 15 (1986)
9. Ettlie, J.E., Bridges, W.P., O'keefe, R.D.: Organization strategy and structural differences for radical versus incremental innovation. Management Science, 682–695 (1984)
10. Henderson, R.M., Clark, K.B.: Architectural innovation: the reconfiguration of existing product technologies and the failure of established firms. Administrative Science Quarterly 35(1) (1990)
11. Van de Ven, A.H.: Central problems in the management of innovation. Management Science, 590–607 (1986)
12. Morgan, J.M., Liker, J.K.: The Toyota Product Development System: Integrating People, Process and Technology. Productivity Press, New York (2006)
13. Hoppmann, J.: The Lean Innovation Roadmap – A Systematic Approach to Introducing Lean in Product Development Processes and Establishing a Learning Organization. Diploma Thesis. T.U. Braunschweig (2009)
14. Gordon, M., et al.: The Path to Developing Successful New Products. Wall Street Journal (2009)

A Tentative Framework for Lean Software Enterprise Research and Development

Petri Kettunen

University of Helsinki
Department of Computer Science
P.O. Box 68 (Gustaf Hällströmin katu 2b)
FI-00014 University of Helsinki, Finland
petri.kettunen@cs.helsinki.fi

Abstract. The current trends in most software development organizations are in striving for high performance while meeting the emergent and even rapidly changing customer needs. Traditional product development models are often ineffective in such respects. Now Lean and Agile software models address many of those particular concerns. However, empirical evidence of their actual performance effects is still scarce and probably many hidden inefficiencies exist in practical software projects. For example the Kanban process model is one of the latest proposals with apparent potential to improve the efficiency of the projects. This paper explores how software development activities and process improvement can be evaluated in such cases. A research model is constructed for the purpose of this investigation. New research hypotheses can be derived and tested empirically with case study projects. By applying the supported hypotheses in practice, the model is intended to be a systematic performance development vehicle for software projects and a provisional framework for the Lean software enterprise transformation research and development.

1 Introduction

Basically every software development organization is nowadays looking for new ways to improve their performance [1], [2]. Often the case is not just increasing the operational efficiency (e.g., productivity) but also – and sometimes even more so – about removing the possible inefficiencies within the current software functions. Moreover, product and process innovation is increasingly a major competitive advantage in most rapidly changing software business areas.

All those needs call for more powerful tools for the software enterprises to master their product development efforts in a rational and effective manner. Current Lean and Agile software models address many of those particular concerns.

However, empirical evidence of their actual performance effects is still scarce and certainly not conclusive [3]. The underlying theory is incompletely developed, making it difficult to draw firm conclusions and consequently suggesting actionable advice for the industrial practitioners.

Currently there is a proliferation of different tools, methods, and even philosophies for development working in different areas and organizational levels. This makes it

P. Abrahamsson and N. Oza (Eds.): LESS 2010, LNBIP 65, pp. 60–71, 2010.

hard for industrial enterprises to link their strategic business goals to appropriate improvement activities, and for the researchers to combine prior work to steer further relevant research.

The purpose of this paper is to tackle that problem in a systematic way by proposing a holistic research model and testing its hypothesis in empirical case study project environments. The model is thus intended to build towards a comprehensive framework for directing, linking, and assessing Lean software enterprise research problems.

The rest of this paper is structured as follows. Section 2 outlines the conceptual background and the related prior research indicating the knowledge gaps and consequent new research needs. Section 3 then presents the research model. Section 4 presents some provisional cases. Section 5 draws the conclusions.

2   Related Work and Foundations

The prior work of the Lean concepts stem from the operations and production management field, but those ideas have subsequently been applied to other areas of product organizations and particularly to software development, too. This section reviews briefly such related work (Sect. 2.1-2.5), highlights the knowledge gaps, and concludes with the consequent research need analysis (Sect. 2.6).

2.1   Lean Enterprise Thinking

Currently there is no one agreed definition of a 'Lean Enterprise'. It can be characterized from different perspectives and at different levels. However, what is commonly presupposed is that the lean principles originate from the production field in the 1950s in Japan (in particular, automotive) [4].

That given, a Lean Enterprise is attributed with a combination of

- high quality products / services
- cost-efficient production / operations
- responsiveness to variations in customer demands

Such outcomes stem from the Lean Thinking principles of [5]

- recognizing the customer values
- developing the production systems for creating the values
- running the production flows accordingly
- controlling the production based on customer "pull"
- continuous improvements striving for excellence

Fundamentally, they are based on competent and motivated people perfecting their work practices and facilities. Such profound elements require deeply shared values and supportive company culture – including specifically the executives and leaders.

Notably there is also a closely-related concept of 'Agile Enterprise' [6]. They have much in common with Lean Enterprises, and the distinction between the two is by no means clear-cut. In general, such agile enterprises put more emphasis on the external interfaces and behavioral effects of the company under turbulent environmental conditions.

2.2   Lean Production

Lean Production (Manufacturing) is an operations management strategy which strive for combining mass production efficiency with flexibility. It is frequently associated with the Toyota Production System (TPS), but it is not limited to automotive industry.

In essence, Lean Production can be described as a 'Japanese' management philosophy coupled with Just-in-Time (JIT) manufacturing techniques [7]. The key to achieve the aforementioned strategic goals is to design the production system to work on short lead times and small yet economically viable batch (order) sizes. That can be realized with Flexible Manufacturing Systems (FMS) and other such modern technologies run by multiskilled people [8]. High product / process quality is an intrinsic trait since the whole production system is sensitive to rework. Lean Production systems are often combined and extended with Lean Supply Chain Management (SCM) methods [9], [10].

Again, there is a related concept of 'Agile Manufacturing' [11]. The characteristic difference between the two is that Agile Manufacturing aims to work even under unpredictable variances in demand, while the flexibility in Lean Manufacturing is more limited to a planned range of product mixes and variants.

2.3   Lean Product Development

Following the principles of Lean Production, it is advantageous to couple the product development functions into the same value chain design. In particular with complex products much of the benefits of the production system depend on the proper alignment of the product designs and the corresponding manufacturing process set-ups (concurrent engineering).

Like in the production field, many of the Lean Product Development approaches originate from the automotive industry (e.g., Toyota Product Development System, TPDS). However, such techniques as set-based design and deferred design decision-making are technology-independent and have subsequently been applied in other industries [12]. Likewise, many of the organizational practices (e.g., Chief Engineers) are basically applicable across industries.

2.4   Lean Software Development

Since the Lean Product Development approaches are basically technology-independent, a consequent trend is to apply them to software product development. However, the intangible and knowledge-intensive nature of software development requires some reinterpretation of the basic ideas – particularly the concepts of value, waste, and flow.

The value of software is realized only when it is executed in the target context. Different software (product) types (e.g., fast-paced consumer goods vs. industrial systems) may then have very different value profiles.

In contrast to the material flows in manufacturing operations, what flows in software product development is knowledge (information). If follows that knowledge creation, transformation, and sharing are core process activities, and people are the actors.

In particular Poppendieck has done some such application [13]. While for instance waiting and defects "wastes" are straightforward to realize in software terms, such key concepts as Work-in-Process (WIP) and unnecessary movement are not so. The underlying key Lean idea is rapid defect detection and removal [14].

On the other hand, many of the more general-purpose product development techniques (e.g., set-based design) and organizational management practices (e.g., empowerment) are readily applicable in software projects [15]. Moreover, certain overarching Lean Enterprise principles could be realized in software organizations, too [16].

In addition, following the principles of continuous improvement, some Lean ideas have been applied to software process improvement [17]. On the other hand, there have also been some attempts to adopt (agile) software development practices for general new product development processes [18].

2.5 Lean Transformation

Currently there is a wide range of different Lean-related organizational and process improvement approaches working in different scopes, at different levels, and even in different time-horizons. In general, they can be categorized as follows:

- Software Process Improvement (SPI)
- Business Process Reengineering (BPR)
- Organizational Development (OD)

For instance most agile software methods address the 'how' at software team level, while the Capability Maturity Model Integration (CMMI) concerns more about the 'what' in product development. However, most organizations require in addition more business- and management-oriented tools in their total Lean improvements – such as BPR and Total Quality Management (TQM) [19], [20]. A Lean transition may require both incremental improvements (Kaizen) as well as conscious radical shifts (Kaikaku). Lean transformations are often not only about traditional SPI, but moreover about more extensive BPR. All those can be managed as OD programs.

Notably, there is also a widely-used term of 'Agile Transformation'. When it focuses mostly on agile software development, it can be considered as a complementary part of the enterprise-level Lean Transformation. However, again, the concepts are not clear-cut.

2.6 Knowledge Gaps and Research Needs

Table 1 distills the key research traits of Lean in different disciplines and areas reviewed broadly in Sect. 2.1-2.5. Notably those are partially overlapping.

Table 1. Lean research inferences for software enterprises

Research Stream	Primary Focus	Key Concepts (Lean/Agile)	LIMITATIONS for Software Enterprises
Lean Enterprise Thinking (Sect. 2.1)	• What is it that makes a lean enterprise?	• systemic value-orientation • workforce-based mindsetting (culture)	• concepts and terms of 'Lean' and 'Agile' currently not all exactly defined
Lean Production (2.2)	• How does production / manufacturing operate there?	• JIT • automation with a "human touch" (Jidoka)	• material flows replaced with knowledge flows • equipment replaced with knowledge work
Lean Product Development (2.3)	• How does new product development join?	• Set-Based Concurrent Engineering	• intangible nature of software creation
Lean Software Development (2.4)	• How to emulate physical production?	• flow and "wastes" in software development	• lack of solid underlying reasoning and analysis
Lean Transformation (2.5)	• How to conduct programs of organizational change?	• continuous improvement (problems, excellence)	• no established pathways for software organizations to follow

There is a need for an aggregating research and development framework. Following that line of thinking, Fig. 1 combines the main issues captured in Table 1.

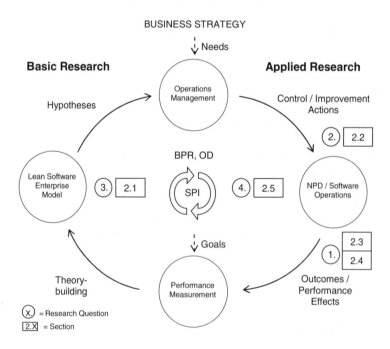

Fig. 1. Lean Software Enterprise research and development cycle

Currently not all those knowledge and capability areas and their relations in Fig. 1 are well understood. This leads to a sequence of research questions like numbered in Fig. 1. Starting from the effects, the principal research problem can be set as follows:

1. How do (successful) software projects contribute to the lean enterprise performance?

When this is known, the software development (projects) can be run accordingly to achieve those desired success effects. This leads to the consequent bridging research question (c.f., Fig. 1):
2. What factors moderate software project performance in lean enterprise context?

The right-hand side of Fig. 1 (applied research) is the prime concern for practicing software-intensive product development organizations. However, in order to really be able to answer the associated research questions (1. and 2. above), certain underlying theory must be built. Although there are general-purpose provisional models for Agile/Lean Enterprises, there is no such established theory for software organizations to date. Therefore, a fundamental research question comes down to:
3. What is a Lean Software Enterprise?

Finally, in order to realize all that, a continuous R&D cycle is needed like illustrated in Fig. 1:
4. How can it be realized (transformation / improvement)?

Such a continuous improvement cycle incorporates both single-loop learning with incremental improvements (chiefly SPI; Kaizen) as well as double-loop learning for even radical changes (BPR; Kaikaku). All those involve organizational development (OD) approaches. Moreover, since the foundation of the Lean philosophy is to foster the culture and people, the improvement activities should consider the organization not only from the traditional process perspective as a mechanical production system but also as a social system. The overall problem-setting addresses thus multiple different disciplines simultaneously:

- software engineering, computer science
- business competence, economics, information systems
- organization management and design, behavioral science

Those considerations raise additional concerns for the research strategy. Agile/Lean software development research has until now been limited mostly to team level, with some provisional miscellaneous attempts to scale them up [21]. However, also the research methods should take into account the elevation from the team level to the enterprise levels.

In particular, the significance and impacts of the different business competence areas need to be scoped [22], [23]. In addition, the organizational leveling must be set up [24]. Different industrial organizations may have different priorities for valid strategic reasons with respect to their Lean Transformation (adoption). This should be taken into account, avoiding overgeneralization in the theory-building.

Considering software product development in particular, this paper does not propose new definitions of 'lean' or 'agile' software development. Instead, the premise is to focus on the performance effects at the enterprise level. Different software methods, practices, and tools provide different effects in such capabilities.

3 Research Model

Based on the related background work and the gap analysis presented in Sect. 2.6 linked to Fig. 1, Fig. 2 proposes an overall theoretical research model for the research problem. Derived from our prior work, it builds on the following line of thinking (top-down perspective) [25]:

- The software product development projects *need* to contribute (positively) to the overall business performance of the enterprise (entity).
- Successful software projects address that *goal* by delivering value.
- Lean methods, practices, and tools are *means* to achieve those software project goals. People (teams) use them.
- On the other hand, there may be some *impediment* factors preventing from applying the means efficiently. They should be eliminated (or at least mitigated).
- Many interrelated factors are necessary *enablers* for making all that happen effectively in practice. They require definite investments.

In addition, the research model incorporates the following key elements of Lean Thinking on product value and product development flows [5]:

- specifying value 'in the eyes of the customer'
- identifying the value stream and eliminating waste
- making value flow at the pull of the customer

Software project performance measurements are generally accepted to include such factors as product quality and development cycle time (lead time). In all, project performance is a multidimensional metric [26]. In the Lean Enterprise context the key performance criteria is the software value, which can be defined in terms of the product service and the cost of providing it over time. The essence of Lean is to produce continuously high value with most efficient utilization of the resources (including time). That is why we put the Value Flow in the heart of the model in Fig. X. Consequently, the development methods and tools (Lean or possibly also Agile) should amplify that on the one hand, and any hindrances (impediments) should be eliminated on the other hand.

Moreover, considering the enterprise (product development entity) level requires elevating from project-level measurements to higher-level business performance metrics – such as profitability, ROI, company stock-market price, and even corporate (brand) image [22]. This calls for linking the software project contributions to the business effects.

Altogether, the elements shown in Fig. 2 comprise a systems model for Lean Software Enterprise (c.f., Fig. 1). The ultimate research aim is now to understand the relationships between those components in order to be able to control and improve the overall enterprise-level effects.

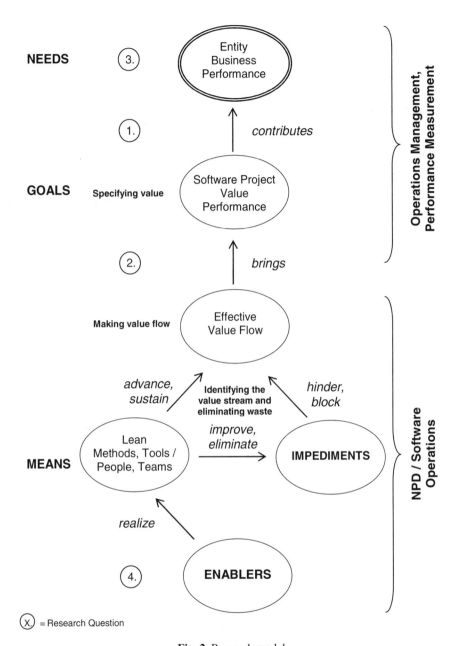

Fig. 2. Research model

Because of the provisional character, the justification of those initial ones is to be validated. Furthermore, possibly more relations and interdependencies may be discovered to enhance the model. Due to the multidisciplinary nature of the problem space spanning from core software engineering to business competence and organizational dynamics, the operationalizing may require interdisciplinary work.

4 Empirical Studies

The research model presented in Sect. 3 (Fig. 2) can be mapped to the R&D cycle shown in Fig. 1 to make new research propositions. This section follows that line of thinking, to investigate some moderating factors of software project performance (research question 2).

Lean Software Enterprise projects should deliver high software value in efficient ways like highlighted in Fig. 2 (flow). We have done some initial investigations in this research area concerning leanness. One case study focused on identifying wastes in one particular software project using the Kanban model [27].

Fig. 3 illustrates the corresponding instance of the research model (c.f., Fig. 2). The project performance (success) is related on the one hand to the Lean tool (Kanban) and the team (people), and to the impediments (wastes) on the other hand.

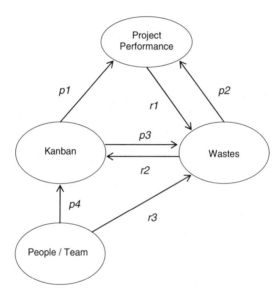

Fig. 3. Kanban case study research instance

The research case provided certain support for the following relations (labeled in Fig. 3):

- r1:   *There may be (observable) wastes in successful software projects.*
- r2:   *The Kanban method does not eliminate all wastes.*
- r3:   *People can identify ("see") wastes when questioned (retrospectively).*

Moreover, the following new propositions could be set for further study (see Fig. 3):

- p1:   *The Kanban method contributes positively to project success.*
- p2:   *Wastes hinder project performance (value flow).*

- p3:   *The Kanban method eliminates (avoids) certain wastes.*
- p4:   *People tend to favor the Kanban process model.*

Another case study suggested that the Kanban model has considerable potential for improving software project work and value-orientation [28]. Like in Fig. 3, an instance of the research model can be constructed. This indicates some support to the propositions *p1* and *p4* above. The proposition *p3* complements the relation *r2* above.

These initial case study findings demonstrate to some extent the applicability of the proposed research model. It may further help setting new research questions, and connecting existing results and observations even retrospectively. However, further evidence is needed to judge that with statistically testable hypotheses, possibly modifying the initial model.

5   Conclusions

This paper proposes a tentative framework for roadmapping and conducting research about Lean Software Enterprises. Like illustrated in Fig. 2, the Lean Software Enterprise performance is expected to be based on continuous delivery of high product value. The software development projects contribute to that. That is the general reasoning for setting the research problem and questions (Sect. 2.6).

While software project success factors have been investigated extensively over the years, their multidimensional relations to the overall product development and firm performance are not well understood. Often the project success is considered only in the local context from the producer viewpoint. However, in the Lean Enterprise perspective more actionable knowledge is needed about the effects from the customer/market viewpoints.

This paper does not advocate any prescribed universal model for Lean Software Enterprises. Instead, the premise is that once the operational characteristics of the software product development are understood, they can be steered according to the specific needs and performance goals of the company. The operational research cycle in Fig. 1 serves those purposes. It is in a way a tool for making the inherently invisible software operations visually recognizable and thereby more easily manageable like in manufacturing [29]. The essence of the Lean Software Enterprise model is continuous flow of high-value software products in sustainable ways (c.f., Fig. 2). This is context- and product-specific, and therefore it is not reasonable to attempt to define one fixed model applicable for every enterprise. That is the way how 'Lean' is framed in this paper.

Since there are no readily available comprehensive models for Lean Software Enterprises (Sect. 2.5), it is hardly possible to take any one particular transformation/improvement template for practical realization. However, again, once the company understands its business-specific needs and strategic goals (Fig. 2), it can direct the OD actions towards those means.

Like presented in the case study (Sect. 4), each relation of the research model (Fig. 2) can be investigated by setting the corresponding hypotheses and testing them in case projects. Furthermore, new relationships are potentially found for further investigation.

Moreover, by analyzing the case study results and inferring them, the underlying theory of Lean Software Enterprises can gradually be developed and practical organizational development tools devised like shown in Fig. 1. This makes it possible to answer stepwise the overall research problem set in Sect. 2.6.

Based on the groundwork done in this paper, future work prospects are as follows:

- Assess for each stakeholder, how they value the product at each stage of the life-cycle, and how that value can be added during the product process.
- What all different areas of business competence does a Lean Software Enterprise model should address at each level of organization? Some typical cross-functional elements are portfolio management and software product lines.
- Which particular realizations of different Lean Software Enterprises require business- and technology-specific implementations? For instance, Lean *Cloud* Software Enterprises strive for defining their product / service value based on the cloud computing models.

In all, a key element of Lean Thinking is "seeing the whole". This should be applied to the research work, too. This paper is a provisional attempt to analyze and direct Lean Software Enterprise research and development in totality. Further work in basic research (e.g., systematic literature reviews on existing models in different disciplines) will strengthen the comprehensiveness on the one hand, and industrial applied research (e.g., focus groups) validate the relevance and bring evidence on the other hand.

Acknowledgements. This work was supported by TEKES as a part of the Cloud Software program of Tivit (Finnish Strategic Centre for Science, Technology and Innovation in the field of ICT). The author would also like to thank Pekka Abrahamsson (University of Helsinki), Maarit Laanti (Nokia Corporation), and Janne Järvinen (F-Secure Corporation) for their influences.

References

1. Schwaber, C.: Corporate IT Leads The Second Wave of Agile Adoption. Forrester Research, Inc. (2005)
2. Scinta, J.: Industrial Research Institute's R&D Trends Forecast for 2008. Research Technology Management 51(1), 19–23 (2008)
3. Dingsøyr, T., Dybå, T., Abrahamsson, P.: A Preliminary Roadmap for Research on Agile Software Development Research. In: Proc. Agile Conference, pp. 83–96. IEEE, Los Alamitos (2008)
4. Womack, J.P., Jones, D.T., Roos, D.: The Machine That Changed the World: The Story of Lean Production – Toyota's Secret Weapon in the Global Car Wars That Is Now Revolutionizing World Industry. Free Press, USA (1990)
5. Womack, J.P., Jones, D.T.: Lean Thinking: Banish Waste and Create Wealth in Your Corporation. Free Press, USA (2003)
6. Dove, R., Hartman, S., Benson, S.: An Agile Enterprise Reference Model (1996), http://www.parshift.com/docs/aermodA0.htm
7. Haverila, M.J., Uusi-Rauva, E., Kouri, I., Miettinen, A.: Teollisuustalous. Infacs Oy, Finland (2009) (in Finnish)

8. Heikkilä, J., Ketokivi, M.: Tuotanto murroksessa: strategisen johtamisen uusi haaste, Talentum, Helsinki, Finland (2005) (in Finnish)
9. Christopher, M.: The Agile Supply Chain – Competing in Volatile Markets. Industrial Marketing Management 29, 37–44 (2000)
10. Heikkilä, J.: From supply to demand chain management: efficiency and customer satisfaction. Journal of Operations Management 20, 747–767 (2002)
11. Kettunen, P.: Adopting Key Lessons from Agile Manufacturing to Agile Software Product Development – A Comparative Study. Technovation 29, 408–422 (2009)
12. Reinertsen, D., Shaeffer, L.: Making R&D Lean. Research Technology Management 48(4), 51–57 (2005)
13. Poppendieck, M., Poppendieck, T.: Lean software development: an agile toolkit. Addison Wesley, USA (2003)
14. Middleton, P.: Lean Software Development: Two Case Studies. Software Quality Journal 9(4), 241–252 (2001)
15. Reinertsen, D.G.: The principles of Product Development Flow: Second Generation Lean Product Development. Celeritas Publishing, USA (2009)
16. Middleton, P., Sutton, J.: Lean Software Strategies: Proven Techniques for Managers and Developers. Productivity Press, USA (2005)
17. Mehta, M., Anderson, D., Raffo, D.: Providing Value to Customers in Software Development Through Lean Principles. Software Process: Improvement and Practice 13(1), 101–109 (2008)
18. Smith, P.G.: Flexible Product Development: Building Agility for Changing Markets. Jossey-Bass, USA (2007)
19. Dybå, T., Dingsøyr, T., Moe, N.B.: Process Improvement in Practice: A Handbook for IT Companies. Kluwer Academic Publishers, USA (2004)
20. Hammer, M., Champy, J.: Reengineering the Corporation: A Manifesto for Business Revolution. HarperCollins Publishers, USA (1993)
21. Kettunen, P.: Agile Software Development in Large-Scale New Product Development Organization: Team-Level Perspective. Dissertation. Helsinki University of Technology, Finland (2009)
22. Messnarz, R., Tully, C. (eds.): Better Software Practices for Business Benefit: Principles and Experience. IEEE, Los Alamitos (1999)
23. Shalloway, A., Beaver, G., Trott, J.R.: Lean-Agile Software Development: Achieving Enterprise Agility. Addison-Wesley, USA (2010)
24. Laanti, M.: Implementing Program Model with Agile Principles in a Large Software Development Organization. In: Proc. Annual International Computer Software and Applications Conference, pp. 1385–1387. IEEE, Los Alamitos (2008)
25. Kettunen, P., Laanti, M.: Combining Agile Software Projects and Large-Scale Organizational Agility. Software Process: Improvement and Practice 13(2), 183–193 (2008)
26. Abrahamsson, P.: Measuring the Success of Software Process Improvement: The Dimensions. In: Proc. EUROSPI. Copenhagen Business School, Denmark (2000)
27. Ikonen, M., Kettunen, P., Oza, N., Abrahamsson, P.: Exploring the Sources of Waste in Kanban Software Development Projects. In: Proc. Euromicro SEAA. IEEE, Los Alamitos (2010)
28. Pirinen, E.: How the Kanban software development method effects the creation of value and the work of a software developer. Master's Thesis, University of Helsinki, Finland (2010) (in Finnish)
29. Goodson, R.E.: Read a Plant – Fast. Harvard Business Review (May 2002)

What Is Flowing in Lean Software Development?

Vladimir Mandić[1], Markku Oivo[1], Pilar Rodríguez[1], Pasi Kuvaja[1],
Harri Kaikkonen[2], and Burak Turhan[1]

[1] Department of Information Processing Science
[2] Industrial Management, Department of Industrial Engineering and Management
University of Oulu, Finland
{vladimir.mandic,markku.oivo,pilar.rodriguez,pasi.kuvaja,
harri.kaikkonen,burak.turhan}@oulu.fi

Abstract. The main concern of the software industry is to deliver more products in shorter time-cycles to customers with an acceptable economic justification. In virtue of these concerns, the software industry and researchers in the field of software engineering have engaged in the process of adopting lean principles. In this paper, we are seeking the knowledge that could help us better understand the nature of flows in software development. We define a generalized concept of the value creation points and an axiomatic system that capture the specifics of software development. Further, a generalized definition of the flow makes it possible to identify super-classes of waste sources. Finally, we define a concept of decision flow, suggesting what a value creation point could be in the software development context. The decision flow is an inseparable part of the software development activities and it carries capabilities of adding or diminishing the value of products.

Keywords: Lean Software Development, Flow, Value Creation Points.

1 Introduction

The main concern of the software industry is to deliver more products (features) in shorter time-cycles to customers with an acceptable economic justification. In virtue of these concerns, the software industry and researchers in the field of software engineering have engaged in the process of adopting lean principles. Lean ideas initially emerged in the manufacturing industry (i.e. the automotive industry). The fundamental idea of lean is to organize production as a series of flows, where the flows are maintained in a such a way that enables continuous value creation to customers through constant motion of work products and activities in the flow. But, what is flowing in lean software development?

Lean software development is mainstreamed with an interpretation of lean thinking [1,2] led by Poppendieck's [3,4] work in this topic. The interpretation takes a view on software development from the lean (manufacturing) angle. Such an interpretation proved to have its merits, as demonstrated with numerous examples [3,4]. However, we argue that the answer to our question from that

P. Abrahamsson and N. Oza (Eds.): LESS 2010, LNBIP 65, pp. 72–84, 2010.

point of view is too mechanical and it blurs the true nature of the software development process.

Therefore, we believe that an interpretation based on an opposite view—*a view on lean thinking from the software development angle*—could contribute to a better understanding of what flowing in lean software development is.

This paper is a quest for knowledge that could help us understand the nature of flows in software development. At first, we will characterize the differences between the manufacturing and the software industries (Section 2.1), and review the principles of lean thinking (Section 2.2). In order to understand basic principles of the flow, we will define a generalized concept of value creation points (Section 3.1), and a system of three axioms that captures the specifics of software development (Section 3.2). In Section 3.3, we will describe how the generalized definition of the flow made it possible to identify two super-classes of waste sources. Finally, we give a suggestion of what a value creation point could be in the software development context (Section 4). In Section 5 we state our final remarks and formulate an answer to the title question.

2   Lean and the Software Industry

Agile thinking became popular in the early 2000s, officially announced in the Agile Manifesto [5]. However, discussions about software development and lean thinking started as early as the 1990s [6,7,8], well before the Agile Manifesto.

The idea of lean in the software industry was mainly promoted by the Agile community, which is not surprising given that agile and lean philosophies have numerous compatibilities and key agile principles are based on lean thinking. The lean community could be considered as process-oriented, focused on large corporations developing really large systems, while the agile community is usually populated with smaller organizations [9]. Besides, while agile development is mainly about how to develop software products in an ever changing world, lean is mainly about how to make organizations deliver as much customer value as possible [10]. Nowadays, there are a number of publications, most notably in Lean Magazine [10,9], that share different lean and agile experiences and analyze disagreement points.

In early discussions on lean and software development, the idea of perceiving lean as a different view of software process improvement was articulated. One of the early conferences on lean and software development was *IPSS-Europe International Conference on Lean Software Development, Stuttgart, Germany in 1992* [6,7]. The speakers[1] of the conference shared a common perception of lean software development, that it is aligned with the objectives of software process improvement (e.g., CMM, TQM, ISO, Bootstrap). Even more explicitly, at that time, Basili [8] made a comparison between different improvement/quality models including lean software development. Nowadays, we can see why software process improvement was considered close to lean thinking, especially due to

---

[1] Mainly extended abstracts with presentation handouts are available in printed form.

the concept of higher maturity. In CMM [11] (Capability Maturity Model) (current version CMMI [12]), the higher maturity levels (L4&L5) are dealing with software process variation and quantitative process management. The main goal is to shrink the process variation, also known as the voice of process (VOP), "inside" the voice of customer (VOC). From the lean thinking perspective, the ability to reduce VOP is a source of value. The main strategies for achieving this are implementation of quantitative management methods (CMMI L4) and optimization of the software process (CMMI L5).

2.1 Manufacturing vs. the Software Industry

The lean paradigm [13] has a holistic view of business, organization, operations, and people, and it is not an exclusive operational-level thinking. The paradigm was one of the main success drivers of the Japanese industry after the World War II [13]. Unfortunately, applicability of the lean paradigm in software development is not that obvious. Let us characterize a few distinguishing points between traditional manufacturing and the software industry. The characterization represents an illustration of two extreme positions. However, in reality, the process can have these extreme forms, but more often it is a combination and variation of the forms somewhere in between these two extremes (e.g., embed systems).

In the traditional manufacturing industry, the end product is a result of carefully planned sequences of actions mainly done by automated machines (pre-programmed robots), though, human presence is required to service or operate these machines. The quality of the end product is mainly dictated by the level of sophistication and precision of the tools (machines) to meet the desired specification tolerance. Tolerance requirements are specified with physical measures (e.g., dimensions, weight, speed, and consumptions). Therefore, the entire concept of quality can be based on the selection principle. For example, by measuring each unit/part and determining if it is within acceptable tolerance limits it is possible to select products of first-class quality.

On the other hand, in the software industry, the entire product creation process fabricates a single copy of a software product, and it is therefore not possible to employ the concept of quality as a selection principle (we do not have a large quantity of end products from where we can select good ones). Furthermore, it is not possible to specify physical measures for a software product, which makes it even more challenging to specify product requirements. Because of these significant differences, the focus has shifted to a process that produces a single copy of a software product. Finally, the software process employs people to create work products while tools are used to service the people. In such a process settings the creativity of people is a dominant factor.

Traditional manufacturing can be organized according to the lean paradigm [13] and it addresses a completely different setting to the software industry. However, the products that are fabricated in factories have to be designed or prototyped. Toyota [14] was among the first to use the lean paradigm for that purpose—lean product development. New product development is a much closer setting to software product development than to traditional manufacturing. Reinertsen [15] characterized the product development process as a decision intensive process. Unlike manufacturing, where "front-loaded" decisions are possible [15, p.38], the product development environments, such as software development, are continuously feeding-in new information that require new decisions.

The concept of a *front-loaded product development process* [16] (slightly differs from front-loading decisions), advocates the use of the best resources up-front on concurrent feasibility projects in order to explore alternatives and to gain knowledge. This is an effective way of reducing alternatives, and reaching the point where a major decisions can be made (e.g., architectural decisions). However, according to Morgan and Liker [16], this approach gives the best results with *derivative product built on existing product platforms*[2]. However, in cases of *revolutionary new products that represent radically different products or technology*, for example, the approach is not so effective [16], and such cases are not uncommon in the software industry.

2.2 Lean Principles of Value, Flow, and Waste

Lean or lean thinking is the English name that western researchers (researches from the Massachusetts Institute of Technology) used to describe the system of organization created by Toyota in Japan (now known as the Toyota Way but originally called the Respect for Humanity System). Originally, the Toyota culture was based on two main pillars: *continuous improvement* and *respect for people* [17]. Although there are direct consequences of this thinking, value and waste were not originally the focuses of the paradigm. When later it was interpreted from a western point of view, influenced by the existing western social-economical system, value became a key component of lean thinking [13].

The starting point for the lean transformation is a defining value [1], which can only be defined by the ultimate customer and is only useful in the context of a specific product. Value is created by any activity in any point of the process that the actual customer is ready to pay for. It can also be seen as the opposite of waste, which essentially means any activity that takes up resources, but does not produce value. The original seven forms of waste identified by Taiichi Ohno, the founder of the Toyota Production System (TPS) [14,18], were overproduction, unnecessary transportation, inventory, motion, defects, over-processing and waiting.

In an effective process the product should *flow* from one value creating activity to another, avoiding the wasteful activities in between. Flow means minimizing the amount of time that any work item is sitting idle, waiting for someone to work on it. If a customer request waits in a queue to be approved, analyzed,

---

[2] Morgan and Liker [16] identified four broad categories of new product development: (1) Revolutionary new products that represent radically different products or technology, (2) Product platform-development projects that require fundamentally new systems and components, (3) Derivative products built on existing product platforms, and (4) Incremental product improvements.

implemented, reworked or tested, then it is not flowing. A key aspect of a lean value stream is the simplification of information flowing within the stream [14]. Both the external information from the customer and the information generated internally, which is needed to complete the work, have to be considered.

The introduction of flow should ideally lead to continuous *single-piece flow*, where the target of value addition is passed on from one machine, operator or actor to another without any queues or waiting in between [1]. In production, this would require minimizing or removing all set-up times to instantly convert from one product specification to the next [1]. In a product or software development context, the removal of set-up times could be identified as the removal of the need for context change within the designers' heads. Achieving this is difficult, as a development organization requires different skills and iterative movement of information between actors. Indeed, Takeuchi and Nonaka [19] have already identified and illustrated this difference with a relay run and the advance of a rugby team, the latter being the preferred option for a product development organization.

When value is specified, value streams are identified, waste generating steps can be removed, and flow can be introduced. Flow is a perfection challenge for continuously identifying value and eliminating waste.

3   Foundations of the Lean Software Development Flow

The software process is vastly dependent on the human-factor, which we will refer to as *actors*. Actors are not only programmers, developers and designers, but also, customers, managers, and business owners. We can identify actors as *stakeholders*, and use the term stakeholders interchangeably with actors.

In order to understand how lean principles can be interpreted in the software development context, we will first define the generalized concept of a value creation point.

3.1   The Concept of Value Creation Points

If we want to maximize the value creation in a flow by utilizing value stream mapping techniques [20] then we should first identify the value creation points in the flow. The value creation point (VCP) is the moment and place where the value is injected, added or created.

In manufacturing, the value creation points are so obvious that there is no need for an explicit definition. Actually, the entire production flow is based on transforming materials to an end-product, for a known customer, where each transformation step is naturally a VCP. For example, cutting a piece of wood according to specifications is adding value to the material, because it transforms a raw material into the leg of a future chair. The entire manufacturing process is transparent (visible and tangible) and therefore controllable. However, in software development, the true production process is a cognitive process, and as such is intangible and difficult to control.

In the following section we will present an axiomatic system that uses a generalized definition of VCP for defining the flow.

3.2 Axioms of the Lean Software Development Flow

The axiomatic statements defined here are relevant for any process that uses the creativity of actors for constructing an end-product, such as in the software development process.

Axioms are a convenient way of formulating and making some trivial and obvious facts explicit, and as such they are not meant to be proved. They are either accepted by the community and used for building theories or they are not accepted.

Axiom 1. *(Source of value)*: The verified knowledge of actors through their own experiences, and the ability of actors to apply it creatively to real-world problems is an intangible source of value.

Axiom 2. *(The flow)*: The flow has to interconnect points of value creation (VCPs) in *time* and *space*.

Axiom 3. *(Feedback)*: The definition and realization of the flow has to support Axiom 1; the flow has to enable actors to gain new experiences and knowledge.

The main difficulty in understanding the software process is the misunderstanding of the role and purpose of actors in the process. The actors can be both the weakest link and the most valuable asset of the process at the same time. It is necessary to reconsider the roles and purposes of the actors in lean terms. Therefore, Axiom 1 clarifies the position of actors in the software process by an explicit acknowledgment of the existence of the intangible source of value.

Axiom 2 specifies the most important characteristic of the flow. If the flow does not interconnect the value creation points then it is impossible to perform value stream mapping and maximization of the value, and consequently identification and minimization of the waste. The *time component* of the flow addresses the importance of the flow dynamics ("flowing of the flow"). When we say *space*, we refer to an organization as a whole, and the points of value creation are distributed throughout the entire organization at different levels.

Learning is the most natural way of expanding knowledge and the experience base, which occurs after engaging actors with real-world problems when they realize the effects of engagement through feedback (Axiom 3).

Here, we presented the axiomatic system of three axioms that capture the most distinguishing characteristics of the software process and package them in a suitable form for further discussions on lean software development flow.

3.3 Super-Classes of Waste Sources

Thinking about the flow as a collection of interconnected VCPs also helps us to understand the sources of *waste*. We can identify two super-classes of waste sources: (1) *interconnections of the VCPs*, and (2) *inability to inject value in a VCP*.

For example, in lean manufacturing, Taiichi Ohno [14] defined seven types of waste. According to our classification of the sources of the waste, transportation, motion, inventory, and delays are the consequence of the interconnections of the VCPs, while overproduction, extra processing steps, and defects are the consequence of the inability to inject value in a VCP.

The generalized definition of value creation points, axiomatic system, and super-classes of waste sources are the abstractions of the fundamental principals that are used to define any lean product development flow. At the same time, the axiomatic system offers a flexibility for further research on exploring what a VCP is in the software development context. The only constraint is that a definition of the VCP should not contradict the axioms, and all concepts should be a logical consequence of axioms and previously derived concepts.

In the following section we will give one possible definition of VCP in the software development context.

4   Decision Points as the Value Creation Points

We consider decision-making as an inseparable process of knowledge and experience codification or transformation activities during a software development process. During the decision-making process, an actor evaluates and examines rationales of a decision. The entire process uses an actor's domain-specific knowledge, experiences, and understanding of the real-world problem or situation (Figure 1, (C)). By its characteristic, this process is a belief reasoning or abduction [21].

Unfortunately, the common understanding is that decision-making is an exclusive right of managers and business owners. In reality, there are different kinds of decisions which are made by different groups of actors. Decisions can be *explicit* or *implicit*. For example, decisions made by managers and business owners are explicit. However, developers are also faced with numerous situations that require decision-making. These decisions are not always explicit, sometimes they could remain hidden in the development process.

However, despite the risk of being misunderstood and this being interpreted as a managerial view of the software process, we will use the term *decision-making* and not abduction or belief reasoning. The main reason for this is that our understanding that people who are making decisions have a responsibility for the consequences of the decisions, while in the case of abduction, this kind of the responsibility is not conceded.

The definition of VCP as the decision point supports Axioms 1 and 3 in the following way:

- Actors have to use their knowledge and experience (source of value, Axiom 1) in order to make decision which will have a consequential effect on product creation.

- The decision-making process embeds *the first feedback loop* (Figure 1, (E)), which represents learning through belief reasoning (supports Axiom 3).
- *The main feedback loop* (Figure 1, (D)) represents learning from the consequences of the decisions. The purpose of decision-making is to achieve the desired effects (results), and when end-results become visible, actors are in position to analyze the quality of their decisions (supports Axiom 3).

The decision point (decision process) takes place in a certain *moment and place* or *point*. We cannot ignore the fact that decision-making is a continuous process that takes place in software development. Therefore, the question of the "granularity" of decisions is important. For example, a few managerial decisions (coarse granularity) made in project gates or milestones are probably not enough to impact and control value creation points (implicit decisions) between the gates. On the other hand, too many decisions (fine granularity) will lead to an explosion in the number of decision points, and those decisions will be trivial. Thus, the value injection will be minimal. The right level of granularity is somewhere in between.

Having defined decision points as VCPs, and according to Axiom 2, we can characterize the flow as *the decision flow*, and, it is conceivable to perceive a software product as a result of numerous interrelated decisions made in certain moments and places by different actors during the software development process.

4.1   Decision Flow

The software development process can be seen as a sequence of interconnected activities, where each activity requires resources (e.g., actors who are performing the activity, tools used for constructing a product, etc.). Such organization of the software process is commonly called a *work flow* (Figure 1, (A)). On top of the work flow, different software development approaches can be defined with the purpose of achieving more effective organization of the activities. One way to organize activities is to group them in strict phases, which would follow in a sequence or waterfall. Other approaches could be iterative or agile-like (Figure 1).

Development approaches (ways how to organize development activities) could help in providing better exposure of the value creation activates, but the ability of the software process to inject (add) value is an inherent characteristic of the process itself and it is not something that is exclusively added by the development approach. Therefore, our view is that a *decision flow* (Figure 1, (B)) is actually behind the work flow and not on the top of it.

According to Axiom 2, the decision flow connects decision points (VCPs) in time and space. Figure 1 represent a schematic simplification of the software process. The decision flow is in reality an entire web of interconnected implicit and explicit decisions. Unfortunately, the problem of the considerably high number of decision points does not allow explicit mappings between the decision flow and the work flow.

Although the conclusion could be that the explicit or more formal decision-making is the key to success, we advise to not use a heavy decision-making

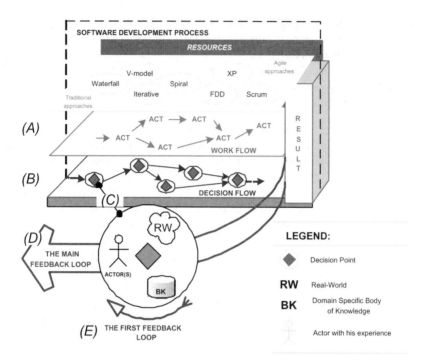

Fig. 1. The anatomy of the software process

theory, which could become the main ballast of a software development process. Therefore, the purpose of the existing and new-coming software development approaches is to enable and encourage decision-making by all actors in a natural way as a part of their activities.

4.2   Some Sources of the Waste in Software Development

The super-classes of the waste defined in Section 3.3, when used for the decision flow, unveil some new sources of the waste.

Avoiding decision-making We associate this waste with the inability to inject value in a VCP. If there are no decisions made (as we defined in Section 4) there will be no adequate transformation of knowledge to the software product or process. The reasons for decision avoidance could vary from organizational issues (actors are not empowered enough) to individual psychological characteristics of the actors.

Limited access to information. In order to make decisions, actors need to have access to the relevant information sources. If they have limited access to the relevant information, they could even make harmful decisions. For example, a product development team could discard some key product requirements (the requirements that can sell a product), due to the pressure created by time to the market deadline. Actually, limited access to information is about the existence of or having information at all, which is a different situation from the case when the information is available but it is distorted.

Noise or information distortion. Interconnections of the VCP can cause distortions in the information in time and space. The time distortion occurs when information is forgotten, not recorded, or is not updated. The space distortion occurs because actors are distributed across different levels or units of an organization, and they represent different contexts and sub-contexts. For example, when an engineer from an operational level communicates information to the manager at an upper-level, the information will be "passed" from one context (engineer) to another (manager). Passing through contexts can have distortion effects due to the interpretation of the information in different contexts.

Uncertainty. We could differentiate several types of uncertainty, like information quality (accuracy), prediction uncertainty, or the uncertainty of decision assumptions. But, for all of them a common point is that a variable or a choice can have multiple possible values or options. The increased number of possible values or options increases the level of uncertainty.

Definition of the VCP as decision points has a logical reasoning, as we elaborated here, and it is maintaining consistence (the axioms are not contradicting each others) and completeness (there are no new concepts created that are not a logical consequence of the axioms) of the axiomatic system.

People, knowledge creation and utilization, and decision-making are closely related. If the people are not respected, the quality of decisions and the level of knowledge creation/utilization will certainly be poor.

Our employment of decision-making for exposing characteristics of the software process and the Agile principle of *postponing decisions as late as possible* could be seen as contradicting each other, but they do not. The flow is supposed to interconnect value creation points in *time* and space (Axiom 2). The *time* means that decisions should occur in the right moment not before and not after. A legitimate question is: what is the right moment? Ballard points out that the decision postponing principle comes from lean [22], and that it means the point beyond which deferring a decisions affects other decisions causing rework. So bring decisions forward, before the point at which failing to make the decision eliminates an alternative. Unfortunately, we do not have evidence to claim that this is the best possible answer.

5   Discussions and Conclusion

A reader could get the wrong impression that the axiomatic system (Section 3.2) is favoring individualism and neglects organizational aspects and structure. Actually, we see the establishment of organizational structures and the institutionalization of processes as a consequence of lean thinking—*maximize value and minimize waste*. For example, we identified *limited access to information* as one source of waste, and in order to minimize it, it is necessary to establish an organizational "space" for knowledge and information sharing and a learning culture (similarly as suggested by [21]).

Furthermore, the concept of software process improvement can be utilized for minimizing different types of waste and maximizing value. The process maturity framework (originating from Humphrey's work [23]) is constructed in a way that helps an organization improve their prediction capabilities when climbing on the maturity scale. Improving prediction capabilities through the institutionalization of software processes at the same time *minimizes uncertainty*, which is exactly one of the waste sources.

The first axiom (Section 3.2), that we proposed, specifies *the source of value*, but it does not define *the value* itself. In order to better understand *the value* in the software development context, we will refer to value-based software engineering (VBSE) [24]. Boehm [24] introduced the seven key elements as the foundation of value-based software engineering. The VBSE framework illustrates the complexity of tasks, which are not trivial, and that are required in order to understand *the value* in the software development context. All those tasks require participation of different actors (stakeholders) across an entire organization and beyond the organization (customers). Only, these actors can utilize their knowledge and experience to make decisions that they believe to be aligned with their understandings of *the value*.

The complexity and difficulty of defining a value in the software engineering context poses a serious challenge for the software metrics and measurement practices. Boehm and Sullivan [25] noted that the measurement of the value as a scalar quantity is rather difficult, if not impossible. This challenge has a profound implication on lean metrics in a software engineering context. Without the ability to measure true value (usually only one aspect—financial—is quantified), an interpretation of the lean metrics will be incomplete (same applies for the waste) by failing to answer the fundamental question—is value maximized and waste minimized? Our concern for metrics is related to the decision flow. Proper metrics are a powerful aid to the decision making process (value creation points), and also metrics have the ability to provide shared understanding among actors.

We see that a true legacy of lean thinking, which could be a valuable contribution to software engineering, is a holistic view of different elements: people, resources, processes, business, which are all part of a single construct, where, the existence of each element is constrained by its purpose.

Our objective was to clarify the nature of the lean software development flow. In order to achieve the objective, we accentuated the role and purpose of actors (people) with explicit statements—axioms. The axioms could be conveniently used for exploring and perceiving related phenomena in the software development context from a human-centric perspective and not from a mechanistic perspective.

What is flowing in lean software development? The nature and diversity of decisions that are scattered throughout an organization prevent a clear picture and an understanding of the flows in software development.

We are not suggesting that a decision flow is the software development flow, but, rather, that it is an inseparable part of the software development activities and it carries capabilities of adding or diminishing value of the software product or process. Therefore, the existing and new-coming software development approaches should enable and encourage decision-making by all actors in a natural way as a part of their activities, while decisions have to be synchronized with a common purpose. In virtue of these needs, we see that further research should focus on metrics and measurement practices in lean software development, particularly exploring methods and approaches that could be used for analyzing value (qualitatively and quantitatively) in the software development context, e.g., business goal-oriented measurement approaches (see [26]) that have the ability to analyze and capture value.

Acknowledgments. This article is based on the work carried out in the Cloud Software program financed by the Finnish Funding Agency for Technology and Innovation (Tekes).

References

1. Womack, J., Jones, D.: Lean Thinking: Banish Waste and Create Wealth in Your Corporation, Revised and Updated. Free Press, London (2003)
2. Womack, J., Jones, D., Roos, D.: The machine that changed the world. Simon & Schuster Ltd., London (2007)
3. Poppendieck, M., Poppendieck, T.: Lean Software Development: An Agile Toolkit. Addison-Wesley Longman Publishing Co., Inc., Amsterdam (2003)
4. Poppendieck, M., Poppendieck, T.: Leading Lean Software Development: Results Are not the Point. Addison-Wesley Professional, Reading (2009)
5. Beck, K., Beedle, M., van Bennekum, A., Cockburn, A., Cunningham, W., Fowler, M., Grenning, J., Highsmith, J., Hunt, A., Jeffries, R., Kern, J., Marick, B., Martin, R.C., Mellor, S., Schwaber, K., Sutherland, J., Thomas, D.: Manifesto for agile software development (2001)
6. Freeman, P.: Lean concepts in software engineering. In: IPSS-Europe International Conference on Lean Software Development, Stuttgart, Germany, pp. 1–8 (1992)
7. Bullinger, H., Fähnrich, K.: Managing lean enterprises and lean software development. In: IPSS-Europe International Conference on Lean Software Development, Stuttgart, Germany, pp. 1–45 (1992)
8. Basili, V.: The experience factory: Can it make you a 5? In: Seventeenth Software Engineering Workshop (SEL), NASA/Goddard Space Flight Center, College Park, MD, USA, pp. 55–73 (1992)
9. Magazine: Learn to be lean: deliver fast in short sprints. Lean Magazine (#4) (2009)
10. Magazine: Fighting muda. are you prepared for the war against waste? Lean Magazine (#3) (2008)
11. Humphrey, W.: Managing the Software Process. Addison-Wesley, New York (1990)
12. Chrissis, M., Konrad, M., Shrum, S.: CMMI: Guidelines for Process Integration and Product Improvement. Addison-Wesley Professional, New York (2006)
13. Middleton, P., Sutton, J.: Lean Software Strategies. Productivity Press, New York (2005)

14. Liker, J., Meier, D.: The Toyota Way Fieldbook: A Practical Guide for Implementing Toyota's 4Ps. McGraw-Hill, New York (2006)
15. Reinertsen, D.: The Principles of Product Development Flow: Second Generation Lean Product Development. Celeritas Publishing, Redondo Beach (2009)
16. Morgan, J., Liker, J.: The Toyota Product Development System: Integrating People, Process, and Technology. Productivity Press, New York (2006)
17. Fujimoto, T.: Evolution of Manufacturing Systems at Toyota. Oxford University Press, Inc., New York (1999)
18. Ohno, T.: Toyota Production System: Beyond Large-Scale Production. Productivity Press, Portland (1988)
19. Takeuchi, H., Nonaka, I.: The new new product development game. Harvard Business Review 2(1), 137–147 (1986)
20. Locher, D.: Value Stream Mapping for Lean Development: A How-To Guide for Streamlining Time to Market. CRC Press, Taylor & Francis Group, New York, USA (2008)
21. Nonaka, I., Konno, N.: The concept of "ba": Building a foundation for knowledge creation. California Management Review 40, 40–54 (1998)
22. Ballard, G.: Positive vs negative iteration in design. In: 8th International Conference on Lean Construction, Brighton, UK, pp. 1–12 (2000)
23. Humphrey, W.: Characterizing the software process: A maturity framework. IEEE Software 2(5), 73–79 (1988)
24. Boehm, B.: Value-based software engineering. ACM SIGSOFT Software Engineering Notes 2(28), 3–15 (2003)
25. Boehm, B., Sullivan, K.: Software economics: A roadmap. In: International Conference on Software Engineering 2000, Limerick, Ireland, pp. 319–343 (2000)
26. Mandić, V., Basili, V., Harjumaa, L., Oivo, M., Markkula, J.: Utilizing GQM+Strategies for business value analysis: An approach for evaluating business goals. In: The 4th International Symposium on Empirical Software Engineering and Measurement, ESEM 2010, Bolzano-Bozen, Italy (2010)

Leadership in Kanban Software Development Projects: A Quasi-controlled Experiment

Marko Ikonen

Department of Computer Science
P. O. Box 68, FI-00014 University of Helsinki, Finland
marko.ikonen@cs.helsinki.fi

Abstract. Useless actions and work in software development projects do not increase the value for the customer. While getting rid of such waste may sound simple, even recognizing the waste is considered a challenging issue. Once recognized with its causes, projects are more aware of the signs of waste: the pitfalls are avoidable by knowing their reasons. On the other hand, self-organization and empowering the teams emerge in a modern Kanban-driven software development project. This makes it relevant to ask whether sacrificing project resources for leadership adds any value. Hence, this paper conducts a quasi-controlled experiment with two leadership settings in order to find out differences between waste, its causes and effects. The results from the empirical analysis show that waste is present in each project but the amount and significance of waste can be reduced with the right leadership even in self-organized teams of Kanban projects.

Keywords: Kanban, leadership, lean software development, management, software process improvement.

1 Introduction

The software industry is constantly searching for new solutions to existing problems [12]. The goals of improvement initiatives range from resolving time-to-market delay to increasing productivity and reducing operation costs. Applying *Lean* production principles to software development [22,23] is one of the newest fashions in the software industry. A key trait in this trend is eliminating all kinds of waste from the development. Consequently, similar ideas for waste removal have been proposed to be adopted for software product development [22].

One of the Lean tools is the Kanban way of managing production operations [18]. Kanban has been applied to software production as a project management process model [9]. It has similarities with and differences to the well-established Scrum method in Agile software development [16].

Our research interests are related to Kanban because of its striving to minimize non-value-adding activities, such as extra processes. Despite this advantage of Kanban, its relation to waste is an area of study that has not received much attention. Regarding the self-organizing team principle, a relevant question in

P. Abrahamsson and N. Oza (Eds.): LESS 2010, LNBIP 65, pp. 85–98, 2010.

order to improve project performance is, whether leadership is still necessary. Therefore, this paper explores how the differences of the leadership style affect waste in Kanban-driven software development projects. The study presents a research model and employs a quasi-controlled experiment research approach [27]. The empirical evaluation is performed based on two Kanban-driven software engineering projects. Altogether, this research endeavor thus suggests practical as well as methodological implications by finding out the need for leadership. The results from the empirical analysis show that waste is present in each project but the amount and significance of waste can be reduced with the right leadership even in self-organized teams of Kanban projects.

The rest of this paper is structured as follows. Section 2 outlines the related conceptual background and presents the research model used in the experiment. Section 3 then describes the empirical research design by introducing the research environment, case projects, and research methods with their evaluation criteria. Section 4 presents the results, followed by elaborative discussion in Section 5. Finally, Section 6 draws the final conclusions.

2 Background

2.1 Waste in Software Engineering Projects

Lean thinking determines *waste* is basically everything that does not add to the customer value of the products [22]. Generally, the following three basic categories of waste-related elements are: (1) non-value-adding activities (NVA), (2) variations (in process quality, cost, delivery), and (3) unreasonableness (overburden). Recognizing waste is one of the most important Lean principles [22]. By applying this principle in software development, such elements can be considered as follows.

Functioning and ability to solve business problems of *partially done work* (inventory) cannot be known until integrated into the software environment. *Extra processes* (NVA), such as unnecessary paperwork, do not add any value but rather consume resources. Resources are also consumed by *extra features* (overproduction) since they have to be tracked, compiled, integrated, tested, and debugged. *Task switching*, such as bouncing between multiple tasks or issues, takes time because of re-orientation. *Waiting* (NVA) does not add value either. *Motion* (NVA) means inappropriate distance to other developers as well as moving of information and knowledge. Finally, small *defects* discovered after weeks are more time-consuming than a major defect detected in a minute [22].

2.2 Kanban Process Model and Leadership

The Kanban process model is one of the key operation management tools in Lean manufacturing [18]. In general, it has three rules: (1) visualize the workflow, (2) limit work in progress (WIP) at each workflow state, and (3) measure the cycle time (i.e., average time to complete one item) [16]. Kanban-driven operations enable to keep the amount of inventories (simultaneous WIP) under control and to balance the overall production flow.

Kanban does not intervene in leadership despite its importance. It is argued that without leadership, even a capable staff head cannot reach goals well enough [17,26]. The lack of a clear authority structure in software development is both a cause of chaos and freedom [13].

Leadership, in general, means the pattern of behavior leaders use to influence others as well as perceived by those being influenced, and can be divided into two basic categories: directive and supportive behavior [3].

This study focuses on the former one which, according to Blanchard, is defined as follows: *"Directive behavior concentrates on what and how. It involves telling and showing people what to do, how to do it, when to do it; monitoring performance; and providing frequent feedback on results."* [3]

2.3   Research Model

This study extends the preliminary research model [11] by tracking the effects and causes of the waste. In other words, the current research model (Fig. 1) focuses on three steps: (1) waste noted in the case projects (i.e., the waste categories from A to F), (2) the effects, i.e., why was it considered to be waste, and (3) the reasons why this waste occurred. This approach enables the comparison of the effects of different leadership styles on waste between the case projects.

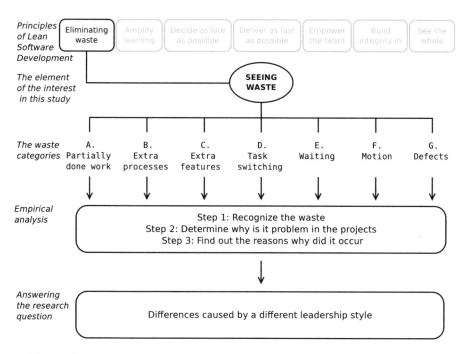

Fig. 1. Our research model including the seven kinds of waste suggested by [22]

3   Empirical Research Design

3.1   Software Factory Research Environment

The *Software Factory*[1] enables software engineering research setting at the University of Helsinki [1]. It is an advanced R&D laboratory environment for conducting software projects. The concept comprises the physical laboratory environment coupled with an operational model from the empirical research perspective. The entrepreneurial aim is to conduct business-driven software development projects for creating new product prototypes and even commercializing them (possibly with spin-offs). This can be utilized as a research platform.

3.2   Case Projects

The proposed cases were two Kanban-based software development projects with controlled variability, something extremely difficult in a business environment. Table 1 presents the variables set as constants for the experiment.

Table 1. The variables set as constants for the quasi-controlled experiment

Project duration	seven weeks
Process model	Kanban
Working time	six hours per day, four or five days per week
Participants' education	Computer Science background
Business life threats (e.g., budget pressures or being fired)	eliminated
Customer type	representatives obligated to commit themselves with time and interaction
Customer experience	experienced technically and in the customer role of software development projects
Product to be produced	product or prototype for real commercial use
Product size	reasonable, must be fitted within seven weeks
Team management	self-organized
Team size	between nine and thirteen members
Support	IT support and external technical consultant without charge

In addition to technical knowledge, each team member had experience in working in a team-based environment. Besides the use of Kanban, no other particular development method was insisted upon. The teams had close to full control within the R&D setting to decide upon the practices used. As a result, both projects chose to use Ruby on Rails (open-source web framework) and to start writing code after a one-week learning session. The observation during the projects and the interviews after the projects verified that the setting of the variables remained except the working time which varied slightly, particularly in

---

[1] 'Software Factory' here means a different concept than existed in the early software factory organizations of the late 1960s and the current software development framework models. The first software factories focused on software production in manufacturing-like systematic ways with CASE tools and component reuse [7]. Some modern software engineering application frameworks have also coined the term "factory" [8]. However, the Software Factory is able to host such facets as well.

project #2. Some members worked longer days while the others worked shorter ones.

More experienced members (called seniors) took responsibility for designs. They also assisted less experienced members (juniors) in technical and practical issues and gave useful advice. In short, the project teams were self-organized.

The team leaders of both projects used directive leadership. Due to the quasi-controlled experiment, the difference was their focus. Leadership in project #1 also focused on process-related issues, such as requiring the team to follow the shared coding style and other rules given. Leadership in project #2, instead, focused only on task-related concerns, such as guiding technically how to do things. The observation during the projects and the interviews after the projects verified that the team leaders really used the focuses set for the experiment.

Both projects had experience in project management, i.e., project #1 did not have a more favorable base than did project #2. This setting enabled us to find out differences in waste between the projects. In other words, the question was, in addition to finding waste, its causes and effects, what are the outcomes of waste in Kanban projects with different leadership settings.

3.3   Research Methods and Evaluation Criteria

Three methods were used for collecting data from the case projects. As Parnas and Curtis [20] state, this approach enabled a more objective view for the analysis than a single method (e.g., interview only).

First, a pre-test questionnaire was used to explore the team members' experiences and skills. While this information was secondary, it provided useful background information to understand the group dynamics and teams' competence. At the end of the projects, the final questionnaire measured the overall project success based on the first and the second dimension of Shenhar's model of project success [24]: (1) project efficiency (meeting schedule (PE-1) and budget) and (2) impact on the customer (meeting functional performance (IC-1), meeting technical specifications (IC-2), fulfilling customer needs (IC-3), solving a customer's problem, the actual use of the product by the customer, and customer satisfaction (IC-4)). The codes in the parentheses, e.g., PE-1, refer to the scores of the selected items presented in Table 9. These items were chosen due to their relevancy in the sense of project content and waste. Both the teams and their customers evaluated the relevant items of the two dimensions.

Second, the author performed a one-week intensive observation session in the Factory in order to study the progress, attitudes, best practices, and waste. During the session, presumptions and perceptions were born which were then validated in the interview session by asking the interviewees whether they agreed.

Third, the most informative one, the semi-structured interview method [21] was performed for collecting data right after the projects ended. Open-ended questions and the semi-structured theme interview technique were used. The questions related to waste were raised in the projects. The framework illustrated in Fig. 1 was applied by generating questions regarding the waste issues under the seven element categories (from A to G). The points of interests in each category were to (1) recognize the waste, (2) track its effects, and (3) find out why it occurred.

Due to a possibility that the interviewees were not familiar with the term 'waste' in the sense of Lean thinking, we used a more familiar way: Regarding waste category B, for example, the interviewees were asked to determine unnecessary work in their project. If they did not find any, we asked them what work should had been cut out of the project in order to reach better results, more efficient progress or time-saving. In this way, waste was finally found. Meanwhile, it became quite obvious whether this waste was a big deal at all. Once found, we asked why it occurred and what the consequences were in terms of time losses or invaluable work.

A total of nine persons from the teams of nine and thirteen were selected for the interviews so that they represented comprehensively the three different roles: juniors, seniors, and the team leaders. This is called a role-based sampling. Each interview lasted about one hour. The interviews were recorded in audio and the answers were categorized into the seven kinds of waste based on the research model (Fig. 1).

4   Empirical Analysis

This section evaluates the case projects and presents waste with its effects and causes that occurred in the projects (Section 4.1). Moreover, the success of the projects is presented (Section 4.2).

4.1   Waste Found in the Kanban Projects

Instead of showing long answers from the interview session, tables from 2 to 8 present the relevant results of the empirical evaluation from the projects by waste categories from A to G (Fig. 1). These results are a consequence of the study strategy and combinations of the three data collection methods (Section 3.3). If a member, for example, said that the retrospections were a waste of time, the author did not believe it without some evidence but rather asked why they are a waste of time. Hence, the tables present only such conceptions that the members were able to justify.

Partially done work. Delays and being stuck with tasks may generate partially done work as they did in project #2 (Table 2). Moreover, this waste can generate another kind of waste: task switching which, in its turn, slowed down the progress (project #2). However, project #1 demonstrated that partially done work may sometimes be appropriate instead of strictly avoiding it.

Related to project #2, the waste presented could have been avoided with the appropriate leadership by demanding that everyone carry out fewer tasks at a time. In addition, by making the team follow the Kanban rule of measurement, delays caused by unfinished tasks could have been avoided thanks to the increased awareness of the work amount of the tasks.

Table 2. Waste of partially done work (1), its effects (2) and causes (3)

Partially done work (waste A) in project #1
1. Some tasks had to be suspended.
2. Re-orientation to the suspended tasks was time-consuming.
3. It turned out that completing some tasks needed other, yet unfinished tasks.
1. The delayed accomplishment of a task prevented some other tasks being accomplished.
2. Members who were producing these tasks needed to be blocked, were forced to suspend them, which created task switching (waste D) in addition to partially done work.
3. The work realization of the blocking task turned out multi-tenfold compared with its estimation.
Partially done work (waste A) in project #2
1. Tasks not finished for the customer demos delayed the schedule.
2. Production of these tasks continued after the demos at the expense of other tasks being finished.
3a. Work estimations were not done for the tasks since the team did not believe in making them realistic.
3b. The realizations of the task durations were not measured either. Thereby, validating the reality of potential estimations would not even have been possible.
1. Several tasks that related to different subjects were assigned simultaneously to one person, which slowed down the progress.
2. Re-orientation to the partially done tasks, as well as task switching (waste D) generated, took time after members were already focusing on new tasks.
3. Members were stuck with tasks and they decided to assign to other tasks.

Extra processes. Showing straightforward in project #1 in Table 3, extra processes could have been avoided by planning things in advance. Regarding project #2, lack of interaction and communication in their different forms resulted in many extra processes and even another kind of waste: waiting. More effective leadership and stricter discipline inside the team could have eliminated these kinds of waste reported in project #2.

Extra features. Despite the minor extra features reported in Table 4, both teams complied with the prioritization of the tasks well, which resulted from appropriate leadership.

Task switching. The case of project #1 shows task switching (Table 5) is an option for waste of waiting. In project #2, the large WIP limits caused task switching, which, in its turn, was closely relatedto partially done work. In both projects, asking for help generated task switching. This kind of task switching can be seen as an investment for a project: when juniors are helped, they learn so they do not have to ask the same things again (project #2). Also, helping each other solves blockages, thus keeps every member efficient, which is an advantage for the project (project #1).

Regarding the leadership in the projects, the only improvement needed might have been not to let members to ask for help any time and to establish particular tutorial sessions for technical questions and requests for help. The effects of such sessions cannot, however, be derived from this study since such data were not gathered.

Waiting. While many kinds of waste of waiting were recognized (Table 6), the only team-caused issue was the attempt to design the things right the first time (project #2). Lean thinking resists this approach. An appropriate leadership could have helped the team to proceed faster without too detailed designs.

Table 3. Waste of extra processes (1), its effects (2) and causes (3)

Extra processes (waste B) in project #1
1. The processes of Code Review and Quality Assurance were useless in tiny tasks.
2. Unnecessary work does not increase the customer-value.
3. The Kanban board contained the current columns so these operations were done for each task.
1. The first retrospections contained redundancy and took nearly a complete workday from the whole team.
2. Long sessions are exhausting and time-consuming.
3. The content of the retrospections were not prepared well enough.

Extra processes (waste B) in project #2
1. Lack of interaction between the team and the customer generated unnecessary (extra) work.
2. The team had to produce some tasks all over again.
3. After having the first requirements from the customer, the team focused fully on production without ensuring that there were no misunderstandings from the customer. These misunderstandings, however, had occurred, which was not discovered before the next customer demo (i.e., time had been wasted because of the misunderstandings, which could have been corrected with more active interaction with the customer).
1. Absences, which were not announced, generated unnecessary work.
2. The rest of the team had to put efforts on deciding whether the task assignments and reservations of the absentee should be declared free because the tasks are important.
3. Absentees may have been sick or absent for other reasons, or just late, which causes uncertainty regarding declaring the tasks free.
1. Lack of sharing information generated unnecessary work and waiting (waste E).
2a. Some decisions were not based on facts due to the uncertainty.
2b. The team had to choose whether it should wait for potential latecomers to the meetings.
3a. Misunderstandings occurred due to insufficient communication.
3b. The customer was not willing or was not able to provide enough essential information regarding a salient component (produced elsewhere), which generated misunderstandings regarding functionality.
3c. Some members did not inform the team about being late or absent. Hence, the others did not know whether the assigned tasks should be re-assigned in order to complete the tasks quickly.
3d. Some members used an unfinished installation document by accident since the document was not marked as unfinished. This led to erroneous installation, which caused unnecessary work.

Table 4. Waste of extra features (1), its effects (2) and causes (3)

Extra features (waste C) in project #1
1. A few unnecessary features were produced.
2. Unnecessary features do not add value for the customer and waste testing and debugging resources.
3. The customer representatives did not always know what they wanted, causing requirement changes.

Extra features (waste C) in project #2
1. A couple of low-priority (i.e., "nice-to-have" priority) features were produced even though there were high-priority tasks in the backlog.
2. Producing, testing, and debugging of these features took resources.
3. Sometimes, all the high-priority tasks available were too complex for some members, thereby driving them to choose low-priority tasks.

Motion. Only minor waste of motion regarding the projects related to communication (Table 7).

Defects. Some waste of defects (Table 8) happened in project #2 because of slow feedback. Moreover, there was hurriedness at the end of both projects. This was shown particularly in project #2 due to its resources lost by the other waste categories. In addition to shortening the feedback loop, an appropriate leadership could have helped making the writing of tests obligatory.

Table 5. Waste of task switching (1), its effects (2) and causes (3)

Task switching (waste D) in project #1
1. Asking for help from others disrupted working.
2. The advisors' orientation to the problem and re-orientation back to their own tasks took time.
3. Help was asked for in order to solve the problems.
1. Code review generated task switching.
2. Re-orientation took resources.
3. Persons were not allowed to make code review for their own tasks, so they used waiting time by doing other things.

Task switching (waste D) in project #2
1. Asking for help continuously disturbed the progress.
2. All senior members were frustrated about this problem. All of them agreed that asking for help slowed down the project because it interrupted their work and re-orientation took time. Orientation to the problems of persons asking for help took time as well. Spending time on this was time spent away from the seniors' own work.
3a. Juniors needed to ask for help. At worst a senior had to do the rest of a junior's task.
3b. Some juniors liked to make sure they are doing things right and with quality. Unsystematic code review increased asking for help since feedback from the code reviews was insufficient to guarantee the quality and style of code. Moreover, the team did not have shared standards for coding.
3c. There were no rules for disrupting each other so they were allowed to ask for help at anytime.
1. Too high WIPs (Work-In-Progress) disturbed the progress of the project.
2. The "In Work" and "Code Review" columns on the Kanban board gathered many task tickets, which increased task switching, which, on its part, increased the time consumed for re-orientation.
3. At the beginning, WIPs for the "In Work" and "Code Review" columns were large, which tempted members to start a new task and to leave code reviews regarding tasks done by others to later, which led to this 'flood' in the columns.

Table 6. Waste of waiting (1), its effects (2) and causes (3)

Waiting (waste E) in project #1
1. Waiting members busy with other things reduced concentration.
2. Doing a task and simultaneously keeping thoughts clear for the occupied person disturbs working.
3. Members needed to ask about things from each other but the others could have been occupied at that moment so the askers had to wait.
1. The team had to wait for the customer.
2. Being on standby distracts from focus on work.
3. The customer was continually late for the customer demos .
1. The team had to wait for the headsets, ordered at the beginning of the project until the last weeks of the project.
2. Without headsets, watching screen casts was not possible without disturbing others because of audio. Learning and progressing, however, was slower without the screen casts.
3. Delivering the order was not supervised.
1. Hardware problems were solved within a day at worst.
2. Hardware problems disrupt work.
3. The I.T. support had limited resources for the project.

Waiting (waste E) in project #2
1. Making designs on too detailed a level slowed down the project.
2. When attempting to do things right the first time, everything must be foreseen and taken into account, which takes huge resources of time. The team had to wait for detailed designs and could not proceed without them. History has shown that original often plans have to change during projects.
3a. Despite spending a lot of time on foreseeing and consideration, the impossibility of designs may not have been revealed before implementation.
3b. Juniors were not able to contribute to designs so they had to wait.
1. The team had to wait for the customer (similar to the notification from project #1).
1. Waiting members busy with other things reduced concentration.
2. Carrying out a task and simultaneously keeping thoughts clear for the occupied person disturbs working.
3a. Members needed to ask about things from each other but the others could have been occupied at that moment so the askers waited.
3b. Some members did not want to interrupt others when they saw that someone was focused on his or her tasks.

Table 7. Waste of motion (1), its effects (2) and causes (3)

Motion (waste F) in project #1
1. Two members did the same task by accident.
2. Duplicate work is unnecessary.
3. Communication was insufficient.
Motion (waste F) in project #2
1. At the beginning, all the communication between the team and the customer occurred via one member.
2. Although a centralized communication model is helpful in gathering information, it generates useless motion.
3. One of the members was assigned to take care of communication with the customer.

Table 8. Waste of defects (1), its effects (2) and causes (3)

Defects (waste G) in project #1
1. Despite the policy of Test-Driven Development, tests were not necessarily written before the code.
2a. Debugging is harder when the tests do not exist .
2b. Advantages of tests written after the code are harder to see and writing the tests may have been forgotten.
3. Writing tests before the code was not obligatory.
1. During the last week of the project, hot-fixes had to be accepted without comprehensive testing.
2. Defects caused in debugging are hard to detect without testing.
3. The integration tests had been planned to be performed during the last week. Time resources, however, were insufficient.
Defects (waste G) in project #2
1. Slow feedback caused a number of defects.
2. Not interfering in the incorrect development of a task before the task is completed, caused more fixes than interfering with it at an early stage.
3a. Slow feedback was one of the most serious problems in the project.
3b. Juniors could not learn from their mistakes when they were implementing their tasks because of the slow feedback.
1. There was no time to perform integration and stress testing.
2. Without comprehensive testing, bugs have a greater probability to creep into an end product.
3a. Time was running out because of other kinds of waste in the project.
3b. Some radical changes were done up until the end of the project. Due to time resources, these changes could not be tested comprehensively.

4.2   Success of the Projects

Table 9 presents the results of the success evaluation for the projects.

Table 9. The project success scores evaluated by the team leaders, teams, and customers using the Likert scale from 1 (totally disagree) to 5 (totally agree). The selected items of the success dimensions used here are based on the project success mapping of Shenhar et al. [24]. The project met the time goals completely (PE-1). The product met the operational specifications completely (IC-1). The product met the technical specifications completely (IC-2). The product fulfilled the customer needs (IC-3). The product satisfied the customer (IC-4).

project	PE-1		IC-1		IC-2		IC-3	IC-4
	team leader	team average	team leader	team average	team leader	team average	customer	customer
#1	5	4.2	5	4.2	5	3.9	5	5
#2	3	3.9	4	4.0	3	3.6	4	4

Both the team leaders and the teams (including the team leader) evaluated items PE-1, IC-1, and IC-2 while the customers evaluated items IC-3 and IC-4. According to the success viewpoint used, the results show that project #1 was more successful than project #2.

5 Discussion

5.1 Findings

By taking into account the effects presented in the tables from 2 to 8, it can be claimed with no doubt that waste found particularly in project #2 caused a serious loss of time. This loss of time expressed itself mainly as actions considered to be useless for the projects (e.g., the case of "making designs on too detailed a level" in Table 6) or as lack of actions (e.g., the case of "lack of sharing information" in Table 3). According to the project success evaluation (Table 9), this finding shows the importance of leadership in Kanban projects. In practice, the right leadership would have saved time by avoiding waste.

The results reveal one of the dual characteristics of Kanban: it allows working without a formal project manager in order to avoid waste but insufficient directive leadership creates waste. In general, Jurison [14] shows that leadership, one of the critical success factors, is needed to keep the team focused throughout the project. Conradi and Fuggetta [5] agree: improving processes cannot be forced from the outside.

Using the seven categories of waste as the lenses for an analysis, it is likely that most of them are apparent in any software development project. A difference is the attempt to minimize the impact of existing waste. Even though Kanban strives for reducing the NVA work, waste may still creep in despite effective leadership as shown in the case of project #1.

In addition to this finding, the study explored causes and effects of the waste by following the research model (Fig. 1) based on the seven kinds of waste suggested by [22]. Avoiding waste brings value for customers since it saves time. An early step in this value-adding operation is to recognize the indicators of waste. The study recognized several sources of waste with their reasons and demonstrated their consequences to the case projects.

While some waste is not avoidable with either style used in the experiment, causes and damages of the waste differ with different leadership. As a conclusion, the amount and significance of waste can be reduced with the right leadership in self-organized teams of Kanban software development projects.

5.2 Validity of the Study

The study has conducted a research model based on best practices [22], i.e., something that we have a reason to believe might be true. In this case, we assumed software development projects contain waste. Hence, we observed the case projects by being aware of what we are looking for. After this observation, with a widened understanding, the interview session was performed in order to validate the observations made and, further, take another point of view to make more findings. Parnas [20] prefers this type of experimental design because of its higher practical value than an inadequate one-method design of studies.

Due to the numbers of constants set up for the experiment (Section 3.2), performing it in an uncontrolled business environment would have questioned the validity of the findings. While a new Lean trend in the business environment encourages not to eliminate variability [23], we were able to estimate the meanings of causes and effects in our study more clearly without certain noise. I.e., the variability was controlled.

The team size and complexity of the product being implemented, however, varied between the projects. Except the matter of competence differences between the teams, waste that was found did not disrupt the comparison of the teams. The fact that project #2 ignored some common rules is an example of such a variable unrelated to the complexity and team size.

All the data are based on the perspectives and opinions of the team members about success and waste, and on the author's observations. Regardless, perspectives and opinions without any evidence, as stated in the beginning of Section 4, were ignored. The findings are thereby based on the established perspectives and opinions, not on the raw data itself.

We do not maintain that the findings are one-to-one with industry but rather that, given specific circumstances, they indicate a trend explaining the project success or failure when a particular set of indicators, including leadership, are searched for. While measuring the damage of waste to the projects precisely (e.g., losses in workdays) was out of the scope of the study, time losses caused by waste were clearly evident.

Finally, the approach of the experimentation strategy used in this study has been favored [15,25] as well as validated [10,19] in the literature.

6   Conclusions

Recognizing waste and thereby minimizing its impact on projects can save resources and accelerate lead-time. Thus, significant actionable opportunities can be reached for practical use. According to the results of this study, waste can be tracked in Kanban-based software development projects based on the research model (Fig. 1). This action enables finding out the causes and effects of the waste. As a conclusion based on the quasi-controlled experiment, amount and significance of waste can be reduced with the right leadership in self-organized teams of Kanban software development projects.

An interesting issue is the problems detected beyond the waste. Lack of communication, for example, is one of the most common reasons for having problems in a project [2,4,6]. It is not, however, waste but rather a shortcoming. This finding suggests that, in addition to waste, it is important to beware of such insufficiencies in order to improve project performance.

Acknowledgments

This work was supported by TEKES as a part of the Cloud Software program of Tivit (Finnish Strategic Centre for Science, Technology and Innovation in the field of ICT). The author expresses his gratitude to Professor Pekka Abrahamsson and to Petri Kettunen and Fabian Fagerholm for their contribution on this research. The time devoted by the Software Factory teams is greatly appreciated.

References

1. Abrahamsson, P.: Unique infrastructure investment: Introducing the Software Factory concept. Software Factory Magazine 1(1), 2–3 (2010)
2. Addison, T., Vallabh, S.: Controlling software project risks: an empirical study of methods used by experienced project managers. In: Proceedings of the 2002 Annual Research Conference of the South African Institute of Computer Scientists and Information Technologists on Enablement Through Technology, SAICSIT 2002, pp. 128–140. South African Institute for Computer Scientists and Information Technologists (2002)
3. Situational Leadership® II - The Article. The Ken Blanchard Companies (2001)
4. Boehm, B.: Software risk management: Principles and practices. IEEE Software 8(1), 32–41 (1991)
5. Conradi, R., Fuggetta, A.: Improving software process improvement. IEEE Software 19(4), 92–99 (2002)
6. Curtis, B., Krasner, H., Iscoe, N.: A field study of the software design process for large systems. Communications of the ACM 31(11), 1268–1287 (1988)
7. Cusumano, M.: The Software Factory: An Entry for the Encyclopedia of Software Engineering. Number WP#BPS-3268-91. Massachusetts Institute of Technology, Sloan School (1991)
8. Greenfield, J., Short, K., Cook, S., Kent, S.: Software Factories: Assembling Applications with Patterns, Frameworks, Models & Tools. Wiley, Chichester (2004)
9. Hiranabe, K.: Kanban applied to software development: From agile to lean (2008), http://www.infoq.com/articles/hiranabe-lean-agile-kanban
10. Höst, M., Regnell, B., Wohlin, C.: Using students as subjects – a comparative study of students and professionals in lead-time impact assessments. Journal of Empirical Software Engineering 5(3), 201–214 (2000)
11. Ikonen, M., Kettunen, P., Oza, N., Abrahamsson, P.: Exploring the sources of waste in Kanban software development projects. In: Proceedings of the 36th EUROMICRO Conference on Software Engineering and Advanced Applications, SEAA 2010, IEEE, Los Alamitos (2010)
12. Jacobson, I.: What they don't teach you about software at school: Be smart! In: XP 2009. LNBIP, vol. 31, pp. 1–4. Springer, Heidelberg (2009)
13. Jensen, C., Scacchi, W.: Collaboration, leadership, control, and conflict negotiation and the netbeans.org open source software development community. In: Proceedings of the 38th Annual Hawaii International Conference on System Sciences, HICSS 2005. IEEE Computer Society, Washington (2005)
14. Jurison, J.: Software project management: the manager's view. Communications of the AIS 2 (September 1999)

15. Kitchenham, B., Pfleeger, S., Pickard, L., Jones, P., Hoaglin, D., Emam, K., Rosenberg, J.: Preliminary guidelines for empirical research for empirical research in software engineering. IEEE Transactions on Software Engineering 28(8), 721–734 (2002)
16. Kniberg, H.: Kanban vs. Scrum – how to make the most of both (2009), http://www.crisp.se/henrik.kniberg/Kanban-vs-Scrum.pdf (January 18, 2010)
17. Kotter, J.P.: Leading change. Harvard Business School Press, Boston (1996)
18. Liker, J.: The Toyota Way. McGraw-Hill, New York (2004)
19. Madeyski, L.: Test-driven development: An empirical evaluation of agile practice. Springer, Heidelberg (2010)
20. Parnas, D., Curtis, B.: Point/counterpoint. IEEE Software 26(6), 56–59 (2009)
21. Patton, M.Q.: Qualitative evaluation and research methods, 2nd edn. Sage, Thousand Oaks (1990)
22. Poppendieck, M., Poppendieck, T.: Lean software development: An agile toolkit. Addison Wesley, Boston (2003)
23. Reinertsen, D.G.: The Principles of Product Development Flow: Second Generation Lean Product Development. Celeritas Publishing, Redondo Beach (2009)
24. Shenhar, A.J., Dvir, D., Levy, O., Maltz, A.C.: Project success: A multidimensional strategic concept. Long Range Planning 34, 699–725 (2001)
25. Tichy, W.: Hints for reviewing empirical work in software engineering. Journal of Empirical Software Engineering 5(4), 309–312 (2000)
26. Watson, T.: Organising and Managing Work – Organisational, managerial and strategic behaviour in theory and practice. Prentice Hall, Pearson Education, Harlow (2002)
27. Wohlin, C., Runeson, P., Höst, M.: Experimentation in software engineering: An introduction. Kluwer, Boston (2000)

Distributing a Lean Organization:
Maintaining Communication While Staying Agile

Sebastian Meyer, Eric Knauss, and Kurt Schneider

Software Engineering Group, Leibniz Universität Hannover
Welfengarten 1, 30167 Hannover
{sebastian.meyer,eric.knauss,kurt.schneider}@inf.uni-hannover.de

Abstract. Distributed software development teams are common-place today. One good reason for distribution is the need to combine special skills or competencies from different locations. However, integrating skills flexibly is both a technical and a communication challenge. Lean and agile projects depend on direct communication. In this contribution, we investigate how agile teams can be distributed by adding a "remote partner" – and still maintain agile advantages. We analyze communication using the goal-question-metric paradigm (GQM) and apply it to a programming project, part of which was distributed. We discuss our insights on the minimal set of additions (technical and organizational) that are required to turn distributed while staying agile.

1 Introduction

Software development is a complex process. With the rise of new technologies, frameworks, and new hardware like mobile phones, software development becomes an even more complex challenge. Developers who are skilled in every aspect of software development are rare. It is more common to build a team that consists of specialists. Each one of them focuses on one aspect and strengthens the whole team in that area. Each aspect requires specific knowledge. Therefore, knowledge has become one of the core values for an organization.

Some problems cannot be solved with the in-house capabilities of an organization or an organizational unit. In this case another company or team can fill gaps in the knowledge spectrum. Geographical distribution of the resulting team is a frequent consequence. The setup of teams that cannot be co-located and their integration into a common development process can turn into a major organizational nightmare. In a traditional (e.g. waterfall) process, outsourcing and its variants demand their own dedicated subprocess – which has to be managed. In the context of a lean organization the additional bureaucracy for starting the distributed subprocess and for integrating the new developers into the development team is considered waste. In order to stay effective and lean, the coordination effort needs to be minimized.

2 Our Lab Setup

Carver et al. [1] discuss chances and challenges of using students in software engineering experiments. Accordingly, it is difficult to study project variations in industry

P. Abrahamsson and N. Oza (Eds.): LESS 2010, LNBIP 65, pp. 99–103, 2010.

settings: In an industrial setting, parallel work for the sake of understanding is too expensive and rarely accepted by the developers/management. In addition, student projects can be better instrumented, measured and investigated.

Therefore, we initiated the Global Software Engineering Lab (GloSE-Lab) as part of our multi-site GloSE research project. In GloSE-Lab, master students from different universities in Germany explore problems and possible solutions in a distributed project environment. In this lab, we aim at evaluating research questions from industry. In this case, we focus on evaluating setup costs for distributed software development projects. We choose our eXtreme Programming course because a) this course is designed to be as realistic as possible (as described in [2]) which enhances external validity and because eXtreme Programming is very communication intensive. This allows us to observe many communication situations. As shown by Poppendieck, XP is also able to reduce the wastes in Software Development [3].

3   Goal-Question-Metric Approach for Measurement

We used the GQM method [4] to answer the following questions:

- Which additions are necessary to work in a distributed setting?
- With these additions, is it possible to stay lean?.

Our goal is to understand the communication in distributed XP from the viewpoint of an XP coach and the developers. The GQM method helps to systematically derive questions from measurement goals, as well as baseline hypotheses about the expected outcome.

3.1   Questions and Hypotheses

Question 1: How much Coordination Overhead is needed in a dispersed[2] XP Project?

Hypothesis 1: We assume that communication in a dispersed XP project needs considerably more technical and organizational effort than in the co-located case and has influence on the question, whether the project stays in time and budget.

Metric 1.1: Measure how much time it takes to setup and initiate each communication channel.

Metric 1.2: Measure which activity uses which channel.

Metric 1.3: Count how often each activity is done.

Question 2: Does a dispersed project need more communication (situations, time per situation) than a co-located one?

Hypothesis 2: We assume that one stand-up meeting per day is enough, as in the co-located case but that it will take more time (approx. 50 % more) compared to a co-located setting.

Metric 2.1: Count the number of stand-up meetings during the project.

Metric 2.2: For each stand-up meeting measure its length.

---

[2] A project is called "dispersed" if different essential roles are located in different locations, so that no meaningful task (e.g. story card) can be completed at one location alone.

Question 3: In relation to forced rituals (e.g. planning poker [5]): Do developers contribute in communication situations and do they initiate communication by themselves?

Hypothesis 3: We assume that the developers contribute less than in a co-located project. Furthermore, we expect very few self-initiated communication situations. Rituals like planning poker or 5-point-evaluation improve the situation.

Metric 3.1: Count Skype and video calls initiated by the developers.

Question 4: Do dispersed teams document more information items per story card than co-located teams?

Hypothesis 4: We assume that they document about 50 % more than in a co-located setup. Video channels decrease amount of documented information items and allow to value interactions over documents.

Metric 4.1: Count the number of documented information items per story card in each team.

3.2 Measurement Results and Interpretation

Metric 1.1, 1.2, 1.3: The above-mentioned metrics results are shown in Table 1. Continuous communication between Coach and developers is not shown. The channels were

Table 1. Measurement results for Metrics 1.1,1.2, and 1.3

Channel	Metric 1.2		Metric 1.3				
	Initialize	Setup Time	Planning Game	Standup-Meeting	Dev. - Customer	Dev. – Dev.	Coach – Dev.
Voice	30min (setup)	1min (start skype)			X	X	X
Video		1h forerun (get conference rooms) + 10 min (init connection)	X	X			
Shared Story Cards	1 h (create accounts, dev. training)	15 min (setup notebook and beamer) + 4 min (log-in all sites)	X	X		X	X
Desktop Sharing	2 h (create accounts, training of developers, init structure)	2 min (start and login) + 2 min (login others, get control)		X	X	X	X
Shared Whiteboard		3 min (login all sites)	X	X	X		X
Shared Tracking Information		3 min (start and login all sites) + 1 min (share file)	X	X			(X)
∑ setup time[3]	-	-	36 min work / 1 h time	40 min work / 1 h time	4 min	19 min	19 min
Occurrences	1	63	3	5	31/8[4]	16	const.

---

[3] Assuming parallel setup of tools.

[4] 31 discussion between the onsite customer and the Hannover team, 8 discussions between the onsite customer and the Clausthal team.

always active, therefore minimizing the initialization time. Obviously, the overhead to initialize the communication infrastructure is higher than in the co-located case where no additional setup is required. But this has to be done only once before the project starts. The initiation of communication has just a slightly overhead compared to the co-located case. The most time consuming setup phases affect video-conferencing and shared story cards. Establishing these channels took ~130 min per day, which supports hypothesis 1: This time considerably adds to the workload on both sites.

Metric 2.1, 2.2: A stand-up meeting was conducted each morning of the respective work day (see Table 2) by each team. The average length of a stand-up meeting was 28:32 minutes. The average length of a stand-up meeting in the local case was 15 min. These results support hypothesis 2, distributed stand-up meetings take more time.

Table 2. Measurement results for Metrics 2.1 and 2.2

Date	25.06.10	26.06.10	27.06.10	28.06.10	31.06.10
Length	19:48 min	31:29 min	26:00 min	27:32 min	37:52 min

Metric 3.1: During the block-week, the developers actively initiated 16 Skype calls and no video conference. While the co-located team and parts of the distributed team that where on the same location communicated a lot, few communication between the distributed locations could be observed, which supports our hypothesis 3

Metric 4.1: For each team, we counted the total requirements raised by the onsite customer during conversations. Based on this, we checked which of these requirements where documented either directly on story cards or as additional documents. Table 3 suggests that additional requirements coming from the customer are much more difficult to see and write down when the customer is not physically present. It *seems* that having to use tools for writing down requirements makes a significant difference to writing them down directly. More in-depth investigations will be necessary to substantiate or falsify our explanation. However, the result of this measurement stands in contrast to hypothesis 4.

Table 3. Measurement results for Metric 4.1

	Co-Located Team	Dispersed Team
Requirements total	135	127
Documented Req.	54	28
Not documented Req.	81	99

4   Conclusion

Our goal was to understand the communication in distributed XP projects. We wanted to identify which additions to the agile practices are necessary to work in a distributed setting. In particular, we wanted to find out whether it is possible to stay lean under these circumstances. Most of the support tools we used can be set up and operated in a reasonable time. The necessary additions are voice and video communication as well as tools for sharing desktops, story cards, whiteboards, and tracking information. Supposedly simple technologies like whiteboards or story cards are very difficult to substitute in a distributed settings.

The overhead for initializing the tools has to be spent only once when a project is set up. In follow-up projects, this overhead decreases. Even some of the additional set-up time can be cut down (e.g. setting up the beamer only once). Nevertheless, setup time remains a major issue. A technical difficult communication channel that needs complex and expensive systems that are not available all the time requires much more organizational overhead. This effort can be reduced by having a rigid schedule, but this also reduces flexibility and agility. The use of a video conference system clearly helps in situations like planning games or stand-up meetings. Still, bringing together teams that don't know each other demands intensive moderation of these meetings. Rituals helped to make the remote group feel less like spectators and gave them the opportunity to actively contribute to group meetings. While believing that it is possible to stay agile even in a distributed setting with only the above-mentioned additions in place, we also like to stress out that distributed communication needs much more attention and focus than communication in a co-located case. The addition of many small time amounts to setup and keep the channels running adds to the coordination effort of managing the different skills in an agile team. This makes distributed communication feel much more intense.

Acknowledgement. We thank Andreas Rausch, Sandra Lange, and the students of Technische Universität Clausthal for conducting this distributed XP lab together with us. This work was funded by the GloSE (Global Software Engineering) project, State of Lower-Saxony.

References

1. Carver, J., Jaccheri, L., Morasca, S., Shull, F.: Issues in Using Students in Empirical Studies in Software Engineering Education. In: METRICS 2003: Proceedings of the 9th Intl. Symp. on Software Metrics, Sydney, Australia, pp. 239–249. IEEE Computer Society, Los Alamitos (2003)
2. Stapel, K., Lübke, D., Knauss, E.: Best Practices in eXtreme Programming Course Design. In: Proceedings of the 30th Intl. Conference on Software Engineering (ICSE 2008), Leipzig, Germany, pp. 769–776. ACM Press, New York (2008)
3. Poppendieck, M.: Principles of Lean Thinking. Technical Report, Poppendieck. LLC (2002)
4. van Solingen, R., Berghout, E.: The Goal/Question/Metric Method: A Practical Guide for Quality Improvement of Software Development. McGraw-Hill Publishing Company, New York (1999)
5. Molokken-Ostvold, K., Haugen, N.C.: Combining Estimates with Planning Poker–An Empirical Study. In: ASWEC 2007: Proceedings of the 2007 Australian Software Engineering Conference, Washington, DC, USA, pp. 349–358. IEEE Computer Society, Los Alamitos (2007)

Experience Report:
Product Creation through Lean Approaches

Henning Rudolf[1] and Frances Paulisch[2]

[1] Siemens AG, Industry Sector, Industry Automation Division,
90475 Nürnberg, Germany
[2] Siemens AG, Corporate Technology, System and Software Initiative
80200 München, Germany

Abstract. This paper describes how lean approaches should be interpreted for the creation of software-based systems and includes an experience report on how that understanding of lean is applied in a project at a Siemens business unit. The case study addresses issues relating to the portfolio and product management, architecture, product lifecycle management processes and people and organization related issues.

Keywords: lean, product management, product development, product lifecycle management.

1 Introduction

Siemens is a global electronics and electrical engineering company, operating in the industry, energy and healthcare sectors. Siemens, with its presence in over 190 countries, its roughly 405,000 employees working at 1,640 locations and its 176 R&D facilities [1], serves a wide variety of customers in diverse businesses with unique challenges.

Due to the nature of their products, many of the Siemens organizations have had a strong orientation towards hardware, electrical engineering, or mechanical engineering. But software is increasingly becoming an important, often dominant, factor in the success of their products and this trend towards software is increasing rapidly. Consider, for example, that more than 60% of our enterprise-wide sales are based on software-based products, systems and plants and that Siemens employs approx. 20,000 software engineers worldwide. The System and Software Initiative of Siemens is set up to take advantage of cross-business unit synergies, in particular regarding increasing the effectiveness ("building the right product") and efficiency ("building the product right") of the development of our software-based systems. Although the business drivers in each of our various business units are somewhat different, there are also many similarities across our businesses. High quality and providing high value to the customer are important goals. Many of our product development teams are set up as geographically distributed teams, product line engineering and the use of platforms is common, and we have well-established and mature development processes. Our product lifecycle management (PLM) approach defines how we develop products in a particular organization.

P. Abrahamsson and N. Oza (Eds.): LESS 2010, LNBIP 65, pp. 104–110, 2010.

Yet we continue to strive for further improvements to our product lifecycle management. We think that there is potential in applying some of the main ideas of "lean", adapted for product development, as one possible way of further improving product development. Often the improvements are ones that would be useful anyway, but the "lean view" is sometimes useful in making them more visible. Section 2 describes our view to applying lean ideas to product creation, which includes both product management and all phases of product development. Section 3 describes a specific case study and resulting insights of applying these techniques in a business unit of Siemens. Section 4 closes with some general lessons learned.

2 Lean in Product Creation

Lean has its roots in the manufacturing area. The high-level goals of lean (manufacturing) can also be applied to the definition and development of software-based systems. But one must also be aware that there are significant differences between manufacturing and product creation (product management and development). According to Reinertsen [2], manufacturing deals with predictable and repetitive tasks, has homogeneous delay costs and homogeneous task durations whereas product development deals with high variability, non-repetitive, non-homogeneous flows and different projects have different delay costs and different loads on resources. Also Cockburn [3] sees significant differences that stem from the fact that what is moving through the "production" is not something physical, but rather information, in particular decisions that over time become clarified. Furthermore, due to the nature of product development, there are many more feedback/correction loops than in manufacturing. Even the time-scale is different, with product development often taking many months as opposed to minutes/days common in the manufacturing space. And most importantly, because the nature of what flows through the process is information and knowledge, it is an even bigger challenge than in the manufacturing space to convince the people and to achieve the necessary change in mindset that is required.

Our approach for software-based systems is based on that of Poppendieck [4], including "Systems Thinking" (the importance of the end-to-end flow and optimizing the whole rather than the parts), "Technical Excellence" (including striving to have decoupled architecture, the importance of early automatic system integration, encouraging prototyping as they lead to valuable knowledge and must not be considered waste), "Reliable Delivery" (managing the workflow in particular to optimize the overall throughput rather than the utilization of particular roles by keeping the amount of work in progress smaller and more even). "Relentless Improvement" (analyzing the root cause of problems encountered and addressing them), as well as "Great People" and "Aligned Leaders" reflecting a culture with a common goal, each empowered to make improvements in their area in an open collaborative atmosphere and to have a product champion willing to take on the end-to-end responsibility for the business success of the product and who strives for close interaction with the team. Siemens has a long history of process assessments and improvements and most organizations have well-established mature processes that help ensure that responsibilities are clear and that we achieve a high degree of predictability. The lean approaches described in this paper are built on top of such a mature process-oriented foundation.

Creating Value: We continuously strive to increase the value of our products. This is typically difficult to measure, especially as there are many different direct and indirect "customers" or other customer-like stakeholders involved, see also [5]. It is very important here to have an excellent understanding of the problems that the customer is addressing and thus what the customer really needs rather than only considering what the customer says they need. For example, often there may be an innovative new way to address the customer's real needs and to some extent this is a "push" idea and not just a "pull".

The long-term stability of our products, based partly on our platform strategy, is another way we create value. In particular one must be sure that also the quality attributes (sometimes called non-functional requirements) such as performance, flexibility, usability, scalability, and reliability are not overlooked when considering the value for the customer.

Avoiding Waste: Waste in lean terminology can be further broken down into "necessary" and "pure" (or unnecessary) waste. Ideally, we want to avoid any kind of waste, but in particular we want to avoid pure waste. As an idea of what kinds of waste exist in product creation, here our mapping for software development, similar to [4], based on seven kinds of waste in manufacturing. The category "necessary" waste includes things like establishing an organization-wide common terminology and processes, these help the organization have a quicker understanding across roles and help to create the products with higher predictability. The types of waste in software development include:

- Waiting: e.g. through unclear responsibilities, insufficient process/tool integration, lack of parallelization, insufficient infrastructure (e.g. computer/network too slow)
- Extra processing steps: unnecessary or too-detailed process steps
- Defects: Re-work (i.e. having to do an activity a second time that could have been avoided, for example due to finding defects or inadequate involvement of all relevant stakeholders)
- Transportation: Inadequate transportation of information across interfaces (e.g. manual transfer of information between roles due to incompatible processes or tools, lack of common understanding)
- Overproduction: e.g. delivery of features that the customer does not need, overly-complex products, too many variants instead of doing systematic reuse
- Inventory: creation of artifacts that are not used downstream (e.g. effort invested in the definition, effort estimation, review of requirements or features that are not realized)
- Motion: unnecessary transfer of persons due to inadequate relationship between the roles (e.g. lack of direct access to necessary information, having to multi-task between too many projects, insufficient communication between sites).

Continuous Improvement: Continuous improvement is one of the main pillars of the Toyota Production System [6] which has, at least in the past, been one of the main sources of information in the area of lean. Constant improvement is not the task of a special process group but instead in everybody's DNA. Standards are important, but need to be seen as a basis for further improvement. All people in the organization need to have the right education and mindset to drive improvements. The role of management is not simply to manage with targets. Instead they should "go-and-see" and personally help solve concrete problems on the doing level.

In order to also continuously improve across the company, we have established a cross-business unit community for addressing topics of lean in the area of development and engineering. We have regular meetings to synchronize on topics of common interest for example having a common training program and a common general framework and to share good practices across Siemens and also with external contacts. Through the diversity of the businesses and the nature of lean itself, it will not be the case that a single solution or "one-size-fits-all" approach will work; instead one must agree on a common framework and apply this intelligently as needed in the various business units. The following case study is one that has been presented, for example, in this community and shared with others across Siemens.

3   Case Study – Lean PLM @Siemens

The business unit in this case study has ~8.500 employees and is a market leader in industrial automation, serving customers with production facilities in discrete (e.g. automotive) or process industries (e.g. pharma). Automation consists of 3 elements:

1.   Sensor (collects the state of the outside world – the shop-floor)
2.   Actor (influences the outside world, e.g. a motor driving a conveyor belt)
3.   Control logic (controlling the actors based on the signals of the sensors)

This specific business unit is active in the area of control logic, yet has to coordinate PLM projects with other Siemens business units developing sensors & actors. Although the customers perceive the offering mostly as hardware, there is a large amount of software necessary. The customer value is best realized when a well-aligned and working system portfolio of hard- and software is delivered.

The challenges when building such complex systems are different from the ones encountered by typical automotive companies including Toyota. One crucial challenge is, for example, the compatibility of hardware and software components: once an automation hard- or software component is sold to a customer, these components are in use for decades in customer specific configurations not controlled by the OEM (in this case Siemens). This compatibility is a major driver of customer value and needs to be treated differently from automotive companies with their modularization and platform approaches.

In order to better serve the customers and to provide them with more customer value, former stand alone products are united in a system approach named "Totally Integrated Automation". While this creates tangible benefits for the customers, it increases the dependencies of the internal development.

3.1 Motivation for Lean

The project in this case study was motivated by a strong belief in continuous improvement. Lean was already a proven concept in manufacturing and helped that the unit's plant won the "Best Factory / Industrial Excellence Award 2007" organized by

French business school INSEAD and the German business school WHU [7]. The plant's success is powered by a culture of continuous improvement, in which everybody in the plant is educated, empowered and active.

With this background, a dedicated project was initiated at business unit level with the aim to increase the value generated in its own product lifecycle management (PLM). Lean was considered as one useful approach but the ultimate aim was improvement. Although there was much experience in manufacturing, the question remained how much of this know-how could be transferred to product management and development.

3.2 Approach Taken

Based on initial interviews with main stakeholders in PLM, it was obvious that the challenges had to be addressed from different perspectives. Similar to the star model for organizational design [8], a project setup by four dimensions was chosen.

Fig. 1. Project structure and the core questions

According to lean thinking, people doing the actual work should be empowered to improve their own work environment [4]. Based on this notion, the different modules were staffed with people from all levels in the PLM organizational hierarchy to ensure that we are close the real problems (Gemba) and have no late handovers of project results to key decision makers. As an important first step, a baseline was created covering the initial set of hypotheses: *Portfolio* including requirements engineering determined patterns for economical success and identified root causes. In *Architecture, technology & products* the dependencies of product structures and the degree of component reuse was made transparent with the method Design Structure Matrix (DSM) by Eppinger [9]. *PLM process* created value stream maps for selected development projects and initiated problem solving based on the A3-method – for both methods see Poppendieck [4]. *People & organization* made current project structures transparent and identified improvement topics based on personal interviews with people doing the actual work. This "Gemba" – go & see – created a common picture of the real situation. Some initial hypotheses were proven wrong and other challenges surfaced.

In parallel to the root cause analysis (shown in fig. 2 as point 4), one module built up the know-how on lean and practices used by others (points 1-3). Using best-practice sharing, companies often simply try to copy practices from others. This is similar to early attempts to implement lean in manufacturing. In the early 90s companies started to use simple, mechanistic practices and were disappointed that e.g. implementing only Kanban cards as standalone tool (a method for visual process control) did not provide the expected benefits.

The essence of lean is to first analyze own root causes on a working level by empowered employees and in parallel define own principles and build up knowledge. A mere data pool of lean practices is not helpful. Based on guiding principles and own root causes, the discussion on the proposed future state should be initiated.

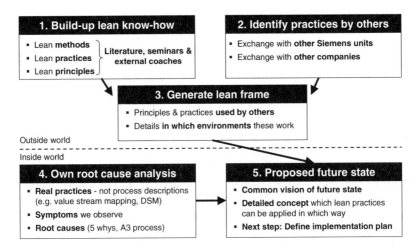

Fig. 2. Structure chosen for the initial project phase

3.3 Proposed Concepts and Insights from the Case Study

Among many others aspects, the two main changes initiated by the project were: 1) a value-oriented requirements process and 2) an iterative development process with product quality (= delivering a customer function) in each development increment. The value-oriented requirements process with a matrix representing value and effort ensures that both large functional departments – product management and R&D – interact early in the process on a high level regarding which product elements should be further elaborated. This ensures that the work going into detailing the requirements is value adding, since it can be completed based on the available R&D capacity. The iterative development will be focused even further on customer value in the future. Progress will be measured based on working code and the fulfillment of customer needs.

These changes may not seem radically new and in many ways are in line with practices proposed by Agile or Scrum. Yet it was important for our organization to start with lean: Scrum first states practices and rules to follow. Only after mastering these practices should people be allowed to modify the rules [10]. Agile – like Lean – clearly states values, yet most of these values refer to the work on a team level and less to a bigger organizational scope. Lean complements Agile and Scrum: it starts on an organizational level with clear principles. Only practices suitable for the concrete problem and its root causes are applied. That does not mean that lean is a cherry picking exercise – quite the contrary – certain elements only work if others are implemented, yet practices should always be based on the root causes and not be copied blindly. Lean is a constant striving towards improvement; it demands a certain attitude and is an undertaking without a defined end date. The lean journey started in this Siemens business unit as a project is now eagerly adopted by one major development project to adopt lean principles and refine the proposed practices.

4 Conclusion

Although lean is not the only way of achieving improvements in product creation, it is one that encourages a holistic approach which we find beneficial. It is critical to be aware that one cannot translate the ideas of lean in manufacturing one-to-one to product creation, but the approach does provide benefits. The holistic approach opens doors when addressing the various improvement topics with management and also can help reduce the barriers to communication across the team. The attention to the people topics, encouraging persons to be active in continuously improving the project also has a not-to-be-underestimated impact on the motivation of the team members. Software development is a knowledge-based activity and strongly dependent on the persons involved; on the one hand this shows great potential but on the other hand is the challenge in achieving the culture change across a whole project or organization.

References

1. Siemens, A.G.: http://www.siemens.com/about/en/worldwide.htm
2. Reinertsen, D.: The Principles of Product Development Flow. Celeritas Publishing
3. Cockburn, A.: Keynote Agile 2009 (2009)
4. Poppendieck, M., Poppendieck, T.: Implementing Lean Software Development: From Concept to Cash. Addison Wesley, Boston (2006)
5. Chase, J.: Measuring Value in Product Development, The Lean Aerospace Initiative Working Paper Series WP00-05 (March 2000)
6. Ohno, T.: The Toyota Production System. Productivity Press (1988)
7. Best Factory 2007 (2007), http://www.beste-fabrik.de/
8. Larman, C., Vodde, B.: Scaling Lean & Agile Development: Thinking and Organizational Tools for Large-Scale Scrum. Addison Wesley, Upper Saddle River (2009)
9. Eppinger, S.D., Whitney, D.E., Smith, R.P., Gebala, D.A.: A Model-Based Method for Organizing Tasks in Product Development. In: Research in Engineering Design, vol. 6, pp. 1–13. Springer, London (1994)
10. Schwaber, K.: Agile Project Management with Scrum. Microsoft Press, Redmond (2004)

Huitale – A Story of a Finnish Lean Startup

Marko Taipale

Huitale, Hiilikatu 3
00180 Helsinki, Finland
marko.taipale@huitale.com

Abstract. We in Huitale have implemented a lean product development process. As a result Huitale has a workflow that is predictable within acceptable variance. We can change the direction of the business at any given time but stay grounded in what we have learned. We can adjust the product roadmap visibility according to our business needs. In addition we have achieved exceptional quality. In past three years we have had two production bugs. The implementation of lean development process requires discipline and experience.

Keywords: lean product development, agile software development, Kanban, Scrum, eXtreme programming, lean startup.

1 Summary

There is on-going buzz about lean startups [1], agile and lean software and product development in the industry [2]. However there is very few descriptions how software product companies have applied the lean principles in order to match the demand for their product and improve the development lead and cycle times. We in Huitale have implemented a lean product development process. For past few years we have been able to predict the lead times for new features and adapt our business model according to the market needs [3]. In addition we have built capability for releasing our software everyday for thousands of consumers with extraordinary quality: we have had two bugs in past three years. We have noticed that it takes discipline and experience to implement continuously improving process.

2 Background

Huitale Ltd is a provider of lean and agile consulting and a product development company. Last three years Huitale has been developing a national consumer portal Nextdoor.fi to enable individuals and companies to buy and sell house holding services online. Currently the portal is having over 30 000 unique visitors every month and 2 000 active users. The people working for Huitale have several years of experience in agile software development, lean product development, Scrum, Kanban and eXtreme programming practices and the company is continuously improving its processes by experimenting new ways of working.

P. Abrahamsson and N. Oza (Eds.): LESS 2010, LNBIP 65, pp. 111–114, 2010.

3 Product Development

Our product development process [3] starts by a signal from development saying that there is only two Minimum Marketable Features [4] left in product development queue. This signal initiates a discovery of three themes from the customer development [5] channels, competition analysis and internal innovation. We spent two hours time box on figuring out which themes are worth of investing the upcoming month. Once the themes are discovered we start working on features by brainstorming them for each theme. We limit the number of features to seven in order to keep the buffer small but still big enough to ensure the flow for next month. The brainstorming session including formulating of MMFs takes two days and it ends by putting the items into Product Qeueue in prioritized order.

Once we have the items in the queue and there is room in the downstream for upcoming work we start defining the highest priority MMFs as READY. The definition of ready is:

- No immediate blocker for developing the MMF
- If MMF has impact on language content the content is available. It might not be final.
- If MMF has impact on look & feel the content is available (GUI layouts, graphics etc.). It might not be final.
- If MMF has impact on emails sent to the users the email templates are available. They might not be final.
- If MMF has impact on reports the expected changes are communicated.
- If MMF has impact on third party services/integrations the expected changes are listed. List might (and usually is not) final.
- We have set measures for MMF to decide later on if we should keep the feature or drop it

At any given time we can have two items defined READY to be pulled by to development. The Work-In-Process limit for development is also two. Developed items must pass our Definition of Done to get done. Our definition of done is:

- MMF can be released
- code has unit tests and automated acceptance tests [6] that execute successfully
- code passes tests in CI environment
- code is refactored and the design is simple
- code passes automated QA checks (checkstyle, pmd/cpd & whatnot)
- new feature is documented (if applicable, sometimes for third parties)
- peer review is done (if applicable, sometimes for critical paths)

Once a MMF is done it will be released to production within next 24 hours with help of our Continuous Deployment [7] environment.

4 Teams

We have moved from single Product Owner model to a Problem and Solution team model as part of process improvement. Problem team is lead by CEO and consist

CTO, Sales and Marketing Director and User Experience Designer. Problem team uses tools like customer development, business reports and metrics to find out what problem we should be solving for our customers and users. Solution team is lead by CTO and consists of developers and User Interface Designer. There is no separate "testers" or "operations". These roles are carried out by the solution team members as part of their development roles. The mission of solution team is to build whatever required by the problem team and provide insights, data and feedback to the problem team and customer development process.

These teams overlap for a reason. The idea is to avoid communications via documents and encourage rich communication between all the parties. We have also involved subcontractors for various roles in the teams. Both the teams are at least somewhat distributed.

5   Results

Our workflow is predictable within acceptable variance and we can change the direction of the business at any given time. We can adjust the product roadmap visibility according to our business needs.

We have continuously done daily releases of Nextdoor.fi to production for past three and half years. The public beta consists of minimum set of features and was developed in 120 man days from which 70 was used to developing the features and 50 for user interface. The environment for Continuous Deployment and operations were developed during the product development incrementally by the solution team. The lead time from idea to production is currently 8 days on average. Smallest MMFs take less than 3 days to pass through the workflow.

The site has now over 30 000 unique visitors per day, over 2 000 active users and it has proven to deliver value for its users. Nextdoor.fi is still released to production every day. The production system has 24/7 system and application monitoring with daily backups and automated system rollbacks in case of unsuccessful deployment. The business reports and metrics for the whole and each feature are generated on every 24 hours.

Continuous Deployment and Integration environment executes over 550 automated acceptance tests through the Graphical User Interface to the database and integration points. The overall test coverage is over 80% for all the code including custom maintenance tools and over 85% for all the application code. During past three years we have gotten two production bugs from which one was reported by the users and both were reported by the application monitoring. Both bugs were fixed within less than one hour from the time they were reported.

We have no employees or owners working on operations nor do we have single tester.

6   Lessons Learned

According to our experience discipline is the key factor on executing, implementing and improving the lean product development process. Visualizing the workflow and measuring both lead time and cycle times is very beneficial on finding subjects for improvement. Applying tools like root cause analysis [8] helps finding actionable issues. For a product company it is also important to have mechanisms to validate the product vision and have metrics to figure out if your product is actually valuable to anybody.

References

1. Ries, E.: What is lean about lean startup,
   http://www.startuplessonslearned.com/2009/12/
   what-is-lean-about-lean-startup.html
2. Wikipedia: Lean Software Development,
   http://en.wikipedia.org/wiki/Lean_software_development
3. Taipale, M.: The Huitale Way,
   http://huitale.blogspot.com/2010/03/
   huitale-way-our-value-stream-map.html
4. Scotland, K.: The anatomy of an MMF,
   http://availagility.co.uk/2008/07/07/the-anatomy-of-an-mmf/
5. Blank, S.: Customer development for web startups,
   http://steveblank.com/2010/02/25/
   customer-development-for-web-startups/
6. Koskela, L.: Acceptance TDD Explained,
   http://www.methodsandtools.com/archive/archive.php?id=72
7. Ries, E.: Continuous deployment in 5 easy steps,
   http://radar.oreilly.com/2009/03/
   continuous-deployment-5-eas.html
8. Wikipedia: Root cause analysis,
   http://en.wikipedia.org/wiki/Root_cause_analysis

Kanban and Technical Excellence
or: Why Daily Releases Are a Great Objective
to Meet

Markus Andrezak[1] and Bernd Schiffer[2]

[1] mobile.international GmbH, Kleinmachnow-Dreilinden, Germany
mandrezak@team.mobile.de
[2] it-agile GmbH, Hamburg, Germany
bernd.schiffer@it-agile.de

Abstract. mobile.international is Europes biggest online automotive market. At mobile.international Product Development is coordinated and orchestrated with Kanban. One major, enabling objective of mobile.international is to release daily. This paper is about the companys way from their successful Kanban implementation to a smoothly running and effective value chain on the technical level. We will discuss how the different levels of technical skills impact Kanban and its results in a positive or negative way and why daily releases supports progress in the right direction on each level.

Keywords: Kanban, Experience Report, Technical Excellence, Daily Releases, Small Releases.

Kanban is a new software development approach based on lean principles. In this approach software development is seen as a continuous flow of software as tickets from the idea to satisfied customers. The limitation of work in progress also known as Limited WIP is Kanbans mechanism to control the software flow. Limited WIP helps to identify and eliminate bottlenecks to expedite the flow, as stated by the Theory of Constraints.

Kanban is a change agent towards lean values that fits most environments. It especially fits such organizations that are not ready for a revolutionary shift. Indeed, Kanban is designed to enable a continuous evolutionary change. Therefore it attracts an audience which is not overtly mature regarding its adoption of lean and agile practices.

It is only natural that Kanban, after an initial improvement, stalls a little, as more deep cutting changes have to be made gradually.

Kanban strives for low transaction and coordination cost. Coordination cost is covered by process improvements by means of visualization and coordination on the Kanban board and the underlying communication topics. A large part of the optimization of coordination cost can be reached by discipline in committing to Kanbans WiP-Limits. This means, reducing coordination cost is a relatively short term lever on optimizing the system. A proxy for low transaction cost

P. Abrahamsson and N. Oza (Eds.): LESS 2010, LNBIP 65, pp. 115–117, 2010.

(with all involved risks of proxies) is lead or cycle time (time from ordering a requirement to its delivery in other words its actual development time). For the remainder of the paper we consider the influence of technical excellence on lead time.

In product development (PD), lowering transaction costs works mostly on the technical level: Ultimately, one would like to lower the transaction costs to the level where very frequent (daily) or even continuous deployment (automation of each single, checked in feature by a chain of automated testing etc.) is cheap.

Such a level of frequent releases and deployment is only possible via a very smoothly running and continuously improving value chain on the technical level: technical excellence from initial development through deployment: Fully Automated Continuous Builds & Test: software releases with just one click Continuous Integration: single piece flow on code base level Configuration management aided by Feature Flags: separation of features for releases with a specific feature set without the need for branches (just HEAD as known as just one branch) Continuous Learning: frequent training of teams and individuals with coding dojos and katas Incremental Design: fluent, decoupled architecture which grows with and stays flexible towards requirements

In this session we want to describe how the positive effects of Kanban and its predictability are hindered if transaction cost is too high and how to get out of this situation.

We will discuss how the different levels of technical skills impact Kanban and the positive and negative impacts on the results.

Lets look at a typical development situation: What if one team member has created a big construction area in the code, whereas another team member just gets a developed and already tested ticket approved and wants to release now? What if one team wants to release its module which depends on another module, and that other module is not ready to be released right now?

Lets start with development: If your development work is bad, you end up nowhere and Kanban makes this brutally visible in many ways: Bad development quality in the sense of too many errors built in destroys your ability for fast lead time as too much rework needs to be done for features. Features are developed, they fail testing and are handed back over to development etc. Common sources of error are poor specification, too many handovers (non-collaborative environment), sloppy coding or an insufficient architecture. The worst effect on Kanbans predictability is given by expedite tickets that have to be fixed right away as they are impact the platform. There are several sorts of expedite tickets, but all are bad for the predictability as, by definition, they discontinue the flow in a Kanban system. Some are introduced by immaturity of the organization (e.g. legal requirements to be done on short notice) or immaturity of product development (high impact development errors to be corrected).

An insufficient architecture, especially one with a high degree of coupling, leads to errors as side effects and inflexible code structures, which leads to fear of refactoring, which leads to ... and so on. This makes decoupling of the architecture a high priority.

Complex configuration management with long feedback cycles hidden in too many branches leads to a high rate of random errors through rebasing and thus has a tremendous impact on quality and speed. Our aim is to get closer to the trunk. Our tool of choice are feature flags, wherever we dare to use them.

Continuous build and test is the basis to achieve fast feedback on any system level during development. Any issue in the consistency of the process or the integrity of the systems leads to misleading and slow feedback which prevents any fast release cycles. This topic is closely related to the necessity of a high level of automated test coverage. But this does come for a price again, as this can only be achieved with the right architecture, because otherwise establishing and maintenance of automated tests is impossible or too costly, which would again make fast release cycles impossible.

For all these topics, Kanban does not tell you what to do. Kanban does not even tell you that you need these. Kanbans value is, on the other hand, that it makes these issues painstakingly visible.

As in all lean and agile processes, Kanban requires a constant improvement of process topics and technical expertise, going back and forth between these areas again and again.

As Kanban only makes the transaction cost, lead time and the underlying issues visible, of course most of the mentioned improvements make sense in most agile and lean product development environments, regardless of the applied method.

mobile.international is Europes biggest online automotive market, serving 1.5 billion Page Impressions (PI)/month, 55 million visits/month for 1.4 million ads and 33.000 dealers in the automotive sector.

mobile.international has a very successful implementation of Kanban. The implementation of Kanban first involved the maintenance of the international products of mobile.international. Now it covers the maintenance of the German main product as well. Further, the whole product development organization is steered via an enterprise Kanban board, balancing the needs of feature, architectural and innovation work. Further, the company is now managing its product portfolio based on Kanban. And still there are countless opportunities for improvement, located at the code level. Their next goal is to release at least daily.

In the presentation of this session, the speakers show mobile.internationals efforts to release daily. Also we discuss several techniques to achieve the goal of releasing daily, some of which have already been applied, and some of which are planned.

Clean Delivery:
An Experience Report of Collaborative Lean Software Delivery

Christian Blunden[1,2]

[1] ThoughtWorks, London, UK
cblunden@thoughtworks.com
http://www.thoughtworks.com
[2] ThoughtWorks Ltd, 9th Floor, Berkshire House,
168 - 173 High Holborn, London, WC1V 7AA,
United Kingdom

Abstract. Stuck in the purgatory of an immature "Agile" IT department and old world project management office, facing up to eighteen month lead times on analysis and sign off, off shoring contractors and people new to Agile. These are the experiences of how we created a bubble of effectiveness through applying systems thinking and radical changes in delivery process. The result was a clear success with practically zero defects and a model of future development within the company.

Keywords: Lean, Agile, Collaboration, Systems Thinking.

1 Introduction

1.1 Context

This section provides a context on the state of our client's organisation when we (Thoughtworks) arrived and to set the scene as to what needed changing. When we arrived, we were met with an immature Scrum/Waterfall hybrid model and over the following year with hard earned successes and big failures, turned into a bearable XP(Extreme Programming)/Scrum agile model. Although there was still little buy in from the upper management or delivery leads.

Internally the departments were siloed and split in different locations and each suffered from their own problems. Development had low experience and capability and were the blamed for the continual breakage of the live web site and project delays and failures. Project management governed by numbers and only served upwards and would only become involved in delivery once it had left both development and QA and was on the path to release.

Quality Assurance (QA) was almost solely external contractors and concentration of effort was late cycle inspection, leading to last minute heroics to "get out the deployment". Separation of Development and QA, resulted in walls full of red defect cards and a bug tracking system that would fill with issues, rarely fixed by developers who had little visibility and context or were simply lost in

P. Abrahamsson and N. Oza (Eds.): LESS 2010, LNBIP 65, pp. 118–123, 2010.

the system. A final "Release" QA team could turn away deployments if they did not "feel" they were ok to continue.

A long and painful standing relationship with an external middle-ware supplier, caused much conflict and delays in all projects. Planning of project deliverables was typically split such that external suppliers finished months (up to a year) before the client had even begun development. Resulting in mismatched or missed requirements, rework and integration hacks put in place to bypass delays for fixes or changes to be made. This was so common place that client developers now accepted that this was inevitable and communication had stopped between the two company's development teams.

Business stakeholders were completely removed from development process and requirements were delivered through technical specifications (specs), containing information often beyond the comprehension of the Business Analysts (BA) writing them (ie: database or web service definitions). A "Gated" sign off process of specs would take in excess of eighteen months and specs were out of date by the time they reached development.

1.2   The Issues That Needed to Be Solved

- waste from red cards (defects)
- absence of quality (work was tossed over the fence)
- balance throughput from developer to QA
- communication and handover (business to BA to developer to QA to ops)
- mistrust and poor code from offshore contractors
- ad-hoc and infrequent visits from business sponsors due to travel commitments
- waste from scrum based agile ceremonies
- work effectively with external middle-ware supplier.

2   Solution

My final project with this client was used as a test ground for the solutions used below and were a result of both upfront radical change before project commencement and continual learning and process improvement throughout. All were used without permission from management and in some cases were hard won within the team. I have collectively called these practices Collaborative Lean (Clean), from the combination of Agile human interaction and lean focus on reducing waste through optimizing flow.

As I see it, flow in software delivery comes from reducing the information boundaries in handover whilst trying to balance the information gap between those handovers through collaboration.

2.1   A New Story Wall

The current story wall which was made of at least six columns (Ready for development, In development, Ready for QA, In QA, Ready for Showcase, Done) was enabling throwing things over a wall and thus departmental silos. This was creating handover and waste through piling up inventory of story cards, work waiting in queues and over processing of work due to context not being known. Handovers, queues and re-work were massively reducing the flow of work through the pipeline.

The radical upfront change was to reduce this to four columns (Ready, In delivery, Ready to showcase, done). Note that the critical change here is recognising that development and QA are a single activity, quality is be built into the process. This change must be accompanied by working in threesomes and single story flow outlined below.

One further horizontal lane was added allocated to re-work (defects) and expediting new functionality. Cards placed in this column were not allowed to be started until the root cause of their creation was understood. This became a crucial opportunity for us to learn why they had eventuated and what could be done to prevent this in the future.

2.2   Micro Inception

Specifications represented inventories of information, they also crystallised over production and processing of information as requirements inevitably changed over the course of their creation. Whilst it was not possible to undo the creation of the out of date specification we had been given, which was over a year old, we needed to refresh the requirements and demonstrate a light weight.

A decision was made from the team to drop the spec and run a rapid requirements gathering exercise with the project stakeholders as the source of truth and the spec as just another source. Stories were broken out into major feature areas and prioritised (using Moscow) within each feature group (as described by Jeff Paton's Feature Map). The minimum feature set formed the goal for release 1.

2.3   Threesomes

The soloing of developers and QA had created a barrier for communication and waste as described above in the new story wall. It was common that defects created by QA would pass back and forth several times, creating waste in excessive motion and transportation of both information and workers. Siloed teams also meant that there was waste within the latent skills of team members unable to easily share knowledge or poly skill sets.

Recognising that pairing of developers (an agile XP technique), was a good thing, it was decided upfront to extend this idea even further and get developers and QA's in threesomes and developers, QA's and business analysts in threesomes. To achieve this the story was iteratively delivered (reducing batch size) to QA in chunks around acceptance criteria (story requirements). Effort shifts where it is required the most, if development is the constraint, QA focusses on cross cutting concerns such as performance or to upcoming analysis. If QA is the constraint, then dev effort is concentrated on automating tests or tasks from tech wall. Additional developer capacity was used to process technical debt in code. A wall of cards (tech wall) was devoted to parked technical issues which could be played when slack time occurred in the system.

The delivery threesomes were mirrored by off shore team who worked as developer pair plus QA. This ensured a greater level of quality and communication equal to the onshore team. To enable this to happen, the off shore team was initially co-located to work in this method.

2.4   Single Story Flow

Because developers could simply push "finished" work over the wall to QA, this created the problem of over production and information inventory where dev complete work could sit waiting, whilst a tester became available.

To solve this problem single story flow was introduced, where only a single story can be "in delivery" between the developer pair and QA at one time and another can not be started until it is signed off by the analyst or product stakeholder. This implicitly balances the throughput between developers and QA and again recognition that this is a single activity.

2.5   Continuous Showcase

Bi-weekly "showcases" resulted in waste both through re-work from incorrectly implemented requirements or missed features and over processing and production when excessive work (also known as gold plating) is performed beyond the point of stakeholder acceptance. We also had the wasted time of booking a long meeting slot (over two hours), which may or may not be required, causing time in-efficiency for stakeholders.

Again here we were looking to reduce the batch size after the first showcase revealed need to rework a story which should have been caught sooner. First was to continuously showcase during iterative story development from dev to QA and BA, this had a regular cadence of usually every hour. We then showcased completed work to stakeholders whenever they were passing through and lasted as long as they needed to (often minutes).

2.6   No Defect Policy

Having the ability to raise defects meant that QA's did, naturally. The fact was that red cards were causing waste, sometimes through over production in that the defect was acceptable or in changed requirements. Also through, unnecessary motion of information, the back and forth caused by the in-effectiveness of communicating through a ticketing system.

A mantra of "work slower to go faster" was adopted, where single story flow was enforced and all effort was placed in reducing the re-work. The net effectiveness gain of no rework, meant we could work slower and more methodically, which lead to less defects a positive re-enforcing feedback system. Another critical aspect was that we removed defect tracking, it was not possible to raise a defect forcing people to collaborate.

2.7   The Studdle (Story Huddle)

Another problem was the batched bi-weekly (up to four hour) iteration planning meetings (IPM), used to discuss, estimate and plan the upcoming stories. This resulted in waste through information inventories and eventual re-work if the information was forgotten if a story was begun as late a two weeks later, and wasted time from unused meeting allocation (over production).

The solution which was adopted after re-work was encountered in early iterations, again, was to reduce batch sizes. The IPM was dropped and a rough plan of stories "as-is" was taken at the beginning of the iteration. Throughout the iteration as stories were started, the entire team would huddle to "sign-on" and acceptance criteria debated with the most up to date information presented. Slack time was used by QA's and developers to help BA's ensure acceptance criteria had met satisfactory standard before huddles.

2.8   Continuous Retrospective

A further attempt to cut batch sizes was to reduce bi-weekly (or monthly) retrospectives, two hour long meetings used to reflect and improve upon incidents within the past development cycle. Further, to try and reduce the inventory of information built in peoples memories, which generally had time to perish over time.

A retrospective wall was introduced to collect issues, positive feedback and questions. A retrospective wall item would trigger a discussion at the next morning stand-up, a quick daily catchup attended by all team members, offshore members (via Skype) and business stakeholders.

2.9   Treating External Suppliers as Partners

The break in flow caused from the breakdown in communication and relationship from the external middle-ware suppliers was immense. Integration work was constantly blocked due to defects, completed work was frequently over specified meaning over production and development teams left waiting for fixes and information. Inevitably, client integration code was hacked around the incorrect middle-ware solutions rather than waiting for suppliers to return with patches and fixes to the defects.

It was critical that relationships were improved with the external supplier, we decided to treat them like an internal partner. This meant working much closer, developer to developer communication was essential, by passing the handover of ticketing systems and project managers. Regular communication over instant messaging and Skype became common place and external supplier team members were invited to morning stand-ups. Furthermore, code and processes were shared (such as automation test suites) to help improve the quality of the delivered middle-ware code. This lead to far few blockages and delays experienced by the client team.

3   Further Experience

This same Clean delivery method was used on another client, however with very different variables. This time with a mature agile team, highly capable (developers, QA, BA, PM), "green field" project, no integration points and responsive client. Essentially what you my consider the perfect agile environment.

What we found was, ironically, this method much more difficult due to fighting deeply ingrained standard XP practices and significantly different constraints, in particular the developer effort early on while ramping up project velocity. At times we found it necessary to break single story flow so that the QA was not starved of work. Increased slack time of QA lead to increased frustration.

4   Conclusions

Whilst no definitive measurements were taken, our team was clearly more effective than the other teams, enough so to gain the attention of IT management (including Head of Delivery who rejected change) who regularly enquired out of interest to how the method was going. The project was undeniably considered a rare success, in spite of fixed deadline and shifting scope, multiple external integration points and new off-shore teams. I have since been contacted by the Business Analyst from the client, who has been selling the message back to the rest of the department and they are embracing the push to further adoption. Also surprisingly, we also saw a much greater level participation and engagement from weaker members of the team due to a higher level of collaboration and reduction in frustration due to more better flow of work.

So what went wrong? Adoption was hard won, I had many long and painful discussion and debates to convince team members to work in this way and I was a constant driving force for adoption. I believe that some of these practices (such as single story flow, and Studdles) would require a committed and experienced coach to have similar debates to drive acceptance. Whilst continuous retrospectives worked well for very menial day-to-day issues, unfortunately, did not entirely solve the real problem of continual improvement and is no substitute for people getting together and reflecting.

I would finally conclude that, despite the catchy name, Clean is not meant to be packaged method for success but rather I want to illustrate the thinking around the problem and how a solution was derived.

Beyond Budgeting – Track Summary

Peter G. Bunce

Director, BBRT

Beyond Budgeting is about rethinking how we manage organizations in a post-industrial world where innovative management models represent the only sustainable competitive advantage. It is also about releasing people from the burdens of stifling bureaucracy and suffocating control systems, trusting them with information and giving them time to think, reflect, share, learn and improve. It is about transferring responsibility and power from the centre to the front line units; putting employees first, customer second and the hierarchy third. Above all it is about learning how to change from many leaders who have built and managed 'beyond budgeting' organizations.

The word 'budgeting' is not used in its narrow sense of planning and control, but as a generic term for the traditional command and control management model (with budgeting at its core). In this context it describes both a management culture and a performance management system. This might become clearer when you understand how Dr Jan Wallander, architect of the management model at Swedish bank Handelsbanken, saw the problems of budgeting. "The basic idea in the Handelsbanken model is *decentralization*," noted Wallander. "If the issues are studied from this viewpoint, the abolition of budgets emerges as a mere detail, something simple and obvious; one of several aspects of the basic idea."

The BBRT (Beyond Budgeting Round Table) is an independent, international research and shared learning collaborative. It is a network of member organizations with a common interest in transforming their management models to enable sustained, superior performance. Two of its founders, Jeremy Hope and Robin Fraser, undertook the initial case-based research in which they identified the new model and later explained it in their book *"Beyond Budgeting"* published by Harvard Business School Press in 2003. The BBRT's research continues with its outputs (e.g. case studies and papers giving insights into the model and how to implement it) being shared internationally among our expanding global network.

The Lean & Agile principles have much in common with Beyond Budgeting. Lean & Agile challenge traditional beliefs about how to best run business support projects, while Beyond Budgeting challenges traditional thinking about how to best manage organizations. Both arrive at very similar conclusions. Complex knowledge organizations operating in uncertain and dynamic environments need agile and flexible processes, supporting fast and value-driven decisions.

The Beyond Budgeting movement believes that organizations will only realize the full potential from Lean & Agile when this becomes the way we run our organizations, and not just our projects.

P. Abrahamsson and N. Oza (Eds.): LESS 2010, LNBIP 65, pp. 124–125, 2010.
© Springer-Verlag Berlin Heidelberg 2010

The papers presented in this track describe several real commercial case studies in organizations that are on the journey from command-and-control to learn-and-adapt. Also why the Beyond Budgeting management model enables Lean & Agile to realize their full potential and how new Lean & Agile project management techniques can help with changing management models.

Beyond Budgeting: A Performance Management Model for Software Development Teams

Garry Lohan, Kieran Conboy, and Michael Lang

National University of Ireland, Galway
{Garry.Lohan,Kieran.Conboy,Michael.Lang}@nuigalway.ie

Abstract. The Beyond Budgeting performance management model enables companies to keep pace with changing environments, to quickly create and adapt strategy and to empower people throughout the organisation to make effective choices. We argue that this performance management model may be ideal for agile software development. Although drawn from different disciplines, both are designed for a customer-orientated, fast-changing operating environment and the Beyond Budgeting model suggests a useful overall framework for research in the performance management of agile software development teams. This paper uses the model as a lens to examine the performance management of agile software development teams within a large multinational. The findings show that some traditional performance management processes (most notably the budgeting process), which were designed to aid in the performance management of software development teams may impede the performance of agile teams due to their suitability adherence to the requirements of the systems development lifecycle model.

Keywords: Beyond Budgeting; Agile Methods; Organizational Agility.

1 Introduction

Continued uncertainty and rapid changes to business and technology environments have meant that a software development team's ability to respond to changing user or customer requirements has become increasingly critical. As a means to respond to these changes the software development community has moved from a traditional, plan-driven, structured approach to more agile development methods, which has had a huge impact on the way software is developed worldwide [1-3].

These newer methods of producing software are not always compatible with traditional performance management models (PMMs) [4-6]. As agile methods grow in popularity, it is important that the management control in the organization be set up to complement an agile way of working. An innovation from the accounting literature called "Beyond Budgeting" has shown great promise as a performance management model for a changing business and operating environment [5, 7-12]. This model is conceptually similar and appears to align well with agile methods [5, 11, 13, 14]. The research objective of this paper is to examine how the Beyond Budgeting model is being applied in the field of agile software development.

P. Abrahamsson and N. Oza (Eds.): LESS 2010, LNBIP 65, pp. 126–138, 2010.

The paper is structured as follows: The next section explores current thinking on performance management and performance management models and introduces the Beyond Budgeting model; the research methodology is then outlined; and the fourth section highlights the major findings of this research, followed by a discussion and conclusion outlining the importance to research and industry.

2 Performance Management and the beyond Budgeting Framework

Performance management models are complex and intertwined, but research tends to ignore the interdependencies between controlling mechanisms and concentrate on simplified and partial areas of the overall PMM. The literature in the area of PMM and management control systems (MCS) increasingly recognizes the need for research to be based on more coherent theoretical foundations [12, 15-17]. The tendency to focus only on specific aspects of control systems, as opposed to a more comprehensive and integrated approach, has led to some spurious findings, ambiguity and a potential for conflicting results [15]. There have been calls for a more integrated approach which includes the interdependency between different control mechanisms operating at the same time in the same organisation [18].

Ferreira and Otley [12] and Broadbent and Laughlin [17] have worked on conceptualizing performance *management* and distinguishing it from performance *measurement*. They have developed research frameworks that are especially useful when researchers seek to gain an insight into the types of performance management techniques being utilized by organizations. These frameworks are generic in their construction and encompass the whole spectrum of operating environments, from command and control to a more decentralized environment. While the Beyond Budgeting model could be classified within either of the aforementioned frameworks, it is specifically designed for a turbulent, changing business environment. This makes it a suitable PMM for agile software development and means it can be viewed as a standalone framework for research in the field of performance management.

In recent years there has been a move from the bureaucratic, hierarchical organization, -considered ineffective in the context of increased competition brought about by globalization, deregulation, the emergence of powerful developing economies, and development in information technologies, -towards flatter, leaner and more responsive structures [19]. Many authors have raised questions about the efficacy of existing systems of management and government, which first came to prominence during the industrial era, calling now for new models in the context of the modern knowledge economy e.g. [20, 21]. Others have questioned the budgeting process and its value in the post-industrial era [5, 22-27].

The Beyond Budgeting performance management model was formally introduced in 2003 as an alternative to the traditional command and control type performance management models, which were usually based on budgetary control mechanisms. Beyond Budgeting is more orientated towards fast changing operational environments and utilizes a sense and respond type of control mechanism, which allows an organisation to keep pace with fast changing environments [10, 28-32]. The emergence of this new concept coincided with the emergence of agile methods and both concepts share many similarities with both having a distinctly agile or adaptive perspective [5, 11, 13, 14]. The model consists of six leadership principles and six process principles when taken together and used in an holistic manner help improve performance management within an organization [5, 10]. Figure 1 lists the twelve principles are they are outlined in the Beyond Budgeting Round Table (www.BBRT.org).

Leadership Principles	Process Principles
Customers: Focus everyone on improving customer outcomes, *not on hierarchical relationships.*	**Goals:** Set relative goals for continuous improvement; *do not negotiate fixed performance contracts.*
Organization: Organize as a network of lean, accountable teams, *not around centralized functions.*	**Rewards:** Reward shared success based on relative performance, *not on meeting fixed targets.*
Responsibility: Enable everyone to act and think like a leader, *not merely follow the plan.*	**Planning:** Make planning a continuous and inclusive process, *not a top down annual event.*
Autonomy: Give teams the freedom and capability to act; *do not micromanage them.*	**Controls:** Base controls on relative indicators and trends, *not variances against a plan.*
Values: Govern through a few clear values, goals and boundaries, *not detailed rules and budgets.*	**Resources:** Make resources available as needed, *not through annual budget allocations.*
Transparency: Promote open information for self-management; *do not restrict it hierarchically.*	**Coordination:** Coordinate interactions dynamically, *not through annual planning cycles.*

Fig. 1. The Beyond Budgeting Performance Management Model

3   Research Methodology

3.1 Site Selection

SCC is a large multinational oil and gas firm with an internal information systems division that builds customized software solutions, mainly for internal clients. The organization started moving from a traditional command and control model during the 1990s and in 2005 began the process of implementing the Beyond Budgeting model. As one of the earliest adopters of the Beyond Budgeting model and an early adopter of the Scrum methodology, the organization presented an excellent opportunity to gain an insight into how the Beyond Budgeting model is being operationalized.

The development teams within the organization had traditionally worked with waterfall development and the transition to agile development processes raised questions on the suitability of the surrounding supporting processes. Organizational structures, which had supported the use of the waterfall method, meant that the emphasis on traditional project management practices needed to be changed to support the more agile way of developing solutions. In many cases, the end user was not the direct customer of the development team. The teams studied were often part of a larger umbrella group and therefore their customers were more often than not an internal downstream function of the organization.

3.2 Data Sources and Analysis

A literature review of each principle from the Beyond Budgeting framework formed the basis of an interview protocol used in this study [33]. Data were collected through a variety of methods: unstructured and semi-structured interviewing, informal meetings and follow up communication via email and commentary of findings. The study was conducted within the IS division of SCC which builds customized software solutions for internal and external clients. Ten formal interviews were carried out with personnel from four different Scrum projects and in three different locations. Four of those interviewed were external consultants hired to become part of a Scrum team once the project had kicked off. The other six interviewees spoke as Scrum masters although some were previously project managers whose role had been redefined to suit the Scrum methodology. Several of these were Scrum masters who were responsible for a large number of teams.

All transcripts were recorded and transcribed entirely. The transcriptions were imported into NVivo for coding. Reflexive remarks and memos made during both the interview stage and the analysis stage helped to interpret the data and lead to the identification of emergent themes. Precautions were taken to corroborate the interpretations made [34, 35]. Responses were checked for representativeness by examining them across participants. For example, team members' reports of their experience with their customers were checked against the reports from other team members and the Scrum masters. The participants in the study also provided commentary, correction and elaboration on drafts of the findings and framework.

4 Findings

The Beyond Budgeting model is an holistic management model suited to an agile environment. A previous literature review discussed each principle of the model and how they may be operationalized in the context of agile software development [33]. This section focuses on the results of this case study that examined how each principle was or was not being operationalized in a real world setting. What is working well and what is not working well is examined under each principle of the Beyond Budgeting model.

4.1 Customer Focus

Where project teams were involved in larger umbrella programs, a Scrum of Scrums took place on a regular basis. This helped disseminate customer knowledge information. There are no specific knowledge repositories utilized to store customer knowledge gathered over time (which could be used by other teams working with the same customer at a later date) and inter team knowledge sharing needed improvement. Filtering of customer requirements through customer proxies or product owners was a cause for concern for some team members. In some cases, team members were encouraged to get requirements from the product owner and not individuals they might know from the customer side. One Scrum master gave the reason for this: *"These are individuals, they do not represent the business need, the product owner represents the business need. So it's really about channelling this into one person who is there to ensure that this is what the business needs and it's not the preference of one aspect of the business."*

Getting and using feedback at the end of each sprint was standard across all teams. However the level of customer or in many cases, proxy customer involvement was very hit and miss with some teams having a great customer relationship and other getting minimal input from their customers. As one Scrum master put it: *"It's the first time I've seen such a close relationship* [with the customer]. *You could say that we've been lucky to have this group as an internal customer, of course they are more motivated to get Scrum up and working and we have a lot of commitment, but its not a default that everyone is as committed"*

Another Scrum master agrees that the organization is committed to providing good quality service and say that the reason for implementing Scrum was because: *"We wanted to be more customer focused and deliver business value faster"*

4.2 Organization

While there were operating guidelines within which the team was expected to operate, the team members had quite a lot of freedom to make decisions and try out new ideas that could improve the performance of the team. The following quote from one team member illustrate this: *"Yeah, the team is pretty much allowed to do whatever we feel would improve the quality of the code, the quality of the process, increase the efficiency, as long as we are able to justify why we would like to spend 5 or 10 hours on an activity, that is usually fine."*

Members were consulted regarding decisions made on new team members or training requirements but they would not necessarily have much control over the final decision. Operating guidelines and decisions such as using the Scrum methodology were, as one team member stated: *"mandated from further up the food chain".* Larger decisions regarding major project milestones, resourcing, methodologies and project roadmaps were made during the project initiation period when the major stakeholders got together and formulated a high-level project plan.

4.3 Responsibility

The onus on coaching team members and enabling members to think and act like leaders lies mainly with the team itself and the Scrum master. While SCC is striving to fully embrace the Scrum concept and develop long lasting teams who share responsibility, this is not yet happening. One reason for this could be that most of SCCs projects involve hiring consultants for the duration of the project or product lifecycle. One Scrum master tells of how the organisation is trying to develop a sense of shared responsibility: *"We are working hard on this… … We are developing the Scrum teams to take more responsibility. But again when you are talking about Scrum teams which are more or less staffed by consultants, they don't have the same kind of responsibility, they are very responsible people but they are doing it according to a contract"*

The main obstacle to long lasting teams appears to be the budgeting process. As one Scrum master states: *"Sometimes you get a budget that is: you need to run this for 13 months and that ends on Dec 1. But then along the way somebody says, ah but we should get another phase on it but we can't get a budget for it so we will start on Feb 1. Then you get a gap, what do you do in the meantime? We have a really good team, should we just dismantle it and try to assemble it in 2 months?"*

Many of the team members are hired as consultants for a specific project. High-level project goals are already in place and the team's priority is to achieve those goals. The use of short-term contracts may hinder the development of long lasting, high performing teams. One Scrum master highlights the problem with yearly budgets and why it is reasonable to assume there may be some myopic thinking among team members: *"We only have a short horizon here; we only have a budget for the rest of the year which means we can't think any longer. That, at least, is what we are being told, even though we know a lot of the task will probably go on the next year"*

4.4 Autonomy

Generally, team members felt they had a lot of autonomy when it came to their daily work. Members participated in daily stand-ups, iteration meetings, retrospectives and show-and-tell sessions and felt that their input was listened to and valued. While team members felt they had a certain amount of autonomy or were empowered to carry out their daily tasks, Scrum masters were somewhat more sceptical with one Scrum master wondering about the organisations support for Scrum: *"So how do we get the whole organization to support it, how do we define roles and responsibilities in our government structure that actually fits the ambition of delegating responsibility further down in the organization"*

Autonomy is also about team members feeling that their input and work is valued by the organization. On one project, it was the confidence in the product owner that left team members unsure of the value of their work. They felt that the product owner filtered requirements and suggestions and the value they contributed was diluted because of this. One team member had this to say: *"The product owner filters the users in such a way that I feel we don't get the requirements which could be beneficial to the users to actually have implemented"*

Confidence in the product owner was sometimes not very high but generally, team members felt that they were carrying out important work and that this work was valued. A Scrum master explains the probable reason for this: *"The product owner has made some effort in creating a vision, so I think they* [the team] *are not only making bricks, I think they know what kind of cathedral they are going to build"*

4.5 Values

Generally, the teams work within a set of operating guidelines that are usually decided during the project initiation. A technological roadmap is set out at the beginning of the project that outlines the goals and major milestones of the project. One Scrum master describes the process: *"Many of the participants in the Scrum teams are actually developing the target and the mission together with the product owners, so they are actually involved in developing it but decisions are not taken by the Scrum teams, they are taken by the product owner and asset owner, but its mostly based on recommendations and input from the teams"*

This roadmap is communicated clearly to the teams and they have an opportunity to make further suggestions or recommendations. This is essentially, what the Beyond Budgeting principle is recommending. However, while detailed rules are not used for governing, yearly budgets still play and important role and have a big affect on the behaviours of the teams.

4.6 Transparency

There was a consensus within all the interviewees that they had all relevant information they required for their daily operations. The organization has formal mechanisms in place, such as coordination workshops and demo sessions, to help promote a wider understanding and transparency among teams, but as one Scrum master says: *"Our intention is good, we would like to think in an holistic perspective and think integration and ensure everyone has the same understanding and so on, but the amount of work makes us focus on what is closest to us and that is the small group of people we are working with and that also goes for the Scrum teams"*

The teams all appear to be happy with the Scrum methodology and the transparency it offers through either the project management tool or charts on wall spaces used by some teams. A Scrum master tells how transparency is complemented and teams are getting up to date information: *"We are sending out newsletters to the project team where we inform them about what has been reported to the steering committee, regarding whether we are within or beyond target and what kind of actions have been agreed to get us on target with time or whatever. They know about some of the largest risks we have and any mitigating actions and so on. So they have a good feeling on how the project is performing"*

4.7 Goals

The goal setting process for team members is an informal process within SCC. Many team members are hired as consultants for specific projects and come into the team with a specifically requested skill set. The move to agile has seen Scrum masters and project manager's focus more on behavioural skills as one Scrum master makes clear: *"When I select team members the next time I will be much more focused on how they actually behave inside the team and to have really clever people is not that important"*

Project roadmaps are already in place when a team is assembled and project milestones outlined. The team members see these as their main goals and within those boundaries they decide, as a team, along with the product owner their shorter-term goals. Within the project duration, most team members felt that their Scrum master would informally speak with them regarding their short-term individual goals. Some senior stakeholders may have their own personal goals but generally, the team is viewed as having a team goal. A Scrum master explains: *"The goals are the Key Performance Indicators (KPIs). Every single department has their own KPIs, process owners have them, line managers, asset owners, everybody has them, and on project as such, we are measured on timely delivery and quality and all that. It does not go down to every single individual on the project. I would say it is fairly informal how this happens in a Scrum project when it comes to each individual"*

4.8 Rewards

Group rewards schemes are not carried out within SCC. All those interviewed seemed to appreciate being part of a team working towards specific goals, i.e. project milestones, go-live dates etc. Groups were rewarded to some extent' for example one Scrum master says: *"The team gets the applause definitely from the customers and those who lead the project when everything goes well"*

   The person to whom the team member is reporting carries out individual reviews. This person is expected to give an objective insight into the performance of the team member. As the team members are consultants with different companies, their individual reward packages were different and were not discussed during these interviews. In many respects, the reward system is in line with the Beyond Budgeting principle, because although the team targets project milestones, these targets are set only by time and there is room for de-scoping if required. Team members are reviewed based on relative performance and both technical and behavioural factors are considered. The review is not carried out by peers as recommended by Beyond Budgeting and is therefore open to the subjective opinion of the reviewer (generally the Scrum master).

4.9 Planning

Once a project roadmap is decided upon and project milestones or decision gates are set then the team has considerable flexibility to change interim plans. The ability to re-prioritize the functionality being delivered is one of the main differences between a Scrum project and a traditional waterfall project. A Scrum master explains the planning process: *"It's the product owner, who at all times defines what is in the scope, so the only thing we can promise is that we can start the project at one time and stop it at another time. If we are keeping to that time schedule then we can deliver within this cost estimate but whatever you get for that money within that timeframe is basically up to the product owners and asset owners to prioritize* [with input from the team].*"*

   Again, working with the Scrum methodology means the teams planning process is both inclusive and flexible. The following quote from a team member illustrates this point: *"That's why we are running Scrum, because we can adjust moving forward, instead of working for a year and going to the customer and saying this is what we have delivered and they say that's not what we asked for. That's what I like about Scrum"*

4.10 Control

Once the budget has been established for a project then, that is deemed as the boundary condition. For team members the key performance indicators are to meet the project milestones that indicate that the project is running within budget. All projects require a high level of quality and de-scoping of functionality may happen in order to meet milestones within budget. One Scrum master explains how their team stays within the budget boundaries: *"We have been able to hold cost exactly at budget and quality we uphold by taking out of the box as much as possible"*

Although not linked to the project timeline, it may be worth noting, that in order to comply with IT SOX requirements the project management office requires an information risk assessment to be carried out after each sprint. This is linked to key controls for confidentiality, reliability and integrity of the information and is done by asking some key questions each month when solutions are put into production.

4.11 Resources

The budget for projects is fixed and when new resources are needed then the Scrum master will decide with other stakeholders what to prioritize. Functionality may be reduced or team members may be removed from the team to keep within the budget. There are mechanisms through which additional resources can be acquired which were not within the original budget a particular team.

The current process within SCC means that high performing teams may lose team members during the duration of a project in order to keep within the budget. This is not in line with the objective of having long lasting teams. One Scrum master shows how the fixed budget has a negative impact on performance: *"They were good* [the team], *they were doing so well and they were delivering excellent IT products, but they knew they were coming to an end, that was a challenge. They were probably at their peak... ...We really saw how good a team can be if they're allowed to stay in the same team for almost 2 years, they were doing so well"*

4.12 Coordination

The organization has mechanisms in place such as intranets, video conferencing facilities, knowledge wikis, etc. designed to encourage continuous interaction. Workloads often mean that teams only interact with those they are involved with in their daily tasks. Scrum of Scrums are used to improve inter team communication. One Scrum master gives his view: *"I still think there is quite a lot that could be benefited for better coordination between team at a team level and perhaps more importantly some improved communication between the product owners"*

There was a consensus that communication and coordination could be improved but the organization does appear to be trying to develop a good communication environment especially when teams are co-located. Some found informal outings very beneficial with one team member noting: *"When it's informal then it's easier to get to know people and then it's much easier to go and ask for help next time"*.

5 Discussion

Although the Beyond Budgeting model is designed as an holistic performance management model with each principle interacting with, and supporting the other principles, implementing it as such, is not always feasible. It is clear that SCC has a motivated and enthusiastic IS department who are fully embracing the Scrum concept. Team members are generally happy with the Scrum environment and the support they receive. More experienced Scrum masters or former project managers have some issues regarding the support for the concept of agility coming from areas such as project management and line management. Many feel that these areas are improving and need to continue to improve to create a truly agile environment. One senior Scrum master states that they have seen what he calls *"organizational transition lock"* when it comes to defining roles and responsibilities in the organizations government structure that actually fit the ambition of delegating responsibilities further down the organization and having self-managing teams. There is a sense that the Scrum methodology could be turned into just another methodology that feeds into the traditional project management structure of fixed budgets and quarterly reporting.

The project budget is still the dominant factor affecting team performance management in SCC. There is considerable flexibility in the project scope but the budget is still the bottom line. Teams that are performing well generally disband at the end of a project lifecycle even though they may be performing well. The main influencing factors appear to be the project budget and the way the project management is structured. In order to create long lasting teams it may be better to focus more on the product and have teams working on a product rather that on a project-by-project basis. More of a focus on the product, rather than a number of individual projects to be staffed and resourced individually, may allow for the creation of longer lasting teams.

The use of consultants gives SCC considerable flexibility to create and disband teams when a project begins or ends. This has the negative affect of inducing myopic thinking among team members who are working on a contract-by-contract basis. Another issue here is the length of time it takes to get a team working well together within the Scrum methodology. One Scrum master estimated that it took 12 weeks (3 * 4week sprints) to get a team working well together. Creating and disbanding teams according to the budget or project timeline creates problems for the Scrum masters who are often the interface between the Scrum team and other functions outside the team, such as the staffing department (line management), the project management office and the business units. Core teams with expertise in many areas, which may be expanded by consultants as required, may be the way forward. If these teams were to become long lasting teams focused on products rather than single projects at a time, then SCC can move easily onto the next step of its implementation of the Beyond Budgeting model.

6 Conclusion

The Beyond Budgeting model was first introduced in 2003 as a management model, which empowers employees with the responsibilities, authority, and support they need to create value for the organisation, with the minimum amount of control required to ensure they are operating within organizational boundaries. This case study develops the model and adapts it for use within the context of Scrum teams operating in a large organization. We contend that it is the optimum management model for a Scrum team and examined how it is being applied in practice, what is working and what needs improvement. The implications for theory and practice are discussed below.

6.1 Implication for Theory

As an holistic performance management model, the Beyond Budgeting model covers the entire spectrum of performance management. Many different theoretical bases are utilised, e.g. customer focus, decentralization, autonomy, governance, goal setting, relative performance evaluation, group rewards, control theory, dynamic resources, etc., all of which can be considered under the broad umbrella of performance management. Further research can establish which aspects of the model will work and in what context. For example, will the model function effectively if group reward schemes are or are not in place or if peer reviews do or do not take place? Are there cultural issues to be considered which will determine the effectiveness of the model? This paper outlines how the Beyond Budgeting model can be used to examine the performance management techniques of Scrum teams and how these techniques are assisting or impeding the effectiveness of the teams.

6.2 Implications for Practice

The Scrum methodology is fundamentally similar to the Beyond Budgeting model. This paper highlights the issues Scrum teams have when it comes to operating efficiently in an environment where supporting processes are not always complementary to a Scrum way of working. By examining each principle separately and highlighting how it is currently being applied within SCC, we show a way forward in the design of performance management systems which are particularly suited to an agile way of working. We believe that all the principles of the Beyond Budgeting model complement the Scrum methodology and for organisations who wish to use Scrum then the Beyond Budgeting model represents a suitable and complementary performance management model.

References

1. Conboy, K.: Agility from First Principles: Reconstructing the Concept of Agility in Information Systems Development. Information Systems Research 20(3) (2009)
2. Conboy, K., Fitzgerald, B.: Toward a conceptual framework of agile methods. In: Zannier, C., Erdogmus, H., Lindstrom, L. (eds.) XP/Agile Universe 2004. LNCS, vol. 3134, pp. 105–116. Springer, Heidelberg (2004)
3. Dybå, T., Dingsøyr, T.: Empirical studies of agile software development: A systematic review. Information and Software Technology 50(9-10), 833–859 (2008)
4. Boehm, B., Turner, R.: Management challenges to implementing agile processes in traditional development organizations. IEEE Software 22(5), 30–39 (2005)
5. Bogsnes, B.: Implementing Beyond Budgeting: Unlocking the Performance Potential. J. Wiley & Sons, New Jersey (2009)
6. Qumer, A., Henderson-Sellers, B.: A framework to support the evaluation, adoption and improvement of agile methods in practice. Journal of Systems and Software 81(11), 1899–1919 (2008)
7. Davila, A., Foster, G., Li, M.: Reasons for management control systems adoption: Insights from product development systems choice by early-stage entrepreneurial companies. Accounting, Organizations and Society 34(3-4), 322–347 (2009)

8. Drury, C.: Management and Cost Accounting. South-western, London (2008)
9. Hansen, S.C., Otley, D.T., Van der Stede, W.A.: Practice Developments in Budgeting: An Overview and Research Perspective. Journal of Management Accounting Research 15, 95–116 (2003)
10. Hope, J., Fraser, R.: Beyond Budgeting: How Managers can Break Free from the Annual Performance Trap. Harvard Business School Press, Boston (2003)
11. Poppendieck, M., Poppendieck, T.: Leading Lean Software Development: Results Are Not the Point. Addison-Wesley, Upper Saddle River (2010)
12. Ferreira, A., Otley, D.: The Design and Use of Performance Management Systems: An Extended Framework for Analysis. Management Accounting Research 20, 263–282 (2009)
13. Ambler, S.W.: Architecture and Design. Dr. Dobb's Journal (2008)
14. Highsmith, J.: An Adaptive Performance Management System. Cutter Consortium Executive Summary (2006),
    http://www.infoq.com/resource/articles/
    Adaptive-Performance-Management/en/resources/apms0606.pdf
15. Chenhall, R.H.: Management control systems design within its organizational context: findings from contingency-based research and directions for the future. Accounting, Organizations and Society 28(2-3), 127–168 (2003)
16. Covaleski, M.A., et al.: Budgeting Research: Three Theoretical Perspectives and Criteria for Selective Integration. Journal of Management Accounting Research 15, 3–49 (2003)
17. Broadbent, J., Laughlin, R.: Performance Management Systems: A Conceptual Framework. Management Accounting Research 20, 283–295 (2009)
18. Abernethy, M.A., Brownell, P.: Management control systems in research and development organizations: The role of accounting, behavior and personnel controls. Accounting, Organizations and Society 22(3-4), 233–248 (1997)
19. Berry, A.J., et al.: Emerging themes in management control: A review of recent literature. The British Accounting Review 41(1), 2–20 (2009)
20. McFarland, K.R.: Should You Build Strategy Like You Build Software? MIT Sloan Management Review 49(3), 69–74 (2008)
21. Manville, B., Ober, J.: A Company of Citizens. Harvard Business School, Boston (2003)
22. Schmidt, J.A.: Is it Time to Replace Traditional Budgeting? Journal of Accountancy 174(4), 103–107 (1992)
23. Dugdale, D., Lyne, S.: Budgeting. Financial Management (14719185), 32–35 (2006)
24. Howell, R.A.: Turn Your Budgeting Process Upside Down. Harvard Business Review 82(7/8), 21–22 (2004)
25. Cassell, M.: Budgeting and more. Management Accounting: Magazine for Chartered Management Accountants 77(8), 22 (1999)
26. Kennedy, A., Dugdale, D.: Getting the most from BUDGETING. Management Accounting: Magazine for Chartered Management Accountants 77(2), 22 (1999)
27. O'Brien, R.: Living with budgeting. Management Accounting: Magazine for Chartered Management Accountants 77(8), 22 (1999)
28. Fraser, R.: Figures of hate. Financial Management (14719185), 22 (2001)
29. Hope, J., Fraser, R.: Take it Away. Accountancy 123(1269), 50–51 (1999)
30. Hope, J., Fraser, R.: New ways of setting rewards: The beyond budgeting model. California Management Review 45(4), 104–119 (2003a)
31. Hope, J., Fraser, R.: Who needs budgets? Harvard Business Review 81(2), 108 (2003b)
32. Hope, J., Fraser, R.: Who needs budgets? Response. Harvard Business Review 81(6), 132 (2003c)

33. Lohan, G., Conboy, K., Lang, M.: Beyond Budgeting and agile software development: A conceptual framework for the performance management of agile software development teams. International Journal of Information Systems (under review), St Louis (2010)
34. Miles, M., Huberman, A.: Qualitative Data Analysis. Sage, London (1999)
35. Yin, K., Robert: Case Study Research: Design and Methods. Sage, Thousand Oaks (2003)

New Approach for Managing Lean-Agile Development: Overturning the Project Paradigm

Juha Rikkilä

Aalto University, School of Science and Technology
PO Box 11000, FI-00076 Aalto, Finland
juha.rikkila@kolumbus.fi

Abstract. Project management has lived long through a growing criticism of not delivering to expectations. When agile development and lean management approaches are now emerging to product development, this paper assesses their impact to current practices of project management. It is indicated that the very basis of the project management has shaken, and new management approaches need to be developed to accommodate the agile development in contemporary product organizations. A proposal is made for the outline of such an approach. In conclusion the changes in business management needed to enable this new approach is discussed.

Keywords: project management, assignment management, planning, lean management, agile, leadership.

1 Introduction

For years project management has been the main means for development and delivery of products and solutions, with defined content, within given schedule and budget, and on the quality level as expected. But for several years criticism has been growing because of worse than expected performance.

The very core of the project management is the project plan that contains, to put it simply, the complete understanding of content, quality, cost and schedule of the work at hand. That is, the topics a project manager ought to know thoroughly about the work in order to be successful. The topics he doesn't know well enough ought to go to risk management plan. It is assumed that these are few and the fewer the better. In essence these two types of plans are the ones projects are managed with, though sophisticated project management models and knowledge bases can list many other plans needed for project management.

"Plans are nothing; planning is everything." (Dwight D. Eisenhower) is quoted often in project context. Planning is the means to find out and understand the task before starting actions of doing it. However, the business world is accepting more and more uncertainty. It is recognized that it would take too long to dig all uncertainty out. That many facts about tasks can be found out only after effort has been spend on completing preceding tasks. Executing tasks and planning the work proceed parallel.

Agile approach has rethought many of the project management practices on team level. For example SCRUM model by Ken Schwaber [1] is built on the idea of 2-4

P. Abrahamsson and N. Oza (Eds.): LESS 2010, LNBIP 65, pp. 139–150, 2010.

week sprints that are planned and managed accurately. Managing the overall product or system goal is based on overall idea of a product and continuously evolving backlog of requirements. Another agile approach, Feature Driven Development (FDD) [2], is based on features instead of sprints, but implements the same idea of planning and implementing in short steps. Both leave the overall end result rather undefined and let it change as needed. In general, having an overall goal and current backlog of requirements, and then planning in short steps within teams while proceeding, characterizes agile approaches.

Management practices over several teams are much fuzzier. Agile approaches don't give clear answers to that. So when several teams work towards a common goal of producing a product or a system release in six to thirty six months the management of this effort is organized in traditional way. Project and program management is often used as the model. Yet these practices are clearly in conflict with agile practices.

This paper analyzes this conflict and builds a proposal of a more suitable management model.

2   Project Management under Pressure

Project management is very well established as a discipline to organize and manage work. For years its position has been unquestioned though often it has been argued not to deliver to expectations. Many different types of developments has taken place to perfect it further. On top of project management a concept of program management has been widely used in product development. It provides a management framework over several projects having the same goal, e.g. developing a product release and related services and support functions for customer deliveries.

Process improvement approaches emphasize the completeness of processes and maturity of their implementation. For project management a good source for checking completeness is the project management body of knowledge (PM-BOK) [3] by Project Management Institute. The CMMI model [4] by Software Engineering Institute or the ISO15504 standard [5] can be used for assessment of maturity.

In order to strengthen the management of uncertainty, risk management has grown to be a study branch of its own. One very comprehensive study and description of risk management as a practice can be found in Jyrki Kontio's dissertation [6]. Further research of managing uncertainty has been done by several people. For example Huchzermeier and Loch [7] use financial market's option pricing theory and applies it to R&D uncertainty management. Fenton et al [8] apply Bayesian Networks tools in analyzing project risks. Ilkaev [9] uses simulation over project PERT chart. Common to these is that they assume having a sufficient project plan as basis for the analysis.

2.1 Market Pressure

Overall, one could say project management is thoroughly understood and well established as the practice to organize work. However, it is the market place and especially some segments there that are evolving towards behaviors that are in contradiction with the project management principles. Using the Kano model[1] for categorizing whole market segments, this paper discusses about excitement driven markets as contrast to performance driven markets. What distinguishes these two is the amount of uncertainty. In performance driven markets customer requirements are well understood and most of them can be defined before work starts. Technology to be used in products is largely verified and uncertainties are few. Development organization is also well established or at least competent resources are sufficiently available for allocation. Plans can be done with sufficient accuracy and uncertainty can be accommodated under risk management.

In excitement driven markets none of this is true. Customers are unsure and their needs evolve and change continuously. Often they need to see some solutions before they have any opinion and then it evolves when solutions evolve. Barry Boehm [11] [12] called this IKIWISI (I Know It When I See It). Similarly technology may be innovative but often uncertain and options are not easily comparable. What comes to resources, organizations want to keep their options open where to allocate their scarce resources at any point of time. Yet, profits of early entry to the market before competition urge companies to take high risks and start efforts to provide the markets. The question is how much planning effort is value adding and at what point it will become waste of time and effort. How to plan doing something that will reveal itself only after lots of effort is spend on it already?

2.2 Business Pressure

In many product organizations internal business management creates a pressure on keeping accurately to plans and keeping costs down. Especially if the business performance of the organization is not on an expected level the latter becomes rigorously enforced. Rigor is often built with process management, standardizing and assuring them vigorously. Goals are set and commitments are given having this rigor firmly in mind. Rewarding locks the organization tightly to following the plans.

When realities of the market place collide with this rigorous internal management style, result is often friction and conflicts between the management and the development teams, and significant losses of opportunities in the market place. Further, effort is wasted on reworking on plans. Agile approach is seen a good response to market pressures but project disciplines with predictability and control is desired for business reasons. So compromising some of both to make them match is considered a way to solve the conflict. The outcome is often less than satisfactory.

2.3 Frictions, Conflicts, Lost Opportunities and Waste

When compromising the project management, outcome is often more overall plans, content with buffering of expected new requirements, resource locking for anticipated

---

[1] Kano model [10] classifies product characteristics (or features) into three categories: threshold, performance and excitement. Threshold features are a must without which product is not accepted. Performance features are what customers use to make rational choices, the better and more comprehensively implemented, the more likely the product is selected. Excitement features are not expected but when found they will impact strongly on customers to select the product.

areas and leaving quality assurance late. When compromising the agile development, outcome is often a large and badly prioritized backlog, restricting management over teams and work plans, ridged resource allocations, and weak co-operation between teams. Yet, commitments must be given and kept. When put this all together, there is plenty of room for distrust and shortsighted action. Some of the consequences are described below.

Requirements and Change Management. There is initially a need to collect all requirements in order to do the planning and to give commitments. So lots of guessing takes place and large backlog is created. It becomes cumbersome to understand the whole and set priorities. Teams start to work on random topics. Consequently product tests can start late because of functionally fragmented integration results. Due to the size of the backlog, loose prioritization and dependencies between items it becomes difficult to identify and drop unnecessary items in the backlog. When some necessary requirements will not be unimplemented some unnecessary will. Further waste is generated when waiting for initial requirements and when waiting change decisions and prioritization of requirements.

Planning and Management. Initially lots of planning takes place in order to get decision of starting the work. Later on this leads to the situation that project managers call "the planning hell". In order to keep plans up to date project managers have to plan and replan time after time after every change. In addition commitments and contracts may need to be revisited, possibly even renegotiated. Let alone updating project content related documentation. During the work teams find problems early and management may feel overloaded with issues. They want to get involved and consequently erode the authority of teams to solve issues. It also generates management overhead and delay in work when collecting data, reporting and deciding again and again. This may decay situation even further and management may enforce tighter planning over teams leading to further inefficiencies in agile teams.

Cost management. Frequent public reporting of financial performance puts heavy pressure on cost management. There is continuous need for cutting costs which lead often to two different paths of action. On one hand costs are cut by functions aiming to ensure 100% workload all the time. On the other hand planning is done optimistically showing lower than realistic costs levels and with very little flexibility built in. Consequently critical resources become a bottle neck causing delays and waiting in development work. Further, cutting corners in development process lead to growing technical dept. Heavy and unplanned quality improvement cycles close at the planned delivery date cause further delays.

Resource Management. 100% work load requirement leads to very little time for learning. Teams don't grow to be multi-talented and thus limit the potent of agile approach. Team velocities remain low. Instead, special competencies become a scarce resource and bottleneck in development teams. This leads to sequential work process and waiting. Yet, organizations are often poorly equipped to notice these situations early and manage them efficiently.

Quality Management. Quality management is typically based on PDCA principle [99], Plan-Do-Check-Act. It fits perfectly with plan driven management, but when plans are relaxed also quality management turn out to be difficult. A completely different approach is needed. However, it is not further discussed here but is a topic for a separate paper.

Product and release management. Project and program management is closely linked to product and release management. Any change in one will require reconsideration of the other. Space don't allow that discussion in this paper but is a topic of a separate paper.

2.4 A New Management Approach

World is not black and white. Markets are not strictly either performance or excitement oriented and management is not purely controlling against plan. The market evolution towards excitement orientation is however clear. Agile approach has been widely accepted as the development approach for excitement driven market place. However, it has major implications to its management environment. Particularly project and program management seem to be in severe conflict with it. It has been suggested that these roles should be discarded. The questions then are, where should their responsibilities and authority be allocated at and what part of those can be discarded altogether?

Already 1988 Kotter [13] published his research about the need to develop business management to deal with evolution towards this kind of markets. He promoted development of leadership skills in business organizations. Also Barry Boehm wrote first time in 1988 and several times later about IKIWISI (I Know It When I See It) and win-win between development project and its customers. He considered it evident that users of a system would know late what they actually want, and it is necessary to accept late in order to achieve win-win of parties. He promoted the spiral model.

More recently numerous other approaches have been proposed to relieve the strictly disciplined management practices. Often mentioned are Theory of Constraints by Goldratt [14], and Design Factory by Reinertsen [15].However, the lean management approach has turned out to be the most dominant source when looking for management models for accommodating agile development in a product organization. There are several variations and applications of lean. Womack and Jones [16] define the value to and pull by a customer, and flow and perfection of it. Poppendiecks [17] [18] apply these principles to development of software intensive systems. Hines [19] builds the connection between the lean management and leadership.

3 Proposal Outline

In management studies there has been a thorough discussion about leadership and management and their applicability in different contexts. For this paper the starting point is the definitions by Kotter that is shortly summarized in table 1 below.

Table 1. Management vs. leadership

Management	Leadership
Plans, planning	Vision, strategy, framework
Budgeting	Operational framework
Organizing and resourcing	Networks, coalitions, empowerment
Controlling	Alignment, engagement, coaching

In his book Kotter heavily criticizes the management dominant approach of leading organizations and describes ways to develop the leadership skills. According to him high level of uncertainty requires leadership approach. Over the years similar writings have been plenty. One of the most prominent forums in lean context has been the BBRT - Beyond Budgeting Roundtable [20].

For this paper leadership approach has been taken to replace the project management approach. This has been concluded to mean:

- Vision and values, strategy and rules are preferred over plans,
- commitment, engagement and drive are preferred over control of performance,
- networks, coalitions and alignment are preferred over formal project structures,
- extended decision making is preferred over strict control and change management,
- framework driven execution is preferred over plan driven control of work, and
- steering to the satisfying closure preferred over just checking that all defined actions are closed and items done.

The second source for developing the proposal in this paper has been the lean management approach and principle of optimizing the organization to produce customer value. The third source is the application of some old planning and management methods, techniques and tools into this new context.

3.1 Vision and Values, Strategy and Rules

The purpose of the project level vision and values, and strategy and rules is to establish the goal and set a framework for development. Typically the goal is a characterization of a release and all delivery related work products, in extended product sense. That is, all product, service and context related aspect of a product. It would characterize the full value of the release to its intended user and owner. The framework contains the organizational context and its more long term desires as well as the goal related specifics. Its purpose is to "frame the uncertainty" and enable the empowerment of teams for decision making. Vision and values set aim on satisfaction of all three stakeholder groups, customers, business stakeholders and development stakeholders. Strategy and rules have aim on keeping the direction and performance, and on avoidance of waste. The framework can be considered as the continuously evolving knowledge base of the organization.

3.2 Commitment, Engagement and Drive

In uncertain environment the energy and knowledge of all parties need to in full use continuously. The word "empowerment" is sometimes used to describe this giving authority and expecting the responsibility to deliver. However, it also requires building such a working environment that enables commitment, engagement and drive of all parties. When uncertainty is high it takes individual capability not just to do individual decisions but also work through networks and coalitions to get those decisions done by others.

Commitment and process of committing under uncertainty is a real challenge. Development is the last in the chain where customers commit to acquire, business stakeholders to deliver, and development to make it available and install it into use. In plan driven world this all is done with plans and contracts at the very beginning. In excitement driven market place committing is a gradual process when the details of the final solution emerge during the development. When a customer wants a fixed commitment, uncertainty needs to be buffered in the contract. The product evolution is then the interest of the business stakeholders and the development stakeholders and hidden from the customer. A fixed commitment does not mean development according to a fixed plan.

3.3 Networks, Coalitions and Alignment

When the content is not known at the beginning, decisions and technical competencies needed for the work are also unknown. Resourcing needs to take place during the work, so the capability to involve is a must. Coalition means coming together, agreeing and deciding. Networks mean sharing knowledge, discussing and solving issues intensively but not necessarily all would be involved at the same time. Technically, the advanced social media provide a feasible means doing things globally without physically being in the same place. Operationally capability to create coalitions and networks to the need, often ad hoc, is required. This enables commitment, engagement and drive in the development work by the whole organization. To the extent that is most productive for creating customer value.

When decisions are frequent and fast new knowledge is created often. In order to keep the organization aligned intensive effort is needed to share the knowledge through the networks. Keeping also those up-to-date who have not participated, is a challenge. Proper tools and advance practices are needed to ensure sufficient communication.

3.4 Extended Decision Making

In the plan driven world decisions are made early. There is plenty of time to prepare those decisions and when done, they communicated by writing in meeting minutes or in different project plans. Focus is in doing decisions.

When working with excitement driven markets decisions are done late as they are known late. However, this also means that there is plenty of information available for decision making. The challenge is to have it where it is needed when it is needed. After decisions the challenge is to communicate it efficiently as it is needed for other decisions. That is why the decision making is extended to cover all of collection and communication as well. Coalitions and networks have the key role in making it happen. Networks, whether predefined or ad hoc, collect the stored information and tacit knowledge and prepares it for decision making. Coalitions make decisions and make them known through networks in order to keep the whole organization aligned. Execution based on decisions can start immediately.

In networked organizations the authority, responsibility and accountability of all phases of the extended decision making require special attention. The definition and agreement of them is part of the creation of the framework discussed already above. The speed of their function is essential. Networks must form immediately and coalitions for decisions put up without any delay. Using social media tools for that can be invaluable, but it requires readiness from the organization as well.

3.5 Framework Driven Execution

The purpose of the framework is to enable fast decision making and steer execution. It has two sides: the common organization framework and the development goal specific framework.

The common steering framework contains the essential elements of organization's market and business decisions as well as operational knowledge accumulated of previous experience. The formation and exact content is outside the scope of this paper, but in general terms it provides the basis for business guidance. It links to business strategy, product portfolio, and long and short term plans. It also contains operational guidelines and professional knowledge of developing software intensive products, tightly bound to business and product goals.

Similarly, the goal specific framework is the means to steer work when no exact plans exist. Specifically it contains description of the user value of the extended product that is about to be developed. This framework evolves with decisions done during development. At the end it contains much of the similar things as plans contain in the plan driven world. It may also contain value descriptions of business stakeholders.

The framework is meant to support the use of tacit knowledge and empower the individual decision making. When process databases and best practice libraries are often used to replace consideration, framework is meant to excite consideration. Yet it should support steering towards common organization goals. For example, product technology decisions may be very strict, but the guidance may encourage individual special effort to try different solutions in seeking the best performance.

It is an interesting observation that product related guidelines and operational guidelines start to intermingle. When roles and responsibilities often diverge in plan driven world, causing more handovers and predisposing to communication gaps, in excitement driven world it is desired to keep them together as much as humanly possible. This leads to development of multitalented people using networks and coalitions effetely to achieve the commonly agreed goals. From this point of view frameworks set common ground and common rules for co-operation and performance.

The role of a manager becomes very much that of leader and coach who participates in networks and coalitions to provide support to people and professional knowledge to ensure quality of decisions. But above all, the role of a manager is to ensure steering to the closure and delivery of the desired outcome.

3.6 Steering to the Closure

The most challenging job in development of products to excitement driven markets is steering the development to the closure so that it delivers to the satisfaction of all stakeholders. Initially there is just a vision of the end result and some characteristics of it defined. These characteristics keep on refining over time. It requires continuous management effort to ensure that each decision takes the development work towards the final agreement of what the end result is and when will it fulfill the requirements of a releasing. When this final agreement has been reached the effort to the closure can be started. As all elements are then known, this final phase can be organized as a traditional project, often containing also other related tasks of readying product for the market.

Steering to the closure is heavily dependent on the commitments given initially and over the period of the development work. The stricter the commitments are, the tighter the goal specific framework must be. And the more devoted management to the closure must it be.

4 Assessment and Evaluation of the Outline

It goes without saying that this approach can not live alone within traditional product development. Instead, similar principles need to be applied on product program management and the management of the whole product organization. Overall the challenge is to replace uncertain, unrealistic planning with vision and values, strategy and rules. The framework supports fast decision making. This requires genuine leadership approach which allows real empowerment and engagement of all staff. Keeping direction and firmly focusing on results and releases becomes the core of the management effort.

Will this approach address the current problems in the specified environment? This question is harder to answer. One reason for this is that problem is often expressed with secondary terms, like we did not deliver it in schedule. The ultimate goal is to deliver content to a customer need and in schedule proper for a customer. Often however, for example schedule is made to as the main goal, all management activity focused on it and all rewards paid based on it. The understanding of the real value to a customer and to business itself is not fully recognized. The approach described in this paper is tuned to understand and deliver the real value. But as said above, it can not live without the whole organization living according to these same principles.

What would this kind of a management approach require from each of the three stakeholder groups?

4.1 Customer View

It is often considered a good business practice to acquire fully defined products or systems with fixed term contracts. And when so, project management is a perfect match to it. However, when the uncertainty grows and speed of changes gets high, fixed terms serve badly leading waste and losses in utilization. On the other hand it must be said that open terms without discipline might lead to waste and financial losses, as well.

This paper proposes the agile approach where frequent demonstrations ensure content decisions that maximize the customer value. However, that can not stand alone but requires different approach for business management and development management as well. From customer point of view their involvement in both will grow significantly. If the market is business to business it may require every customer to involve. If it is the consumer market the representation of the different market segments need to be organized. Overall, this involvement would address both the end product related topics as well as the commitment and business management related topics.

4.2 Business Stakeholder View

For the product or system vendors the fixed term approach to business has been dominant as well, both when dealing with customers and when organizing product development work internally. This paper has especially been focused on the latter. For the purposes of this paper markets and customer behavior was categorized using Kano model into excitement, performance and threshold driven markets.

In threshold driven markets cost is the king. If a product or a system fulfils the threshold requirements cost will dictate the buying decision. In this kind of markets the above described way of developing products is out of the question. Best suited management style could be characterized as strictly following the rules, and avoiding costs and deviations as much as possible. Employees are expected to do the things as defined in the work plans.

In performance driven markets the characteristics of product feature implementations drive decisions. The better the required features correspond to user specifications the more probable the customer will accept it. This assumes specifications to be available beforehand which also enables planning of development, i.e. projects. So plan driven management style applies well. Development organization is team oriented and well prepared and willing to project type work.

This paper has discussed about a management approach for excitement driven markets, where many of the even key requirements are not know when work is started. This is either because users can not comprehend or agree on them, or because the technology will reveal itself only after lots of effort and experimentation. Also users will change their minds frequently of already agreed requirements.

The proposed approach builds on vision of the end result and strategy leaving enough room to maneuver with the continuous change of requirements and uncertainty of technology. Business management needs to accurately observe this change and uncertainty and efficiently steer the networks and coalitions to deal with it. Decisions need to be done swiftly, and execution needs to start immediately. The framework for observation and decision making needs to evolve continuously. Even more importantly the development of tacit knowledge in the organization needs to be priority of the management. The performance of the networks and coalitions is heavily dependent on tacit knowledge. Making all this to work requires leadership approach.

4.3 Development Stakeholder View

Organizations in the excitement driven market place have two major challenges in management. On one hand there is the challenge of building an environment of motivation and engagement of employees, teams and middle management. On the other hand it is the challenge of aligning these highly self-fulfilling individuals to common organization and delivery goals as given commitments will require. The approach proposed in this paper has moved the balance of organization performance factors away from processes and tools aspects more to management and people aspects. This is not to say that processes and tools are less important than previously, but it is to say that they must be subordinated to serve the management and people factors.

5 Conclusions

This paper concentrates on the characteristics of the excitement driven market place for software intensive products. Typical to that market is continuous flow of new ideas, new technology and frequent changes of mind. For that environment the traditional project management is too slow, ridged and laborious. A proposal for a new management approach, based on lean management, leadership and agile approaches was done. Agile approaches give the basic patterns of doing the development work, leadership the patterns of management, and lean management the patterns for managing the product development.

The approach proposed here is part of a wider concept, a part of the work to find new means to tackle issues in product development today. It is obvious that the current practices in wide use will be sufficient still for many. However, the market trends and successes of the new players there seem to suggest that new approaches might substantially benefit those organizations which are looking for means to transform their operation.

References

1. Schwaber, K.: Agile Project Management with Scrum. Microsoft Press, Redmond (2004)
2. Plamer, S., Felsing, J.M.: A Practical Guide to Feature Driven Development. Prentice Hall, Upper Saddle River (2002)
3. Project Management Institute, Project Management Body of Knowledge (PMBOK® Guide), http://www.pmi.org/Resources/Pages/Library-of-PMI-Global-Standards-Projects.aspx
4. Carnegie Mellon University, Software Engineering Institute.: CMMI for Development, Version 1.2., CMU/SEI-2006-TR-008 (August 2006)
5. ISO, International Organization for Standardization, JTC 1/SC 7.: ISO/IEC 15504, Information technology – Process assessment, parts 1-7
6. Kontio, J.: Software Engineering Risk Management. In: A Method, Improvement Framework and Empirical Evaluation, Doctoral Dissertation. Helsinki University of Technology, Publisher Suomen Laatukeskus (2001)

7. Huchzermeier, A., Loch, C.H.: Project Management Under Risk: Using the Real Options Approach to Evaluate Flexibility in R&D. Management Science 47(1) (January 2001)
8. Fenton, N., Radliński, L., Neil, M.: Improved Bayesian Networks for Software Project Risk Assessment Using Dynamic Discretisation,
   http://en.scientificcommons.org/norman_fenton
9. Ilkaev, D.: Handling Uncertainty in Project Planning,
   http://www.projectperfect.com.au/info_managing_uncertainty.php
   (first published on July 2005)
10. Agile Software Development.com, Kano model of customer satisfaction,
    http://agilesoftwaredevelopment.com/2006/12/
    kano-model-of-customer-satisfaction
11. Boehm, B., Egyed, A., Kwan, J., Port, D., Shah, A., Madachy, R.: Using the WinWin Spiral Model: A Case Study. IEEE Computer (July 1998)
12. Boehm, B.: A Spiral Model of Software Development and Enhancement. IEEE Computer (May 1988)
13. Kotter, J.P.: The Leadership Factor. The Free Press, New York (1988)
14. Goldratt, E.M.: Theory of Constraints. The North River Press (1990)
15. Reinertsen, D.G.: Managing the Design Factory. The Free Press (1997)
16. Womack, J.P., Jones, D.T.: Lean Thinking, Banish Waste and Create Wealth in Your Corporation. Free Press, New York (2003)
17. Poppendieck, M., Poppendieck, T.: Implementing Lean Software Development. Addison Wesley/Pearson Education Inc. (2007)
18. Poppendieck, M., Poppendieck, T.: Leading Lean Software Development. Addison Wesley, Poppendieck (2010)
19. Hines, P., Found, P., Griffiths, G., Harrison, R.: Staying Lean, Lean Enterprise Research Center, Cardiff University (2008)
20. BBRT - Beyond Budgeting Roundtable (2010), http://www.bbrt.org/

Beyond Budgeting in Statoil

Bjarte Bogsnes

Statoil, Forusbeen 50, N-4035 Stavanger, Norway
bjbo@statoil.com

Abstract. It is both scary and amazing to observe how little management practices have developed over the last fifty years, a period where we have seen groundbreaking innovation in most other parts of business and technology. My sons who now are finalizing their business studies could easily have used many of my own textbooks from thirty years ago, especially those covering budgeting, planning and performance management. Most business schools still teach, and most companies still practice a "command-and control" approach born in a time when the pace and predictability of business environments were radically different, and when the expression "knowledge organisation" did not exist.

Statoil is Scandinavia's largest company. One of it's values reads "Challenge accepted truth, and enter unfamiliar territory". Bjarte Bogsnes will share Statoil's long journey, which by no means is over, towards a new coherent management model which "takes reality seriously" both from a business and people perspective. He will advocate the need for joining forces with HR on this journey, because management processes must be fully aligned with leadership principles and practices. The two communicating opposing messages is a recipe for confused and disillusioned employees. Bogsnes will also argue that organisations will not succeed with their lean and agile efforts on development projects unless lean and agile also becomes the way the organisation, and not just it's projects, is run.

P. Abrahamsson and N. Oza (Eds.): LESS 2010, LNBIP 65, p. 151, 2010.
© Springer-Verlag Berlin Heidelberg 2010

Case Study: The SpareBank 1 Gruppen's Road to a New Corporate Governance Based on the Principles of beyond Budgeting

Sigurd Aune

SpareBank 1 Gruppen, Oslo, Norway
sigurd.aune@sparebank1.no

Abstract. SpareBank 1 Gruppen is a Norwegian holding company that, through its subsidiaries, provides and distributes products in the field of life and P&C insurance, fund management, securities brokering and factoring. The company joined the BBRT in 2008. *Sigurd Aune, CFO SpareBank 1* Gruppen will describe their Going Dynamic (Beyond Budgeting) project. This will include why they needed to change, what they are changing, their progress so far and the challenges that lie ahead.

P. Abrahamsson and N. Oza (Eds.): LESS 2010, LNBIP 65, p. 152, 2010.
© Springer-Verlag Berlin Heidelberg 2010

How the beyond Budgeting Management Model Enables Lean Thinking and the Agile Organization

Peter G. Bunce

BBRT, 745 Ampress Lane, Lymington, Hampshire SO41 8LW, UK
peterbunce@bbrt.org

Abstract. Lean thinking has been around for decades, yet relatively few organizations have adopted and benefited from its ideas to the fullest extent. Even fewer organizations have gone on to become both lean and agile. As the evidence for such radical improvements is so compelling you have to wonder why. Most organizations implement lean thinking as a series of tools and have no concept of agility. Effective lean thinking and agility require organizations to push decision-making and responsibility down to the self-managed teams, yet the way most organizations are designed and managed inhibits changing from hierarchies and command-and-control to these self-managed teams.

This presentation briefly outlines why we need to change from the traditional command-and-control management model to the Beyond Budgeting learn-and-adapt management model. It examines the basic requirements of lean thinking and agility why this learn-and-adapt model is necessary to enable lean thinking and agility to realise their full potential. It explores the visions and principles of the Beyond Budgeting management model, with examples from companies that have adopted many of these principles. Finally it explores some of the practical steps for successful implementation and change management. Peter Bunce is a Director of the Beyond Budgeting Round Table (BBRT), an international shared learning network dedicated to helping organizations move beyond command-and-control. His background is in manufacturing engineering.

P. Abrahamsson and N. Oza (Eds.): LESS 2010, LNBIP 65, p. 153, 2010.
© Springer-Verlag Berlin Heidelberg 2010

Handelsbanken – Our Way

Pekka Vasankari

Handelsbanken, Konstaapelinkatu 4, 02600 Espoo, Finland
pekka.vasankari@handelsbanken.fi

Branch Manager, Handelsbanken Espoo-Leppävaara, Finland

Abstract. Founded in 1871, Handelsbanken is one of the leading banks in the Nordic region, with over 700 branches in 22 countries. It regards Sweden, Denmark, Finland, Norway and Great Britain as its domestic markets. The Handelsbanken management model is acknowledged by the BBRT as almost certainly the best 'Beyond Budgeting' exemplar in existence. This presentation will describe the principles and values of running a multinational bank through good and bad times. Handelsbanken has for decades been successful in applying a decentralized management model. The strong core values and beliefs are the Handelsbanken way to better banking.

P. Abrahamsson and N. Oza (Eds.): LESS 2010, LNBIP 65, p. 154, 2010.
© Springer-Verlag Berlin Heidelberg 2010

Dynamic Management in a Global Telecomms Business

Kenneth Hauge

Telenor, Group Finance, N-1331 Fornebu, Norway
kenneth.hauge@telenor.com

Abstract. Telenor Group is one of the largest mobile operators in the world with more than 40.000 employees situated in 13 different countries across Europe and Asia. The history of Telenor's communication practices can be tracked back all the way to the mid 19th century. The communication services provided was more or less governmentally controlled at that time since. The Telegraph Act that was passed in 1899 gave the Norwegian state authorization to take over the private telephone companies. The Norwegian Telegraph Administration as it was called back then changed its name to Norwegian Telecommunications (Televerket) in 1969 and the productions of communication services, now also included television broadcasting, continued without any competition until 1988 when the Norwegian Telecom's monopoly on the sale of telephone sets ends. In the years past we had seen the birth of new markets of satellite phones and soon the mobile technology was standing in the doorway ready to be introduced to the public. In 1995 Norwegian Telecom changed the name to Telenor and in 2001 Telenor went from being fully owned by the Norwegian state to being publicly listed. After about 150 years of evolution within the telecommunication business we see Telenor as it stands today; a company with interests in many of today's countries around the world and a still continue to be a growing driving force in modern communications.

In addition to its own telephony and broadcast services, the Telenor Group has substantial activities in subsidiaries and joint venture operations. While some are seen as a pure financial investment, others are important in order to support and develop the core business of Telenor. The Telenor Group is dynamic and flexible in its business approach, always exploring new markets and new technologies to make long-term investments. This is part of the reason why Telenor has been able to grow from a national telephone service company in Norway to become the world's 7th largest mobile service provider in less than two decades.

The initiative to begin the journey towards implementing Beyond Budgeting in Telenor was decided by the top management in the Telenor Group, including all the CFO's of the Telenor Group, already in 2007. However, there is still some distance to travel until we have completed the implementation. The first year of the project it consisted of three pilots; DiGi in Malaysia, dTac in Thailand and Telenor Broadcast in Norway. **Going Dynamic** was the name chosen for this ongoing project in Telenor. We found that the existing way of governing was not adequate as the growth in certain markets was higher than anticipated. The budget assumptions and goals we had in relations to these markets were therefore insufficient. Delivering "on budget" was not sufficient in the competitive market, but when everything was based on the budget (follow-ups,

P. Abrahamsson and N. Oza (Eds.): LESS 2010, LNBIP 65, pp. 155–156, 2010.
© Springer-Verlag Berlin Heidelberg 2010

bonus agreements etc) there were limited incentive for the employees to go beyond the budget.

Telenor developed a Going Dynamic management model framework where the focus is strong when it comes to the relationship between establishing strategy and ambition, operationalizing the strategy and dynamic forecasting, reviews & action planning/execution. With this we are hoping to establish a stronger link between the strategy and operations making us able to respond to rapid changes and being able to initiate necessary actions accordingly. At the same time, the developed model maintains the same "level of control" as before (although without budgets). This is a more forward looking management model than previously. The Going Dynamic model increase probability of getting more forward looking financial and operating information as well as removing the yearly budget process. In addition, well defined responsibilities and documented management processes will strengthen and clarify the roles of individuals. Eventually, this kind of cultivation will encourage everyone to perform as business owners and not just following the budget.

Lean Implementation - Lead by Example

Heidi Pschibilla

München, Germany
HeidiPschibilla@gmx.net

Abstract. Successful Lean Transformation achieved through leading by example. It has been noted that the number one secret to success for a successful and sustainably lean transformation is management commitment and support the initiative. This presentation is targeted towards identifying those key elements that management must possess and exhibit in order to support the initiative and drive the right culture change. Heidi's presentation is based on a real case in a European manufacturing company.

P. Abrahamsson and N. Oza (Eds.): LESS 2010, LNBIP 65, p. 157, 2010.

Continue Your beyond Budgeting Journey with Help from Agile, Lean and Scrum

Helge Eikeland

Statoil, Forusbeen 50, N-4035 Stavanger, Norway
heeik@statoil.com

Abstract. Statoil is introducing the so-called "Scrum" method in business support project throughout the company with the goal of achieving better, cheaper and more sustainable results in a shorter time. Scrum is based on the principles of 'lean' and 'agile' and is closely related to Beyond Budgeting. *Helge Eikeland, Statoil* will explain the principles of Scrum and how they are beneficially using it in their Beyond Budgeting implementation.

P. Abrahamsson and N. Oza (Eds.): LESS 2010, LNBIP 65, p. 158, 2010.

Panel: Why Agile, Why Lean?

David Anderson (hosting)

Author, Consultant
dja@djanderssonassociates.com

Kati Vilkki, Alan Shalloway, David Joyce, David F. Rico, and Ken Power (panelists)

The Agile movement started a transition in the software industry. Some say that Agile brings more professionalism to the industry by focusing on the core activities and calling for a redesign of our software development processes in a fundamentally different way. However, it is clear that as Agile gets adopted, not everything is a bed of roses. Many companies are faced with issues that the available Agile methods do not sufficiently address. Lean is another paradigm that is gathering momentum and, according to many, can be the "next step" for the agile methods to step out of the software development environment and step into the larger business context of our industry. Some of the questions we intend to frame in this panel are: Why have companies embraced Agile? Why have companies embraced Lean? What do each of these paradigms agree on and what are the divergences? Why are those divergences important? What does the Lean paradigm change for a software company that has embraced Agile in the past?

David Anderson

David J. Anderson leads a management-consulting firm focused on improving performance of technology companies. He has many years management experience leading teams on agile software development projects. David was a founder of the agile movement through his involvement in the creation of Feature Driven Development. He was also a founder of the APLN, a non-profit dedicated to improving management and leadership in technology companies. Recently David has been focusing his attention on business agility and enterprise scale agile software transitions through a synergy of the CMMI model for organizational maturity with Agile and Lean methods.

Kati Vilkki

Kati Vilkki is currently heading Lean and Agile Transformation in Nokia Siemens Networks. She has M.Sc. degree in Computer Science from Helsinki University. She joined Nokia in 1994 and has since held various management and development positions mostly within product development, R&D and supporting functions. She has headed quality and process management teams, managed SW process and other

P. Abrahamsson and N. Oza (Eds.): LESS 2010, LNBIP 65, pp. 159–161, 2010.
© Springer-Verlag Berlin Heidelberg 2010

improvement programs, driven operational mode development and been the change agent in many different projects. Starting in 2005 the most important improvement action has been introducing lean and agile thinking in large scale product development and in an organization, which has very traditional, water-fallish development back-ground. There has been remarkably change and now agile development is the main street development mode in NSN. Kati Vilkki has also wide experience in organizational and leadership development and in coaching teams.

Alan Shalloway

Alan Shalloway is the founder and CEO of Net Objectives. With almost 40 years of experience, Alan is an industry thought [Innovation Games Trained Facilitator] leader. He helps companies transition to Lean and Agile methods enterprise-wide as well teaches courses in Lean, Kanban, Scrum, Design Patterns, and Object-Orientation. Alan has developed training and coaching methods for Lean-Agile that have helped his clients achieve long-term, sustainable productivity gains. He is a popular speaker at prestigious conferences worldwide. He is the primary author of Design Patterns Explained: A New Perspective on Object-Oriented Design, Lean-Agile Pocket Guide for Scrum Teams, Lean-Agile Software Development: Achieving Enterprise Agility and is currently writing Essential Skills for the Agile Developer. He has a Masters in Computer Science from M.I.T. as well as a Masters in Mathematics from Emory University.

David Joyce

David is an agile coach with 12 years technical team management and coaching experience, and 20 years software development experience. In recent years, using Scrum and XP, David has coached onshore and offshore teams and successfully launched an internet video startup from inception to launch. More recently David has coached teams on Lean, Kanban and Systems Thinking at BBC Worldwide in the UK. David currently works for Thoughtworks as a principal consultant and is a Systems Thinker, Lean practitioner, Kanban coach and certified Scrum Master. David recently received the Lean SSC Brickell Key award for outstanding achievement and leadership.

David F. Rico

Dr. Rico has been a technical leader in support of major government agencies such as NASA, DARPA, DISA, SPAWAR, USAF, AFMC, NAVAIR, CECOM, MICOM, GSA, and MITI for over 23 years. Dr. Rico worked on NASA's $20 billion space station in the 1980s, Dr. Rico worked for a $40 billion Japanese corporation in Tokyo in the early 1990s, and Dr. Rico worked on U.S. Navy fighters such as the F-18, F-14, and many others. Dr. Rico has led, managed, or participated in over 20 organization change initiatives using Agile Methods, Lean Six Sigma, ISO 9001, CMMI, SW-CMM, Enterprise Architecture, Baldrige, and DoD 5000. Dr. Rico specializes in

IT investment analysis, IT project management, and IT-enabled change. Dr. Rico has been an international keynote speaker, written or contributed to six textbooks, and published numerous journal articles on topics such as Cost Estimating, Cost of Quality (CoQ), Breakeven Analysis, Return-on-Investment (ROI), Net Present Value (NPV), and Real Options Analysis (ROA). Dr. Rico holds a bachelor's degree in computer science, a master's degree in software engineering, and a doctoral degree in information systems. Dr. Rico is a Certified Project Management Professional (PMP) and Certified Scrum Master (CSM). Dr. Rico teaches doctoral and master's courses at three Washington, DC-area universities. Dr. Rico has been in the field of information systems since 1983.

Ken Power

Ken Power is a software engineer, architect, and experienced agile practitioner and coach. He has wide experience introducing and applying agile development at all levels in organizations, and across a variety of industries and domains. His technical and research interests include architecture, agile processes, lean development, patterns, systems design, test driven development, and organization design to support productive and effective teams. Ken works with Cisco's Voice Technology Group on development of Unified Communications products, including voice, video and messaging applications. In addition to product development, he is part of the team leading agile process adoption across the organization. He is a Certified Scrum Master and a member of ACM and the IEEE Computer Society.

Fit Manufacturing

Duc Truong Pham[1], Andrew J. Thomas[2] , and P.T.N. Pham[1]

[1] Manufacturing Engineering Centre, Cardiff University, CF24 3AA, UK
[2] Newport Business School, University of Wales Newport, NP20 5DA
phamdt@Cardiff.ac.uk, andrew.thomas@newport.ac.uk,
PhamPT@cardiff.ac.uk

Abstract. With the current global downturn, companies must develop innovative approaches to ensure that economic sustainability is achieved. This paper proposes a Fit Manufacturing Model (FMM) to help manufacturing companies to become economically sustainable and to operate effectively in a global competitive market. The FMM combines the principles of existing manufacturing paradigms with new and innovative management concepts to create a sustainable approach to manufacturing.

Keywords: Lean Manufacturing; Agile Manufacturing; Sustainability.

1 Introduction

The closure of numerous manufacturing companies over the last two years and the resulting loss of thousands of manufacturing jobs prove that the economic battle for survival has become increasingly difficult. Indeed, in the UK, the number of jobs in manufacturing has fallen by around a third in the last two decades (Experian Business Strategies, 2003) and, it is clear that UK manufacturing industry requires successful and sustainable strategies and business solutions capable of overcoming these modern manufacturing challenges.

Over the years, a number of business improvement strategies, methodologies, tools and techniques have been proposed and developed aimed at enhancing the productivity and economic longevity of organisations. Total Quality Management, Business Process Reengineering, Just In Time and "Lean", "Agility" and Six Sigma are just a few changes. Despite the reported success of these initiatives at increasing profits and market share for manufacturers, there are still a significant number of companies battling to keep their heads above the turbulent waters (Hines, 2004). The issue for many organisations is that these proposed solutions, although purporting economic benefits in the short term, fail as long-term business improvement strategies since they rarely become the explicit or even implicit focus of the change initiative in companies (Bateman, 2001). The result of failing to embed the strategy correctly into these companies often is that any improvements are lost as initiatives are abandoned and shop floor employees regress to previous methods of working (Thomas *et al*, 2009).

The implementation of "Lean" is mainly process-orientated and concentrates on the tools and techniques aimed at reducing waste in the system. Although "Lean"

H. Liu et al. (Eds.): ICIRA 2010, LNAI 6424, pp. 162–174, 2010.
© Springer-Verlag Berlin Heidelberg 2010

programmes consider strategy and alignment factors in the form of Policy Deployment, this has usually been poorly implemented and rarely sustained (Hines *et al*, 2004). In most cases, there is very limited attention paid to different leadership styles and behaviour of the employees working within the organisational system and the need for cultivating a culture and employee mindset that will welcome and nurture "Lean" behaviours. "Lean" programmes also rarely give any significant consideration to the role of technology, especially Information Technology, in supporting an economically sustainable system. The lack of a holistic approach to "Lean" implementation suggests that "Lean" is one of the many business improvement models that are piecemeal driven and as such is open to implementation in a variety of different ways with the resulting success being equally varied. In essence, "Lean" focuses on only a small number of conditions necessary for economic sustainability. Unlike previous research which tends to adopt a static approach to economic sustainability, this paper considers the need to move away from the traditional "Lean" approach to achieving economic sustainability and suggests a new approach called Fit Manufacturing as a new paradigm for the future. The paper suggests that "Fit" links in four major manufacturing themes which are: strategy, leadership, process and technology into a cohesive framework to deliver a sustainability solution for industry.

A review of the literature suggests that most organisations only concentrate upon one or two of these themes as a means of delivering economic sustainability (Small, 2006), (Liyanage, 2007) but lack a framework for a more holistic and dynamic perspective on sustaining change. This paper seeks to develop just such a conceptual "Fit" model which helps the interested company to decide how it might achieve sustainable economic change by taking account of each factor and the complex interaction between them.

2   The Need for a Sustainability Perspective

With the demand profile changing, companies must now operate in a less secure and more complex environment forcing their business and manufacturing strategies to cater for a wider range of requirements.

Low cost, highly responsive and flexible product ranges are now essential in order to capture new markets and to become economically sustainable (McCarthy, 2002). Sustainability is about not simply maintaining current operational levels and penetrating new markets in order to replace lost ones, but going further than this by achieving continued growth and development so that a company remains in business well into the future. This may mean that companies will need to move away from long-term relationships between supplier and customer and into shorter-term relationships where high-value manufacture will provide the necessary growth stream. However, to do this, a company must be able to support its manufacturing operations by integrating the traditional strategic manufacturing requirements of "Lean" and "Agility" with business process strategies such as marketing and sales as well as technological and product innovation approaches in order to achieve a sustainable manufacturing environment (DTi Foresight, 2000), (FutMan, 2002). Sustainability in this context is therefore the ability of a company actively to seek new markets, grow and prosper through greater customer and product diversification.

It can be argued that both "Lean" and "Agility" (Dale, 1996), (Vernadat 1999), provide the 'potential' for a company to grow rather than the actual growth and expansion and . Both paradigms provide for greater manufacturing capacity, lower unit costs, greater responsiveness (Christopher & Towill, 2000). However, neither paradigm promotes breaking into new market sectors through pro-actively aligning business process elements such as marketing and innovation in order to win new customers. It is possible for a company to be very "Lean" yet still fail as a business due to the lack of growth opportunities created.

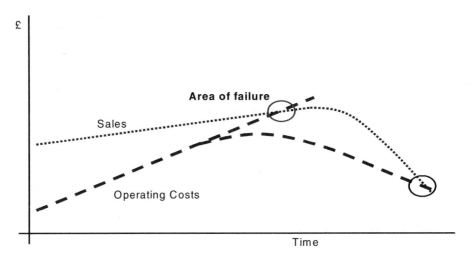

Fig. 1. Cost Versus Sales Analysis – Effect of Simple Cost-Cutting Approach

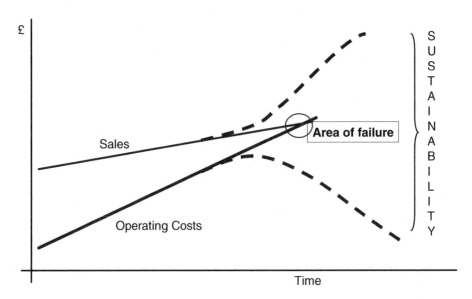

Fig. 2. Cost Versus Sales Analysis – Effect of Creating a Sustainable Organisation

Figure 1 illustrates the effect on a typical company's economic sustainability by simply concentrating upon the "Lean" aspects of a company's operations. Here it can be seen that without developing a strong and sustainable product portfolio to complement the "Lean" initiatives, company sustainability is threatened and the onset of failure is just delayed until such time as the drop in sales finally catches up with the operating costs and then the company becomes economically unsustainable.

Figure 2 shows the sustainability profile achievable using a combined approach towards waste reduction, responsive manufacturing, pro-active product development and increased sales opportunities.

3 A Fit Manufacturing Perspective

Over the years many manufacturing strategies and paradigms have claimed to provide a 'total' solution to the manufacturing problem. Usually, a solution to the efficient manufacture of products is achieved. However, rarely do the paradigms connect all the key elements of a manufacturing organisation in order for that organisation to grow and prosper in a sustainable way.

This disconnectedness of manufacturing practices causes process failures in terms of incurred cost, failing quality or missed delivery. Thus, the paradigms designed to improve these performance measures then act as inhibitors by necessitating additional efforts to maintain existing levels of performance. This is seen to manifest itself in SMEs in terms of specific system failures, incurring suspicion in the production areas, imposing operational limitations, and causing subsequent mistrust of new/modified systems, thus preventing integration of the paradigm into daily operations, which further exacerbates the situation.

The failures are characteristically isolated in occurrence, resulting from a wide variety of specific root causes, but the commonality between them stems from uncertainty caused by instability of the operations management and typically by the interfaces between the various components of it, which are most easily appreciated in terms of the product supply and demand chain. Childerhouse and Towill (2004) demonstrate the effects of traditional improvement thinking by means of the uncertainty circle concept, identifying that an additional level of improvement is required to regain the balance of system capability and customer/supplier influence in the state of reduced uncertainty.

Control can be acheved through a variety of methods to reduce the potential for poor performance, and similarly there are a variety of levels of implementation split between prevention and management. The prevention techniques are closely related to the "Lean" methodology which attempts to prevent the cause of uncertainty. However, one of the implications of the tighter controls is a reduction in flexibility and agility which are widely acknowledged to be among the prerequisites of an effective manufacturing strategy (Babu, 1999), (Azouzi et al, 2009). The management aspects employing buffering techniques (Koh and Gunasekaran 2006) such as safety levels of stock, lead time, capacity, overtime and scope for order rescheduling, may be considered techniques to cope with uncertainty but do not provide the means to reduce it. In addition, the effects of uncertainty can be compounded due to multiple sources (Koh, Gunasekaran and Saad, 2005). Therefore, the key is seen to be the identification of the critical level of uncertainty before further controls lead to unacceptable levels of inflexibility. The structure of the FMM is set to achieve this by maximising the influence of uncertainty reduction techniques while incorporating flexibility to the heart of the model and considering it a key performance indicator (KPI).

As stated earlier, "Lean" and Agility provide an effective platform for the efficient manufacture of products. However, these paradigms concentrate primarily on providing the 'capacity' for greater growth. "Lean", for instance, encourages doing more with less: less space, less raw material, less energy etc. "Agility" promotes the need to be responsive and flexible to customer requirements and so, quick changeovers, time compression approaches, etc, are important issues. These paradigms suggest therefore that a customer base is available for a company to work with. However, what happens when a customer base collapses? How does a company cope with the vacuum left after such an event? "Lean" and "Agility" are then seen as somewhat secondary to the issue of penetrating new market areas that are often alien to a manufacturing company and often occupied by supplier companies with many more years of experience of operating in these markets. What is therefore required is a more 'holistic' manufacturing strategy, one that enables a company to seek new markets and, more importantly, can give prior warning of major changes in current customer trends so that the company can adjust and move into new market areas quickly and effectively by adjusting its core manufacturing capabilities to meet new market requirements.

The proposed Fit Manufacturing Model in this paper ensures that "Lean" and "Agility" are central to its core activities with the aim of the model to create economically sustainable manufacturing companies. Sustainability means being able to achieve long-term growth and prosperity in what is now an increasingly volatile and complex marketplace. In order to achieve this, companies must be able to operate effectively in more than one market sector through penetrating a number of high-value manufacturing markets. In order to work in such diverse market sectors, the company must have at hand the technology platform and innovation culture to break into these areas and have the confidence to operate in such environments. Moreover, a company must ensure that whilst its manufacturing operations are balanced to meet the demand chain needs, it is also critical that its supply chain is developed to the same extent thus ensuring a complete connection between demand chain and supply chain.

Alongside these issues, a company must also make effective use of their Sales and Marketing departments. These departments should work to provide advance warning of customer and global trends advising the manufacturing sections of the company of any potential capacity issues when markets are buoyant and actively seeking new markets that the company's technological systems are capable of working within when markets are low. Also, sales and marketing can provide essential information of a product's positioning on its product life cycle identifying quickly when the product has finally started to move away from its maturity stage and into its decline stage thus triggering in advance the need to develop a new product or service.

It is therefore the integration of a company's manufacturing operations with its respective business, marketing and technology strategies that is required to enable it to achieve sustainable economic growth.

Kaplan and Norton (1996) identify the need for a company to consider a wider set of issues in order to remain competitive in the future. They state that for a company to grow and prosper there must be a more holistic view taken of the company operations rather than simply to concentrate on its manufacturing operations or its financial capabilities. Companies must now create future value through investment in customers, suppliers, employees, processes, technology, and innovation. They go on to identify four major perspectives a company must address. These are shown in Table 1.

Table 1. Four Major Business Perspectives for Sustainable Growth (adapted from Kaplan and Norton, 1996)

Financial	**Customer**
Waste Focus	Customer
Maintenance	Focus
and Control	Environmental
Vision and	dfds
Strategy	
Internal Business	**Learning and Growth**
Strategy	Leadership
Deployment	Continuous
Cross	Learning
Functionality	Teamworking
Technology	Culture and
Social	Empowerment

In proposing a new manufacturing paradigm for industry, it is important that these perspectives are considered and incorporated into its structure. It is proposed that companies should now look at developing a more holistic strategy towards achieving manufacturing sustainability (Hill, 1985), (Thomas & Pham 2004). Implementing a Fit Manufacturing approach rather than applying a purely "Lean" or Agile strategy allows a company to respond quickly to changes in future customer demands since it has, at its heart, an integrated manufacturing and business infrastructure capable of reconfiguring quickly to meet new customer demands.

The aim, then, is to structure a manufacturing operations strategy which aligns the supply and demand characteristics, limits the level of intervention required to manage the interpretation and control at each stage (reduce uncertainty), takes full advantage of the benefits provided by existing knowledge of cost and lead-time reduction to retain a competitive QCD model and enables the company to apply these principles to new business opportunities when they arise. The strategy must have inherent intelligence to control application of the various constituent best practices as appropriate without necessity for a learning period, perhaps by means of a knowledge-based system to associate controls with input data.

The Fit Manufacturing Model proposed in this paper aims to achieve this by integrating Kaplan and Norton's thirteen elements into an operational strategy for growth ensuring that company operations are reconfigured to suit changes in customer demands on a real-time and continuous basis (Beth *et al*, 2003).

4 The Mechanisms of the Fit Manufacturing Model

The proposed model is an integrated approach to the use of key business paradigms to achieve distinct and significant levels of manufacturing performance that are unique to each company. This model does not only develop a company's latent potential to meet new market requirements, but also actively encourages companies to seek new markets and to operate in unfamiliar areas knowing that the technological, human and financial aspects of the company are robust enough to enable it to achieve market breakthrough. Figure 3 shows the structure of the framework and the nature of its integrated system as well as the elements, ßwhich make up the Fit Manufacturing Model (FMM). The first elemental stage of the FMM comprises the '*Core*' elements. It is here that the company's infrastructure is defined and subsequently developed in order to support the FMM. These elements are: Marketing and Sales Integration, Strategy Integration, Financial Integration, and Knowledge and Skills Integration.

Integration is critical to the FMM. Traditionally, companies have incrementally and systematically implemented various manufacturing paradigms (TQM, "Lean", "Agility" etc) in a sequential manner as they become available or fashionable. This leads to an operational environment that is often left fragmented as individual systems are bolted onto existing infrastructures, usually causing internal conflicts within the company as the demands of one paradigm pull against those of another. These conflicts result in a significant increase in system and operational complexity as well as increased project costs and extended project timescales which, in turn, delay the benefits that can be gained from the application of a joint strategic approach (Visionary Manufacturing Challenges, 1998)

The FMM will integrate key business process strategies together with a company's existing and future technology platforms and operational strategies (Katz & Kahn, 1978), (Small, 1999). This integration provides not just a single new business approach but leads to an integrated manufacturing system that combines the systemics of a range of business process concepts (Gonzales-Benito, 2005) into one model that has low operational and systems complexity.

As an independent aspect itself, integration has a net impact on uncertainty management. This can be on several different levels:

- To integrate tighter controls into the daily operations management, which has the effect of reducing the opportunity for error though incomplete information, but at the same time introduces more constraints on the manufacturing system, effectively strangling the creativity and flexibility of the production staff.
- To integrate the various business functions to the fringes of the production system e.g. design, purchasing, etc. The aim of this is to limit the logistical constraints imposed by interface between departments, thus reducing the long-term uncertainty in quality issues, component lead-time, etc.

Further still, integration of the demand requirements and supply capabilities to the intermediary processing functions is the optimum in uncertainty management. However, this could also prove to be the most restrictive scenario by eliminating the opportunity for diversification or movement to markets or suppliers with different characteristics

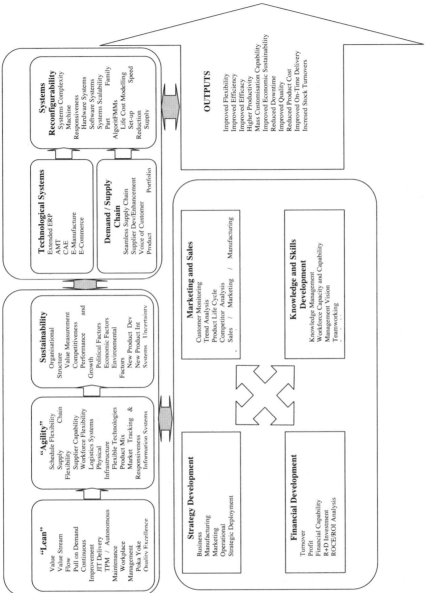

Fig. 3. FMM Manufacturing Structure

The FMM aims to maximise the positive effect of the integration, utilising the elements which can be utilised to control cost whilst neutralising undesirable side-effects of restricting the adaptability of the shop-floor. The measure of success of this often hinges on implementation. Hence, the mantle can fall on the shoulders of the first-line managers. Therefore, it is key that the implementation team of engineers, first-line managers and supervisory staff are well supported and able to consider the integration aspect of the model without being too blinkered in their approach to protect their own interests.

Alongside this, the FMM identifies the need for effective integration of the technologies in order to implement and sustain change. This technology platform includes more than just the machinery and associated systems that convert the raw material into a finished product. It also covers e-commerce at the front end through to the electronic transfer of customer order requests and the complete e-manufacturing facility that takes essential customer data, design data and manufacturing data and drives them forward in a simultaneous manner so that a product can be manufactured quickly and cost effectively. It is the tight integration of these various electronic platforms along with the strategic and business systems that will provide the cost effectiveness and rapid response required to meet customer demands.

Financial Integration: Over the years many companies have traditionally looked at relatively simple cost accounting approaches to monitor the health of their company. The FMM adopts an approach that also requires a company actively to build into their financial procedures two major aspects, namely:

    a)   the need to link technological development and innovation into its cost accounting system.

    b)   the need to tackle and amortise fixed costs through product/customer diversification.

On the first of these issues, the FMM proposes that companies actively plan for the continual upgrading of its technological platform by analysing how much of a its profit is reinvested in new and advanced technologies. Through the continual upgrading of such technologies, new market areas can be defined and the confidence to operate effectively increases due to the knowledge that the company has the technical power to do so.

On the second issue, it is important that a company links and closely monitors its product's life cycle in accordance with the financial performance of the company. Closely monitoring the sales of a product will enable a company to identify early that a product is losing market share. This will enable the company to take corrective action by possibly introducing a new product to their range or enhancing the existing product. Product diversification can provide a company with an opportunity of 'splitting' its overhead and fixed costs into a range of different product lines or customers. Single product manufacturers have the problem that all fixed costs are channeled into one product and thus the weight of the complete company's costs are centred on one product line or customer. Having a wider product portfolio and/or customer base can alleviate this problem and allow for the amortising of fixed costs. If therefore one product fails to perform, it has less overall impact on the company.

Knowledge and Skills Integration: Worker skills and knowledge are important to the performance of any company. For companies that continually enhance their technological capacity as is proposed through the FMM, this issue is seen as being even more critical. A study undertaken by Thomas and Webb (2003) into technology implementation in companies identified that one of the main reasons that companies failed to adopt new and advanced technologies was that the Managing Directors felt that their workforce did not have the technical and intellectual capacity to take on such technologies with the fear that the technology would be under-utilised and thus will not return a cost-effective yield on investment.

The FMM actively promotes knowledge and skills alignment. Through the continual enhancement of a company's technology will come the need to ensure that its workforce is suitably trained. However, this does not extend simply into the manufacturing aspects of the company. Since the FMM promotes the continual development of new and innovative products in order to attract new markets, a company's design and engineering team must also be continually trained to meet market needs.

The *Operational Elements* in the model provide the means by which a company can build upon the Core Elements to create an efficient manufacturing infrastructure. However, they do not act as one-way gates in the system but also as a feedback mechanism to ensure that the Core Elements aligned with the feedback received from them. This two-way approach allows a company to balance its effort undertaken in developing its infrastructure with the results obtained from the operational aspects of the model.

The Systems Elements provide the company with the working interface between it and the customer. This allows the company to respond to customer requirements through connecting the Core and Operational elements with the internal production and design system's capability to balance demand with supply and to reconfigure its manufacturing and operational systems to meet the needs of the customer..

As previously discussed, applying the FMM approach rather than the ""Lean"" and "Agile" strategies in isolation allows a company to respond quickly to changes in future customer demands and provides the capacity for a company to seek new customers and markets. This is because the FMM has at its heart an integrated manufacturing and business infrastructure capable of *reconfiguring* quickly to meet new customer and hence manufacturing requirements (Thomas *et al*, 2008)

Reconfigurability is a key enabler in the FMM and is not simply limited to readily adaptable machine systems but includes the ability to reconfigure the complete company, its manufacturing system including its design system (John *et al*, 2009), technology, logistics, and supply chain (Putterill *et al*,1996) so that optimum responsiveness to customer demand is achieved. Therefore, the ability of a company to balance its demand requirements with its supply capabilities is critical to the FMM. However, regardless of how effective a company's ability to reconfigure, the process still takes time to achieve. It is therefore essential that a company is sensitive to customer trends and movements so that that has the necessary advance warning to be able to take appropriate action at an early stage.

Demand – Supply Balancing: With any organisation that captures new markets, the customer demands and requirements extend not only to the supply company but to its supply chain. Traditionally a company may have only dealt with one type of customer and so has been able over a number of years to transform its supply chain to meet the demands of this customer. However, because with the FMM, new markets and customer/product diversification are seen as critical for survival, a company's supply chain must also respond to the new demands. Central to this approach is the need to reconfigure the supply chain so that its technological and operational characteristics are aligned with the company's demand profile. It is incumbent on the company to ensure that its supply chain becomes responsive to the needs and that the FMM is driven into these supply companies.

Technology and Product Innovation: This is considered to be the cornerstone of the FMM approach. Here, it is critical that a company has the required technological platform that is able to respond to the increasingly complex customer requirements. Also, the development of new and innovative products allows a company to break into new markets and also to stay ahead of its competition in mature market environments. It is through the effective integration of technologies with the capacity to support the product innovation process that real market penetration can be made. The exploitation of new and advanced technologies is critical in today's manufacturing environment. Companies need to reduce product lead times, introduce new products more frequently into the market place and rapidly reconfigure their manufacturing systems as well as ensuring high product quality and low manufacturing costs. Technology, therefore, is a key facilitator in this 'time compression' process (Gonzales-Benito, 2005).

In the light of the model developed, the FMM approach allows a company to prosper in a sustainable manner through the manufacture of high quality products facilitated by an integrated, robust, highly responsive and reconfigurable "Lean" manufacturing system that returns high product quality and reduced internal and external manufacturing costs. It is clear that, with the application of the FMM, manufacturing success can be assured through increased competitiveness and improved long-term sustainability.

5 Conclusion

This paper has proposed a Fit Manufacturing Model (FMM) designed to satisfy the unique manufacturing and knowledge constraints of manufacturing companies. The model leads a company through the complete Fit Manufacturing improvement cycle.

The Fit Manufacturing Model is a solution to some of the challenges not met by the typically partial or inappropriate implementation of existing paradigms. The key advantage is the elimination of some causes of uncertainty which currently constrain the particular system improvements targeted by practices such as "Lean" or "Agility", but also maintaining the level of adaptability required to promote movement to new products, technologies and markets.

The systematic development of a Fit Manufacturing culture is important if SMEs are to survive in the global marketplace. Whilst the development of a specific manufacturing improvement model will obviously aid in the development of the knowledge-driven culture, further work has to be done in order to ensure that this work is diffused to large numbers of SMEs. Therefore, the adoption of the FMM and the associated rate of diffusion of such a strategy into SMEs requires further analysis and development (Ramasesh *et al*, 2001).

Refinement and the subsequent validation of the model will take the form of applying the model in test-bed companies. The results of such a process will inform any changes required to ensure the model achieves optimal effectiveness in different types of SME. Therefore, the test-bed companies should be selected from differing market sectors with different resource capabilities.

Acknowledgements

This work was supported by the European Commission as part of the Innovative Production Machines and Systems (I*PROMS) FP6 Network of Excellence and the "SUPERMAN" ERDF Objective 1 project. Support was also provided by the Innovative Manufacturing Initiative of the EPSRC via its Cardiff IMRC grant. The authors also wish to thank Mr Paul Byard, Mr Paul Bailey and Mr Will Campion of MAS Wales for providing the DTI QCD measuring template for GVA capture.

References

Azouzi, R., Beauregard, R., D'Amours, S.: Exploratory case studies on manufacturing agility in the furniture industry. Management Research News 32(5), 424–439 (2009)

Babu, A.S.: Strategies for enhancing agility of make-to-order manufacturing systems. International Journal of Aglie Management Systems 1(1), 23–29 (1999)

Bateman, N.: Sustainability: A Guide to Process Improvement, "Lean" Enterprise Research Centre. Cardiff University, Cardiff (2001)

Beth, S., Burt, D.N., Copacino, W., Gopal, C., Lee, H.L., Lynch, R.P., Morris, S., Kirby, J.: Supply Chain Challenges: Building Relationships. Harvard Business Review Article (July 1, 2003), Prod. #: R0307E-HCB-ENG

Christopher, M., Towill, D.R.: Supply chain migration - from "Lean" and functional to agile and customized'. Supply Chain Management: An International Journal 5(4), 206–213 (2000)

Childerhouse, P., Towill, D.R.: Reducing Uncertainty in European Supply Chains. Journal of Manufacturing Technology Management 15(7), 585–598 (2004)

Cooper, R.G.: Winning at New Products: Accelerating the Process from Idea to Launch, 2nd edn. Addison Wesley, Reading (1993)

Dale, B.: Sustaining a process of continuous improvement: definition and key factors. TQM Magazine 8(2), 49–51 (1996)

Experian Business Strategies/GLA Economics, Making Sense of the Annual Business Enquiry, GLA Economics, London (2003)

Gonzalez-Benito, J.: A study of the effect of manufacturing pro-activity on business performance. International Journal of Operations & Production Management 25(3), 222–241 (2005)

Hill, T.: Manufacturing Strategy: the Strategic Management of the Manufacturing Function. McMillan Press, London (1985)

Hines, P.: Manufacturing in London: Where Should Development Effort be Focused, Theme Paper No. 5, London Development Agency, London (2004)

Hines, P., Holweg, M., Rich, N.: Learning to Evolve: A Review of Contemporary "Lean" Thinking. International Journal of Operations & Production Management 24(10), 994–1011 (2004)

John, E.G., Davies, A., Hammond, J., Thomas, A.J., Kuznecov, A.: A Conceptual Framework For Deciding Upon The Need For Re-configurability In Manufacturing Systems. In: Proceedings of the 7th International Conference on Manufacturing Research. University of Warwick (September 2009)

Kaplan, R.S., Norton, D.P.: The Balanced Scorecard: Translating Strategy into Action. Harvard Business School Press, Boston (1996)

Katz, D., Kahn, R.L.: The Psychology of Organizations. Wiley, New York (1978)

Koh, S.C.L., Gunasekaran, A., Saad, S.M.: A Business Model For Uncertainty Management. BencFMMarking International Journal 12(1), 383–400 (2005)

Koh, S.C.L., Gunasekaran, A.: A Knowledge Management Approach for Managing Uncertainty in Manufacturing. Industrial Management & Data Sytems 106(1), 439–459 (2006)

Liyanage, J.P.: Operations and maintenance performance in production and manufacturing assets: The sustainability perspective. Journal of Manufacturing Technology Management 18(3), 304–314 (2007)

McCarthy, I.: Manufacturing Fitness and NK Modeling. In: Proceedings 2nd International Conference of the Manufacturing Complexity Network, p. 27. University of Cambridge, Cambridge (2002)

Pham, D.T., Pham, P.T.N., Thomas, A.J.: Integrated Production Machines and Systems - Beyond Lean Manufacturing. Journal of Manufacturing Technology Management (2008), ISSN: 0954-478X

Putterill, M., Maguire, W., Sohal, A.S.: Advanced manufacturing technology investment: criteria for organizational choice and appraisal. Integrated Manufacturing Systems 7(5), 12–24 (1996)

Ramasesh, R., Kulkarni, S., Jayakumar, M.: Agility in manufacturing systems: an exploratory modeling framework and simulation. Integrated Manufacturing Systems 12(7), 534–548 (2001)

Rich, N.: Turning Japanese?, PhD. Thesis, Cardiff Business School, University of Wales, Cardiff (2001)

Salimi.B, New product development in small high tech firms. M.Phil Thesis, University of Calgary (1996)

Small, M.H.: Assessing manufacturing performance: an advanced manufacturing technology portfolio perspective. Industrial Management and Data Systems 99(6), 266–278 (1999)

Small, M.H.: Justifying investment in advanced manufacturing technology: a portfolio analysis. Industrial Management and Data Systems 106(4), 485–508 (2006)

The Future of Manufacturing in Europe 2015-2020, The Challenge for Sustainability, EU FP6 Funded Programme (2003)

Thomas, A.J., Pham, D.T.: Making Industry Fit: the conceptualisation of a generic 'Fit' manufacturing strategy for industry. In: Schoop, R., Colombo, A., Bernhardt, R., Schreck, G. (eds.) Proceedings 2nd IEEE Int. Conf. on Industrial Informatics, INDIN 2004, Berlin, pp. 523–528 (June 2004)

Thomas, A.J., Rowlands, H., Byard, P., Rowland-Jones, R.: "Lean" Six Sigma: An Integrated Strategy for Manufacturing Sustainability. International Journal of Six Sigma and Competitive Advantage (February 2009), ISSN 1479-2494

UK Manufacturing – We Can Make It Better, Final Report, Manufacturing, 2020 Panel. Foresight Manufacturing, Panel Report 2020. DTI, London (2000)

Van Der Merwe, A.P.: Project management and business development: integrating strategy, structure, processes and projects. International Journal of Project Management 20, 401–411 (2002)

Vernadat, F.B.: Research agenda for agile manufacturing. International Journal of Agile Management Systems 1(1), 37–40 (1999)

'Visionary Manufacturing Challenges for 2020', Committee on Visionary Manufacturing Challenges Board on Manufacturing and Engineering Design Commission on Engineering and Technical Systems National Research Council, National Academy Press, Washington, D.C (1998)

Enabling Dynamic Capabilities through Agile IT and beyond Budgeting Practices

Martin Curley

National University of Ireland, Maynooth &
Director, Intel Labs Europe
Martin.G.Curley@Intel.com

Abstract. This paper discusses the confluence of agile, lean and beyond budgeting approaches in the context of Enterprise IT solutions and presents a framework, which helps to achieve synergies from these approaches and avoid sub-optimizations. The paper suggests that lean and agile approaches cannot be used in a vacuum but need to be developed and considered in the context of other critical processes required to sustain and deliver enterprise IT solutions. While agile and lean methodologies certainly provide benefits they can deliver significantly more value when applied in collaboration with an overall dynamic capabilities (Teece et al, 2007) approach. The paper briefly introduces the IT-Capability Maturity Framework (IT-CMF), (Curley, 2004, 2006) and considers a closed loop mechanism to enable a dynamic capability in the context of rapidly changing environments. The paper also presents a five-layer maturity model for managing the Enterprise IT budget which aligns to the principles of beyond budgeting (Hope and Fraser, 2003; Bosgnes, 2009) being considered in this conference.

Keywords: Lean thinking, Sustainability, IT-CMF, Enterprise Solutions, Beyond Budgeting, Agile.

1 Introduction

Information Technology is emerging as one of the most dominant forces changing business and indeed society today. Increasingly we are seeing the collision of Moore's law with all types of business producing great entrepreneurial and business opportunities. Although technology, driven by Moore's law, is advancing at a very fast rate, the management practices used to manage and apply IT appear to be lagging significantly. Arguably agile methods enable businesses to take early advantage of emerging technologies but when agile is used while ignoring other processes required to sustain enterprise IT solutions, then the result can be anything but "lean".

Enterprise solutions and systems are an early adopter of the "Lean" concept but increasingly the concept of "Lean" may need to apply to many disciplines and indeed may have to become a cross-societal value and practice. As this happens lean and agile enterprise solutions and services will be a key vehicle to achieving a "leaner" economy and society where resource and energy efficiency are prioritized equally with product/service functionality and features.

P. Abrahamsson and N. Oza (Eds.): LESS 2010, LNBIP 65, pp. 175–184, 2010.

This paper discusses the IT-CMF leveraging a dynamic capabilities and process maturity approach to help develop and deliver innovative sustainable solutions which are rooted in value creation. Too often enterprise software and solutions (whether developed by agile, extreme or formal methods) are developed without cognizance of what it takes to sustain and improve a solution over multiple years.

Dynamic Capabilities can be defined as "the firm's ability to integrate, build, and reconfigure internal and external competences to address rapidly changing environments" (Teece et al, 2007). Very often the enterprise IT capability can be the platform for which to implement a dynamic capabilities approach for a firm and this is increasingly true as the information content of products and services continues to increase.

The IT-CMF (Curley, 2004; Curley, 2006; Curley and Kenneally, 2009) advocates taking a process approach which includes an integrated set of over thirty processes such as IT Governance, Risk Management, Demand/ Supply Management and indeed Solutions Delivery. Operating a lean and agile methodology without cognizance of the other enterprise IT processes can lead to an efficient software delivery process but an overall sub-optimization in terms of a managed set of sustainable solutions.

Sometimes agile and lean methods are deployed in a vacuum and are not used in an environment where all the processes required to deliver a sustainable enterprise solution are considered. The IT-CMF identifies four macro processes (Curley, 2006) which are required to design, deliver and operate sustainable IT solutions within the context of a sustainable economic model for IT. I argue that agile and lean methods which are used outside the context of some form of dynamic capabilities framework of an organization may lead to sub-optimizations. The IT-CMF is one such dynamic capabilities approach, which ensures that overall agility and value is improved rather than just the software development process and outcomes.

2 The IT-Capability Maturity Framework

The IT-CMF is an emerging blueprint of the key processes encapsulated in the IT capability of an organisation. A core function of the IT-CMF is to act as an assessment tool and a management system with associated improvement roadmaps to help continuously improve, develop and manage the IT capability in support of optimised value delivery. Systematically improving the maturity of critical processes can improve the overall efficiency and effectiveness of the IT capability in delivering value to an organization. The IT-CMF has been developed and extended using a Design Science research process and the highest level artifact includes four macro processes as show in figure1 below.

Fig. 1. Four Macro Processes

The IT-CMF posits there is firstly a *managing IT like a business process (MP1)* which serves to set strategy and enable concurrent control of the IT capability and modify the IT spend or the portfolio allocation of this spend to help ensure IT helps the firm to deliver to its objectives on an ongoing basis. This macro-process focuses on critical processes such as IT Governance (Weill, 2004; Weill and Ross, 2004), Supply/Demand Management (Earl and Sampler, 1999) and builds on Ventrakaman's seminal work   (1997). Ventrakaman introduced a new approach juxtaposing risk propensity (Minimize risk vs. Maximize Opportunity) versus purpose (IT efficiency or Business Capability) of the IT organization and defined four different types of business models for IT, cost centre, service centre, investment centre and profit centre.

Secondly there is a process for *Managing the IT budget* (MP2) which is a critical input to the IT value creation process. The IT budget process controls both the absolute level of budget applied to the IT capability and the allocation to particular portfolios. Budget management is a well recognized component of a management control system. As one moves to high level of maturity one can move to maturity states described in Beyond Budgeting Approaches (Hope and Fraser, 2003)

The IT capability is the production engine of the framework and essentially reflects what IT can do for the firm (Curley, 2004). *Managing the IT Capability* (MP3) concerns an integrated macro process to manage both the Assets/Value chain process of Enterprise IT and the ongoing development workflow and services delivered by Enterprise IT. Capability (Peppard, 2004) refers to the strategic application of competencies leveraging underpinning resources such as technical assets and people. Agarwal and Sambamurthy (2002) identify three primary processes of the IT value chain as Innovation, Solutions Delivery and Services Provisioning. Agile methods for software development are most relevant to the first two of these processes. The IT Capability consisting of the IT assets and the associated value chain is energized and made productive by applying a budget to it.

The *Managing IT for Business Value (MP4)* process is the instantiation of a competitive process identified by Markus and Soh (1998) where value is created through using IT impacts to create competitive differentiation. This is where value is assessed and realized. IT creates value through two fundamental mechanisms – business continuity and business change. Business continuity ensures that the firm can continue to obtain value from its products and services through such actions as process automation, product or service development, services provisioning etc. Business change delivers value when some change in the business model, process or product/services is enabled or driven through IT. Business Change reflects on value created through the IT impacts defined by Sambamurthy and Zmud (1994). These include new/improved products and services, transformed business processes, enriched organizational intelligence and dynamic organizational structures. Lean Methods are very often applied to business continuity solutions to improve efficiency but also a lean paradigm can be applied to the business change portfolio so that future solutions are lean by design. Intel's IT organization has synthesized a lean and a six sigma approach to create an efficient method for developing and transforming automated processes so that they are both efficient and controllable.

3 Improving IT Dynamic Capability and Productivity

In general most organizations want to increase output and agility and indeed this is true of a firms IT capability. Agile and lean methods can make IT software development processes more productive and agile through more efficient use of resources and faster iteration of development cycles to deliver finished software which best meets the requirements. A key objective of a lean and agile development process should be to deliver based on the constraints imposed and optimization of criteria such as fast time to market, minimized cost and highest percentage of requirements met.

In the face of increasing competitive pressure firms want to achieve more output from their IT capability. Dedrick et al (2003) define two mechanisms for increasing the productivity of the IT organization – capital deepening and improving multi-factor productivity. Adopting lean and agile methods are one method of improving multi-factor productivity for the IT organization and indeed the whole enterprise. Beyond Budgeting approaches can lead to significant capital deepening for the IT portfolio. Described below are some approaches for improving IT capability productivity and output;

- Using a different portfolio mix of inputs, weighting investment toward higher performing kinds of IT investments
- Aligning and sequencing investments better so that they better support the goals of the organization
- Improving the quality of the inputs to the IT capability (for example buying computer hardware from a different vendor resulting in potentially improved performance with lower acquisition and total cost of ownership costs)
- Capital deepening: the productivity of IT employees and organization may increase when more capital is provided. Capital could include hardware, software, data centres, use of other related assets acquired through increased investment or budget increases achieved through beyond budgeting approaches.
- Multifactor productivity (MFP): advances in improving the conversion effectiveness of the IT capability through improving the maturity of composite business processes and/or using lean/agile practices can increase the level of output without an additional increase in input

Jurison (1996) identified that IT benefits primary depend not on the size of the investment but on management effectiveness in converting the investment into business results. He also states that organizations differ vastly in their conversion effectiveness. Improving the IT capability to allow improved conversion effectiveness through the use of agile and lean methods is an area which shows much promise.

A key theme then is to improve the maturity of the IT capability by improving process maturity and outcomes to improve conversion efficiency and then modulating and changing the portfolio allocations for different kinds of investments based strategic business alignment and on historical returns to optimize the overall value delivered from the IT capability.

4 Dynamic Capabilities and Continuous Improvement of Value Delivery from the IT Capability

We can achieve agile and lean macro performance from the overall IT capability by exercising and performing closed loop control and dynamic portfolio management of the overall IT development portfolio. In many organizations there is no overall closed loop control of the IT capability and the associated software development workflow therein contained.

An example of an unmanaged, unaligned situation is shown in figure 2 below, with each box in figure 2 corresponding to the macro processes shown in figure 1. Here effectively the IT capability operates in open loop with no connection between output and input. There is no direct connection between IT strategy and the IT budget. There is also no alignment amongst investments or even a concept of portfolio management. Some investments may not only be not complementary but indeed be also competing.

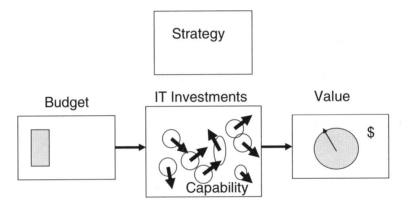

Fig. 2. Unaligned, Unmanaged IT Investments

To improve this situation the following sequence of events and connections is recommended to provide more dynamic and agile control over the entire development portfolio.

1. In the Managing IT like a business process (MP1) the IT leadership/governance and IT strategy processes set the direction for the overall IT capability. This direction setting should be highly aligned to the business strategy and influenced by prevailing business conditions.
2. In the Managing the IT Budget process (MP2) the strategic direction is translated into an IT budget which will create two kinds of value, value from maintaining existing systems and future value from new solutions.
3. The IT Capability (MP3) is the production and manufacturing engine of the IT capability and two primary activities are performed here (a) existing products and services are maintained and provisioned and (b) new solutions are envisioned, developed and existing services are supported, based on the budget applied.

4. In the fourth macro process Managing IT for Business Value (MP4) value realization and assessment happens with IT delivery translating into value. Here the ongoing performance of IT investments should be regularly tracked.
5. The performance of these IT investments should then be fed back into MP1 perhaps resulting in a change in strategic direction based on information on financial return information of investments. IT strategy reassessment will also be considered in the light of changing business strategy and business conditions.
6. Subsequently the cycle starts again with a new budget being determined in MP2 based on the output of MP1. In organizations with high maturity budgeting processes the frequency of assessing alignment of budget to overall needs and the portfolio allocation of the budget can be significantly faster than the traditional one year in many firms.

This continuous operation of the control loop closed at an appropriate frequency is intended to lead to continuous alignment and improvement of the value contribution of the IT capability given a constrained budget.   The application of a dynamic capabilities approach where the loop is closed regularly aims to move IT Value creation from a relatively unmanaged and unaligned state to a scenario depicted in the figure 3 where all IT investments are aligned with strategy and value is continuously improved through active portfolio management, weighting investment more heavily towards the better performing type of investments. For example one might determine that historically IT investments in manufacturing have a higher return than IT investments in Product Design and this one could change the portfolio allocations based on this information to increase the amount invested in manufacturing solutions.

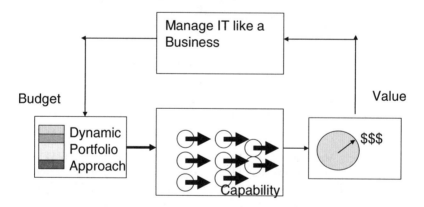

Fig. 3. Aligned and Managed IT Investment

Superior returns from IT compared to other classes of assets or responses to new business opportunities or challenges may lead to an increase of the IT budget, which would correspond to the capital deepening option discussed above. Alternatively improving productivity or efficiency of IT through for example the adoption of lean or agile methods may lead to a reduction in the overall IT budget as more can be done with less. The IT posture of the firm may be a modulator in this kind of decision making.

By applying an IT-CMF approach a "lean" and "agile" paradigm can be introduced to the design, delivery and sustaining of enterprise solutions. This approach which leverages a dynamic capabilities approach (Teece et al, 2007) creates a closed loop control mechanism where the enterprise IT budget and all the moving parts of an Enterprise IT organization are continuously changed and reconfigured to meet the challenges and opportunities of a continuously changing business and societal environment. Obviously having an agile software competency is crucial to achieving a dynamic capabilities approach but this can only make a sustainable difference to the enterprise if agile software is developed in conjunction with an agreed enterprise architecture and that there is sufficient and scalable capacity to meet demand once a solution is deployed.

5   Applying a Capability Maturity Approach

The Software capability maturity model (Paulk et al, 1993) has inspired reuse to several different domains and here I summarize such an approach applied to Managing the IT Budget (Curley, 2004; Curley, 2006). It is the hallmark of a maturity model approach that excellence is achieved incrementally and in the Managing the IT Budget capability maturity curve (figure 4) there are five maturity levels described.

Fig. 4. IT-CMF for Managing the IT Budget

At the initial level, there is no strategy, no budget, no clear operating plan, and no measures of outcome in monetary or service terms. This level of maturity often results in chaos. At the next step, the basic level, the IT organisation is starting to become organised. IT is a cost centre with a formal budget and IT begins to deliver technology more reliably. The intermediate level shows further improvements and taking into account total cost of ownership, the IT organisation formally begins considering the return on IT investments from the IT budget and associated IT investments. At Level 3, IT organizations have introduced systematic cost reduction techniques that focus on reducing the aggregate and unit cost of IT products and services. This is a key strategy for CIOs who have had to take cost out of existing operations to yield savings which can be reinvested in new IT investments. Disciplined reduction of unit costs using lean approaches and other methodologies is very important.

There is of course still room to grow and at the advanced maturity level, the IT budget is considered as an investment portfolio rather than something whose cost should be minimized. At Level 4 the IT budget is increasingly aligned with the long term business objectives of the firm. At Level 4, IT organizations achieve funding and resource amplification. At level 4, IT organizations have expanded their funding options beyond simply CFO funding and are obtaining funding from a number of different sources, perhaps even internal and external to the firm. Funding options may include pay-per-view usage fees, business unit funding, and external funding from supply chain partners or grants from Governments. A key characteristic at this level is budget flexibility where the IT organization is decoupled from the annual budget planning cycle and has adequate reserves and budget flexibility to align spending with key needs and opportunities. At level 4, IT organizations are using savings captured (from systematic cost reduction approaches such as lean) either for new IT investments or returning monies directly to the firm's bottom line.

Level five, optimising, describes ongoing year-on-year improvements to maintain and improve the business value contributions of IT based on a budget which is continuously modulated to adapt to changing circumstances and new opportunities. The successful IT organisation finds itself in a virtuous circle as cost savings provide resources for innovative IT solutions which, in turn, improve business value contributions. At level 5, IT organizations have achieved sustainable economic models for their budgets with optimized capital expenditures and operational expenditures. At this level, the IT organization has delivered scalable services to meet the firm's growth while maintaining a stable IT budget over time. The balance of budget allocation between innovation, solution development and maintenance/support costs has been optimized as well. The growth demands of company are supported using a stable IT budget, with balanced budget allocation across appropriate portfolios based on prior and ongoing value performance. At level 5 IT intensity is actively managed and compared against other key corporate spending categories, whilst the budget is driven by long term organization/business roadmaps and value performance. Also the budget size is appropriate for the organization's IT posture and track record of value delivery. Additionally the IT budgeting process is an adaptive process which is a hallmark of a beyond budgeting process (Hope and Fraser, 2003)

At level 5, the firm has an IT financial model which is quantitatively managed in which the budget is actively managed and balanced to meet ongoing demand and fund new strategic initiatives, with a variety of best practices in place to ensure the IT organization can meet ongoing demand. Strong cost management techniques are also in place and the budget is modulated in a controlled fashion based on strategic posture, context and ongoing performance on IT investments.

By applying an IT-CMF approach a "lean" paradigm can be introduced to the design, delivery and sustaining of enterprise solutions. This approach which leverages a dynamic capabilities approach (Teece et al, 2007) creates a closed loop control mechanism where the enterprise IT budget and all the moving parts of an Enterprise IT organization are continuously changed and reconfigured to meet the challenges and opportunities of a continuously changing business and societal environment. Obviously having an agile software competency is crucial to achieving a dynamic capabilities approach but this can only make a sustainable difference to the enterprise if agile software is developed in conjunction with an agreed enterprise architecture and if there is sufficient and scalable capacity to meet user demand once a solution is deployed.

6 Conclusions

By applying an IT-CMF approach a "lean" and "agile" paradigm can be introduced to the design, delivery and sustaining of enterprise solutions. This approach which leverages a dynamic capabilities approach creates a closed loop control mechanism where the enterprise IT budget and all the moving parts of an Enterprise IT organization are continuously changed and reconfigured to meet the challenges and opportunities of a continuously changing business and societal environment. Having an agile software competency is crucial to achieving a dynamic capabilities approach but this can only make a sustainable difference to the enterprise if agile software is developed in conjunction with other processes which are required to operate a sustainable IT capability. Closed loop control enables the creation of a "Lean" IT capability where continuous alignment of IT investments with overall priorities ensures an efficient use of resources while meeting overall business objectives. Lastly moving forward the IT organization must move beyond budgeting to active value management.

References

1. Agarwal, R., Sambamurthy, V.: Principles and Models for Organizing the IT Function. MIS Quarterly Executive 1(1-16) (March 2002)
2. Bogsnes, B.: Implementing Beyond Budgeting: Unlocking the Performance Potential. John Wiley & Sons, Inc., Hoboken (2009)
3. Curley, M.: Managing Information Technology for Business Value. Intel Press (January 2004)
4. Curley, M.: Introducing the IT-Capability Maturity Framework. In: International Conference of Enterprise Information Systems, Portugal (2006)
5. Curley, M., Kenneally, J.: The IT-Capability Maturity Framework, Innovation Value Institute. National University of Ireland, Maynooth (2009)
6. Dedrick, J., Gurbaxani, V., Kraemer, K.L.: Information Technology and economic performance: A critical review of the empirical evidence. ACM Computing Surveys 35(1) (2003)
7. Earl Michael, J., Sampler, J.L.: Market Management to Transform the IT organization. MIT Sloan Management Review (summer 1998)
8. Hope, J., Fraser, R.: Beyond Budgeting. Harvard Business Press, Boston (2003)
9. Jurison, J.: Toward more effective management of information technology benefits. The Journal of Strategic Information Systems 5(4), 263–274 (1996)

10. Markus, M.L., Soh, C.: How IT creates value, a process theory synthesis. In: Proceedings of the 16th International Conference of Information Systems, Amsterdam, The Netherlands (1995)
11. Paulk, M.C., Curtis, B., Chrissis, M.B.C., Weber, C.: Capability Maturity Model for Software, Version 1.1, Software Engineering Institute, CMU/SEI-93-TR-24, DTIC Number ADA263403 (February 1993)
12. Peppard, J., Ward, J.: Beyond strategic information systems: towards an IS capability. Journal of Strategic Information Systems 13(2), 167–194 (2004)
13. Sambamurthy, V., Zmud, R.W.: IT Management Competency Assessment: A tool for Creating Business Value through IT. Working Paper, Financial executives Research Foundation (1994)
14. Teece, D., Pisano, G., Shuen, A.: Dynamic Capabilities and Strategic Management. Strategic Management Journal 18(7), 509–533 (1997)
15. Venkatraman, N.: Beyond Outsourcing: Managing IT Resources as a Value Center. MIT Sloan Management Review (Spring 1997)
16. Weill, P., Ross, J.: How Top Performers manage IT decisions rights for superior results. Harvard Business School Press, Boston (2004)
17. Weill, P.: Don't Just Lead, Govern. How Top-performing firms govern IT. MIS Quarterly Executive 3(1) (March 2004)

Author Index

Printing: Mercedes-Druck, Berlin
Binding: Stein+Lehmann, Berlin